AF479275

INTERNATIONAL CARTELS IN BUSINESS HISTORY

INTERNATIONAL

The International Conference on Business History 18

CARTELS IN

Proceedings of the Fuji Conference

BUSINESS

edited by AKIRA KUDŌ   TERUSHI HARA

HISTORY

UNIVERSITY OF TOKYO PRESS

This volume is the proceedings of the Third Session of the Fourth Series of the International Conference on Business History, which took place from January 5 to 8, 1991. We would like to express our deepest gratitude to the Taniguchi Foundation for its continuing sponsorship of the conference.

Contents

Introduction

Akira Kudō and Terushi Hara

The International Conference on Business History, popularly known as the Fuji Conference, has been held annually since 1974. The fourth series, which commenced in 1989, takes international business relations as one of its main themes. The 18th conference took place in January 1991 under the title "International Cartels in Business History." In this conference we examined the question of international cartels within the context of international business relations. We took as our topic competition and cooperation between international corporations, using international cartels as a concrete example for examination.

International cartels, in the true sense of the word, did not emerge until the last quarter of the 19th century, and it was in the interwar period that they really came into their own. After the Second World War, they were overtaken by multinational corporations and generally appeared to be on the decline. However, during the 1970s and 1980s yet another change took place. There was a transition in the means of international expansion by large corporations from direct investment to diverse organizational arrangements, into such ways as, for example, the formation of what can be called strategic alliances between large companies. Of course, this cannot be said to be merely a simple revival of the original international cartels, but it can be seen as the reappearance of this kind of organization in an altered form. In this sense the examination of the history of international cartels has a direct bearing on the analysis of the way modern corporations are managed.

International cartels, apart from the obvious close link they have with companies' expansion of their international business, also have a connection with the strategies and structures of large companies in general. However, in spite of this, the study of international cartels using the business history approach, in contrast to economic and political approaches, has until now proved rather insufficient. This is the reason why we decided to undertake a thorough study using the business history approach.

In other words, we re-examined international cartels by looking at, on the one hand, the various related aspects of industrialization, such as domestic cartels, business management, and technical transfer and development, and on the other, the role played by the government with regard to the expansion of business and the economy. To put this in more concrete terms, we analyzed: (1) the circumstances surrounding, as well as the motives behind and reasons for, the formation of international cartels; (2) the formation process; (3) management and functions; (4) the effect of international cartels (especially the influence they had on the management of companies and on the economy in general); and (5) other factors.

The period we chose to cover was the interwar period, as this is when the expansion of the international cartels began in earnest, and it forms the high point of their hundred-or-so-year history. We narrowed our examination down to the manufacturing, and especially chemical and electrical, industries. The areas we covered were obviously Europe, where the international cartels were centered, and the United States, which was emerging as a new power and stood in a unique position regarding the international cartels because of its domestic antimonopoly legislation. Moreover, we also covered East Asia including Japan. What we wanted to do was to draw attention to the mutual relationship between these three areas, or the "triangular constellation." In other words, we wished not only to draw attention to the countries and corporations at the center of the international cartels' activities, but also to give a clear view of the peripheral nations and enterprises involved. In particular, we wished to give emphasis to questions concerning the first Newly Industrializing Economy (NIE), Japan, as a representative peripheral country; for example, the international cartels' strategy with regard to Japan, the policies of the Japanese corporations, and the response of the international cartels.

This volume thus represents a direct continuation of the theme of the initial conference in this fourth series, which had as its title "Foreign Business in Japan before World War II." It comprises a total of ten papers.

Terushi Hara and Akira Kudō's joint paper was written with the aim of presenting the various questions to be discussed at the conference. The authors first gave an overview of international cartels and then the various topics to be debated, such as the setting up and management of international cartels, their relations with domestic cartels, their influence on business management, and legislation relating to cartels. In addition, they presented an outline of relations between the international cartels and Japan and a proposal for a typology of international cartels.

Part I is made up of papers relating to the chemical industry. In his paper, Harm G. Schröter dealt with one of the most extensive and influential international cartels to emerge in the interwar period, the international dyestuffs cartel. He analyzed mutual relations between the European corporations at the center of this cartel in order to clarify its internal structure. Moreover, he also examined relations between these corporations and those enterprises that stood on the peripheries of this international cartel, including Japanese ones, and from this he gave an explanation of the structure of the cartel as a whole. Next Jonathan Liebenau took a fresh approach to the study of international cartels by looking at the problem of how enterprises controlled and used information as a management resource. For material he used the European chemical industry, and especially German pharmaceutical corporations, as a representative research-intensive industry. Moreover, he made use of this to examine in particular the relation between corporate research and international cartels.

Together with dyestuffs and pharmaceuticals, nitrogen fertilizer was a main sector of the chemical industry in the interwar period. Therefore, three papers dealing with the international cartel formed within this industry, from Japan, France, and Belgium, respectively, were also presented. Takeshi Ōshio's paper traced in detail the negotiations between the international nitrogen cartel and representatives of the Japanese nitrogen industry during the time of the Great Depression. He proved that a change in relations from competition to cooperation occurred and explained the reasons for this change from the point of view of both the international cartel and the Japanese corporations. Emmanuel Chadeau looked at the ambivalent relationship that existed between the French nitrogen fertilizer corporations and the international cartel. In his examination of the background to this, he drew attention to the existence in France of different types of enterprises, the movements within the agricultural and military groups, and government policy regarding the introduction of import quotas. Greta Devos analyzed the relationship between nitrogen fertilizer corporations and the international cartel; she examined companies from the Benelux countries, as minor European powers, concentrating on Belgium and Holland. In the same way as Chadeau, she presented the many different factors affecting this relationship, such as the interests of agriculture, and government policy, etc. Moreover, she added her thoughts on the policies employed by the international cartels, such as the payment of compensation.

In contrast to this, John Kenly Smith, Jr., dealt with the U.S. chemical corporations, which had only relatively weak relations with the international cartels. The American companies were able to conduct their business relatively independent of the international cartels, which controlled chemical products that were mainly industrial goods. This was possible because U.S. manufacturers were producers of consumer chemicals, such as polymers; they had a large domestic market and among themselves specialized in different products and processes. He showed that these corporations achieved particular success in product development and innovation.

Part II concerns the electrical industry. Here we have three papers that overlap and at the same time complement each other. Shin Hasegawa's paper dealt with the Japanese heavy electrical industry and incandescent electric bulb manufacturers. He focused on the competition within the industry and the changes in it, in the context of relations between the international cartel and Japanese corporations. He came to the conclusion that the international cartel was unable to exert a direct influence over the Japanese electrical market, and that in fact competition within the Japanese market was furthered by the provision of technological transfers from European and American companies. Renato Giannetti discussed the heavy electrical international cartel and the Italian heavy electrical cartel, emphasizing the existence of structural similarities between them. In relation to this, he raised a number of points, such as the peculiarities of the Italian electrical power industry, problems regarding the government's electrical power policy, and the failure of joint enterprises in the electrical industries. These points all proved of great interest in drawing a comparison with Japan. Leonard S. Reich dealt with General Electric's electric lamp enterprise. He described the history of the company and showed that a high profit was obtained by promotion of its technical superiority through patent and marketing strategies. He indicated that General Electric had a cooperative direct investment policy with regard to Europe, as well as acted as a mediator for those European corporations that formed the international cartel. He also made reference to the opposition shown by the company to the entry of Japanese corporations into foreign markets.

As is usual at these conferences, a comment and response were added at the end of each paper, so as to adequately give the reader an impression of the contents, direction, and atmosphere of the discussions. These were in fact revised to a greater or lesser degree in accordance with the contents of the debates themselves. A summary of the final discussion is included as a final chapter.

As has been indicated, it is to be hoped that the business history approach to the study of international cartels will be built on in the future. In this sense we, as project leaders, are very pleased that in this volume we have gathered together papers in which firsthand data has been used to produce interesting new case studies. Moreover, the balance of intellectual cooperation and rivalry with regard to area and type of industry as presented in the papers has adequately met our expectations. One of the results to come out of the papers is the emergence of a type of international comparison made by using the case of international cartels. For example, comparisons were made between "minor European powers" and Japan: Japan and Italy in the case of dyestuffs; Japan and France, as well as the Benelux countries, in the case of nitrogen fertilizers (within this industry France was classified as a minor power); and Japan and Italy in the electrical industry. Therefore, this provides extremely interesting material for comparative studies. Apart from this, discussion points were raised regarding the differing responses of Japan and the United States to Europe, which was at the center of the international cartels' activities. This kind of international comparison can form not merely a static examination, but can be given a degree of dynamism by the examination of the changes that occurred relating to the cartels. In this sense, it has an important place in the history of international business relations in general.

However, there is some justification in pointing out that, as the business history approach to international cartels has so far been a relatively unexplored area, research in this field, though interesting, also poses certain problems. The degree of success achieved by the authors of this volume must therefore be entrusted to the judgment of the readers. Whatever the response may be, we hope that our approach, in showing various actual examples of international cartels, will provide the groundwork for cooperation and rivalry, in a positive sense, for future research in this field.

International Cartels in Business History

Terushi Hara and Akira Kudō

I. Introduction

This volume examines the evolution of international cartels by focusing on the process of organization as well as rationalization of manufacture and sales in corporations in different countries through the international cooperation and competition that took place. As a definition of cartels we propose the following: "Cartels have been defined as voluntary agreements among independent enterprises in a single industry or closely related industries with the purpose of exercising a monopolistic control of the market."[1] The United Nations, Department of Economic Affairs, gives the following definition of international cartels: "International cartels are of the same nature and serve essentially the same purpose [as national cartels], with the qualification that the contracting parties are located in two or more countries and may be either single firms or groups of firms already combined into national cartels."[2]

Within international cartels, there are both raw materials cartels and manufactured goods cartels. An examination of manufactured goods cartels or, more precisely, industrial cartels is undertaken because raw materials cartels are in many cases affected by the geographical, political, and diplomatic factors of the countries where the raw materials are produced. In contrast, manufactured goods cartels are more strongly influenced by operational factors, such as production technology and terms of sale. Therefore, manufactured goods cartels prove more suitable for a historical analysis of the management of international cartels.

We have limited ourselves to international cartels from the interwar period, the 1920s and 1930s, because it is within the process of economic reconstruction after the First World War, in the 1920s, that the full-scale establishment of international cartels can first be observed. Moreover, this was the period when the world economy began to be reorganized through competition and cooperation on an international level. One of the factors behind the emergence of the international cartels was the imbalance that arose between production and consumption. This was due to the accumulation of surplus production power exceeding demand, caused by the construction or enlargement of production facilities to meet the urgent demand that arose during the war. The international nitrogen and dyestuffs cartels are two examples of cartels that arose in this way. Additionally, with the progressive internationalization of economic activity, a number of international agreements concerning patent rights and production method exchanges were made. Therefore, international cartels were set up in order to assist in the implementation of these international agreements. The incandescent electric light bulb cartel is representative of this type. Furthermore, corporations in various countries, confronted with the intensification of international competition, set up international cartels in order to preserve their domestic markets for domestic producers. The railroad materials cartel is one such example. In terms of the research that has been carried out up to now, analysis that has been done on the managerial history of the international cartels remains insufficient. Full-scale research on this theme remains a task for the future. However, on the basis of the little research that has actually been done, we wish to consolidate what basic knowledge is available to enable debate to take place at this conference.[3]

II. Some Selected Topics on International Cartels

1. Geographical Distribution

There are no conclusive figures available on the number of international cartels in the interwar period. Haussmann and Ahearn emphasized that from 1929 to 1937 42% of all international trade was under the control of international cartels.[4] Hexner considered that the ratio of major products under the control of international cartels in 1937 was more or less the same.[5] At this stage, we cannot specify the total number of international cartels, but we can offer conjectures on the situation as regards their ratio by location, through an understanding of the regional distribution of trade. The ratio by area of export of industrial raw materials, semimanufactured and manufactured goods for 1926, 1929, and 1935 is shown in Table 1. According to this, the percentage of manufactured goods exported in 1935 was 70% for Europe, 13% for America, and just over 17% for the rest of the world. This is, therefore, the reason for the international cartels being centered in Europe at this time.[6] The importance of the European countries becomes even clearer if we look at the number of cartel members by country, as shown in Table 2.[7]

TABLE 1 Share of Europe and the United States in the Total Value of World Exports of Industrial Products, 1925, 1929, and 1935 (%)

Area	Raw materials and semi-manufactured goods			Manufactured goods		
	1925	1929	1935	1925	1929	1935
Continental Europe	24	29	31	47	49	49
Great Britain	5	5	6	25	20	21
Total (Europe)	29	34	37	72	69	70
United States	20	18	15	14	18	13
Rest of the World	51	48	48	14	13	17
Total (World)	100	100	100	100	100	100

Source: United Nations, Department of Economic Affairs, *International Cartels* (New York, 1947), p. 3.

TABLE 2 Number of International Cartel Member Corporations by Country

Country	No. of Participants		
	Direct	Indirect or Partial	Total
France (and colonies)	67	2	69
Germany	57		57
Great Britain	31	9	40
Switzerland	25		25
Holland	20		20
Belgium	20		20
Czechoslovakia	17	3	20
Norway	16	1	17
Sweden	16		16
Austria	15	3	18
Italy	15	1	16
Poland	13	2	15
Finland	10	1	11
Yugoslavia	9	1	10
Hungary	8	3	11
United States	8	3	11
Japan	2	2	4

Source: Laurence Ballande, *Essai d'Etude Monographique et Statistique sur les Ententes Economiques Internationales* (Paris, 1937), pp. 312–13.

2. Membership and Administration

By classifying the international cartels according to differences in the form of membership, the following three forms emerge. The first is where participation was by individual corporations from different countries; the alum cartel, which was set up in 1901 and re-established in 1926, is an example of this type. The second form is where participation was by domestic cartels of different countries; the iron and steel cartel is one such example. The third is where participation was by various forms of organizations such as domestic cartels, domestic or foreign trusts and/or individual corporations; the potassium and rayon cartels are examples of this form.[8]

The administration of the international cartels was entrusted either to a body formed of representatives from the member corporations or to an organization legally independent of the member corporations and their agreement. In the first, day-to-day business was dealt with by the organization's executive office in accordance with decisions made at regular meetings of the members' representatives. More important business was decided at general meetings. This was a system that worked as far as the fixing of minimum price levels and the protecting of domestic markets and such matters were concerned. However, where it had to deal with production quotas, apportionment of orders, and other matters relating to accounting or indemnity payments, the fact that the adjudicators were also, as representatives of the member corporations, interested parties, made impartial administration difficult. This was where the second administrative form, where administration was carried out by groups that were more or less legally independent from the member companies, was more effective. The Société Anonyme Suisse of the aluminum cartel and the Société Allemande GmbH of the rayon cartel are two examples of this. Moreover, within the second form there were cases of centralized consolidated control organs, such as Phoebus of the incandescent electric light bulb industry, being formed by the international cartels so as to be able to perform the administrative functions required. There were also cases of joint sales organizations (comptoir de vente), such as the Convention Internationale de l'Azote in Basel, being set up.

3. Functions of International Cartels

These agreements can be classified on the basis of the following five functions. (1) Agreements regarding production, where a fixed standard rate was set for production; such methods as the individual enterprise production quota, the banning of installation of new equipment in factories, and the payment of compensation to firms whose production had been cut were all used to achieve this. (2) Agreements regarding sales, which were first of all designed to protect the domestic markets of the member corporations and block the advance of foreign corporations into them. The methods used to achieve this can also be said to have served as substitutes for the setting up of import quota systems and protective tariff duties by governments. Furthermore, the export markets were divided among the cartel's member companies. This could be done either by area or amount of exports, but usually a combination of the two was used. In other words, it became a system whereby the export volume and the export markets of a said product were distributed among the cartel members. Where these sales agreements went further, joint sales organizations (comptoir de vente) were set up. These organizations collected together the orders received and distributed them among the member corporations. (3) Price adjustment agreements, which used the methods of compulsory price-setting and indicative price agreements. These agreements included export price-setting, market price-setting by country, and price-setting for specific markets, etc. In addition to this, the method used for distribution of profits between member corporations can be thought of as having the same effect as indirect price adjustments. (4) Agreements concerning inventories, which included cases of buying in of stock by the cartels or stockpiling by member companies, used in order to prevent price falls caused by excess production. (5) Agreements concerning product quality and rationalization, which provided for patent and technology exchanges, joint surveys, and the creation of research bodies.[9]

4. Legal System

If we take a look at cartel legislation, we can see that in the 1930s European countries, which were restricted by the size of their domestic markets in comparison with the American one, showed a fairly tolerant attitude regarding international cartels. In the majority of countries, rather than trying to actually make the cartels illegal, attempts were made to prevent abuses of the system in advance. Additionally, when abuses did occur, efforts to eradicate them were made.[10] Against this background, the most important historical fact to be noted is that in European countries in the 1930s, the general trend was not just to approve the setting up of domestic cartels, but going a step further, to in fact make it compulsory. This change in stance from prohibiting to allowing, and then enforcing, the setting up of domestic cartels, can be said to be what caused the acceleration of the formation of the international cartels.

Before 1930, only Germany and Norway had special cartel laws. But in the 1930s, the following countries set up cartel enforcement laws: Japan (1931), Italy and Hungary (1932), Czechoslovakia and Poland (1933),

Yugoslavia (1934), Belgium and Holland (1935), Bulgaria (1936), Romania and Denmark (1937). Additionally, in Germany the 1923 Cartel Law was revised in 1933, and a cartel enforcement law was set up. In France in 1935, a motion for the Code Marchandean was adopted by the Chamber of Deputies. This organization of markets by each country, through the legal enforcement of cartels, certainly facilitated the formation of international cartels.[11]

5. The Economic Effects

The economic effects of international cartels fall into three categories, as defined by research done by the United Nations, Department of Economic Affairs, namely: effects on cost, effects on price, and effects on trade.[12] International cartels, in contrast to multinational corporations, were formed through agreements between independent corporations and as such did not include a unified cost policy. The membership in cartels of high-cost producers meant that profit had to be obtained by the distribution of markets and price-setting. For lower-cost producers, the elimination of these inefficient producers would have been more beneficial, but as long as they remained members of the international cartels, this proved difficult. Therefore, within those industries in which cartels were formed, high costs were generally maintained. However, at the level of individual enterprises, this was not necessarily the case. Even where temporary price-setting was carried out, those companies that had the desire and capacity to do so tried to reduce costs in order to increase profitability. They usually did so through the implementation of technical advances. Moreover, the economies on advertising through elimination of competition, the reduction of transportation expenses through the distribution of markets, the setting up of joint sales bodies, and so on also had cost-saving effects. International cartels promoted technical progress through the exchange of patents, licenses, and research data. Examples can be seen of international cartels trying to spread new technology and technological improvements among their member corporations as rapidly as possible. These cost-saving effects first became possible where the international cartels had set up central organs from which directives could be given. In the cartel industries as a whole, however, the general result was one of rising costs.

Following this, let us consider the effect on prices. This differed according to whether the international cartel possessed export quotas that were not accompanied by a regional division of the export markets, or whether they were market distribution cartels. International cartels that had export quotas in most cases had a common price policy. The ways of determining sales prices varied. One was to impose a uniform export price on the markets of all member corporations (as in the case of aluminum, mercury, tin plate, phosphate, etc.), while another was to fix the sales price in each export market separately (as in steel cartels). Alternatively, the desired price level could be brought about not by directly fixing the sales price, but by production policies. Within cartels in general, sales prices showed a constant tendency to rise in order to cover the costs of the highest cost producer.

The effect on sales prices of cartels that operated on a market distribution system is as follows. Within these cartels, the system used was one of dividing domestic markets among domestic producers and export markets among the member corporations. The decision on the sales price in the apportioned export market was left up to each individual enterprise; there was no existence of a common price policy. Therefore, according to the degree of monopoly enjoyed by the cartels, price differences arose.

Finally, we have the effects on trade. First, there were cases where international cartels protected internal markets for their domestic producers and prevented the entry of products from other countries' cartels. In such cases, domestic markets were even better protected than through the imposition of tariffs, and the monopolistic position of domestic corporations was further strengthened. Second, we have cases where import quantity limitation agreements were combined with licensing systems, thereby allowing for technical exchanges. Third, agreements over distribution of export markets strengthened the monopoly of corporations in the markets which had been apportioned to them. The countries that were on the receiving end of this, however, suffered difficulties as regards domestic production, and this created unfavorable conditions for their domestic consumers. Fourth, export quota cartels, since competition in terms of product quality remained among the member corporations, in many cases pursued technical innovation rather than aimed for mass production enabling price competition. Finally, if we look at the connection between international cartels and tariff barriers, we can see that corporations from newly industrializing nations in some cases used the threat of protective tariff barriers in their negotiations over membership of the cartels.[13]

6. Subjects Discussed at the Conference

We propose the following subjects concerning international cartels for study and analysis in this volume.

(1) We must describe as accurately as possible the actual facts relating to the research subject of each paper presented here, namely, the various

international cartels. In other words, the production agreements, sales quota agreements, price agreements, technological agreements, and other concrete matters relating to international cartels and their methods of administration.

(2) We need to analyze the relation between domestic and international cartels. In other words, how domestic industries responded to international cartels, the process by which domestic corporations were organized into domestic cartels, and how the latter participated in the international cartels; or in contrast to this, the process by which domestic companies banded together against the international cartels.

(3) There is a need to analyze the effect of the international cartels on the management of domestic corporations. There is also a necessity to clarify the kind of influence not only domestic but also international cartels had on the running of individual companies, illustrating our points as far as possible with actual examples.

(4) There is a need to explain the response of legal systems, governments, industry, and the labor force of each country to international cartels. In addition, it is also necessary to examine the effects of the policies prohibiting cartels in some countries and allowing and regulating them in others, plus the endemic differences in each country's business climate on the management of corporations.

(5) There is a need for an analysis of the effectiveness of international cartels, as well as a requirement to show clearly how the production, sales, technical improvements, etc., of a country changed with the setting up of the cartels.

(6) We must examine not only the cooperative relationships between the corporations of countries within the cartels' areas, but also the competitive aspects of the free market and cartel-free areas.

III. International Cartels and Japan

The above is thus a consolidation of basic facts known about international cartels in the 1920s and 1930s, including the work of past scholars. While fully recognizing that they were above all a European phenomenon, we wish to examine themes concerning the international cartels as looked at from the point of view of Japan, at that time a newly industrializing nation.

1. Regional Characteristics—Japan, the First NIE

A high economic growth rate was one of the characteristic features of modern Japan. Between the two world wars, Japan's annual growth rate surpassed 4%, which was the highest growth figure for any country in the world at that time. Moreover, in terms of speed of industrialization, Japan, together with the countries of Eastern Europe, also stands out. It seized the First World War as an opportunity to begin heavy and chemical industrialization, and the pace of this did not slacken even during the Depression. Japan can thus be said to be the first NIE.[14]

The second salient feature was the strength of economic nationalism. In the 1920s, in Japan, as in other countries, the policy line followed was one of relatively free trade, and the prevalent attitude was one that welcomed direct investment by European and American firms. However, at the same time, policy measures to protect domestic industries, such as imposition of customs duties and limits on the quantity of imports, were also implemented. Moreover, various restrictions were placed on the management rights that could be assumed by European and American companies with respect to enterprises based in Japan. Moving into the 1930s, we find increasing trade protectionism, and the tone changes to one favoring exclusion of direct investment in Japan.[15] Against this background of increasing economic nationalism, Japanese corporations, which formed the backbone of Japan in its emergence as the first NIE, began to strongly assert their independence, both technically and in managerial terms, of European and American corporations. Moving from domination of the domestic market to advance into the Asian market, these Japanese companies became the new challengers to the old order of international cartels.

2. Industrial Characteristics—The Chemical and Electrical Equipment Industries
Taking the chemical and electrical equipment industries as examples of the new industries, even at first glance we can see the existence of distinct differences between the two. First of all, within the chemical industry the protection of technology by a patents system proved rather ineffective. Therefore, enterprises in this industry sought to achieve overseas expansion by exports and licensing rather than by direct investment. In connection with this came the spread of the comprehensive international cartel network worldwide. European companies were the main force in this with I.G. Farbenindustrie (I.G. Farben) at the center, to which were added American corporations.

In contrast to this, within the electrical equipment industry, in addition to exports and licensing, fairly active direct investment and production overseas were carried out, backed up by a viable patents system. American corporations were drawn into the international cartels within this industry too, but these cartels did not have the power of their counterparts in the chemical industry. This was related to the fact that General Electric and the other American corporations within the industry were in fact ahead of the European companies.[16]

3. Vertical Type and Horizontal Type

As well as considering the characteristic features of the country and the two industries, we would now like to give a typology of the kinds of relationships that existed between the international cartels and the Japanese market and Japanese corporations.

In one type of relationship, international cartels and/or a few members of international cartels made individual agreements or settlements with Japanese companies. This is called the vertical type. (See Figure 1.) This type can often be observed in the chemical industry. It did not involve direct investment, but instead the spreading of the intricate net of the international cartels still wider. European and American corporations made individual agreements with leading Japanese companies with respect to the Japanese and Asian markets so that they could gain supremacy in the Japanese market by using these firms and at the same time apply the brakes to Japanese exports to the Chinese and, more broadly, to the East and Southeast Asian markets.

On the other hand, in the electrical equipment industry, where direct investment played a more important role, relations with Japanese companies were more or less governed, or at least regulation was attempted, through direct investment channels. Consequently, within this industry, vertical-type agreements regarding Japanese corporations and the Japanese market do not have much significance. But there were cases of European and American companies reaching accords over the Japanese and Asian market without the inclusion of Japanese companies. These were either in the form of links in the international cartel structure or separate special agreements. They were in both cases of the horizontal type.[17]

In other words, vertical-type agreements were those formed with Japanese companies with regard to the Japanese and Asian markets, and

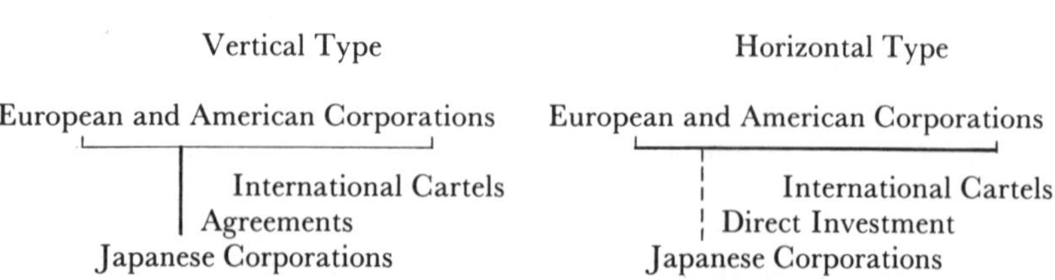

Fig. 1 Vertical Type and Horizontal Type.

horizontal-type agreements were those concerning the Japanese market formed between the international cartels' member companies. Actually, there were also agreements that were a mixture of the two types. Provided that the agreements can be recognized as deriving from one type or the other, they have been included here.

4. Seven Case Studies

Presented here as case studies within the chemical industry are dyestuffs, fertilizers, soda, and synthetic oil; and, within the electrical equipment industry, incandescent light bulbs, heavy electrical equipment, and telephones. These have been selected as being the most important examples both quantitatively and qualitatively, as well as the most representative from within their industries. Moreover, in all cases an international cartel or corresponding structure existed within the relevant industry. (For each case, see Figure 2.)

Dyestuffs. In August 1926, a gentleman's agreement was made between I.G. Farben and the Japanese dyestuffs industry. This was named the Saitō-Waibel Agreement after its signatories. The main points contained in this agreement were the banning in principle of exports to Japan of products that could be domestically produced, and the free export, as a general rule, of those products such as indigo that could not. The agreement thereby laid down a kind of division of labor within the industry. Thus an agreement had been drawn up between I.G. Farben and Japanese companies with regard to the Japanese market. This agreement was an individual one made by I.G. Farben, but if we take into consideration the fact that the company held by far the largest share in the world dyestuffs trade, this agreement can be considered as a vertical-type one. The real reason that I.G. Farben had independently entered into this agreement with the Japanese, and at an early stage in comparison with those developments in other industrial sectors, was closely linked to the fact that the Japanese government had promptly put the import permit system targeting German products into effect early on.[18]

Meanwhile, in Europe, following the German-French agreement made in November 1927, an agreement between Germany, France, and Switzerland was made in April 1929, thereby establishing a three-party international cartel.[19] This cartel very rapidly joined in concerted action with relation to Japan. In October of the same year, the export price to Japan was raised uniformly by 5%. However, Japanese corporations did not follow suit. This was because the growth of the Japanese dyestuffs market, affected by a domestic financial crisis in 1927 and the Depression in 1929,

(1) Dyestuffs—Vertical Type
Dyestuffs Cartel, I.G. Farben and American Corporations

        Saitō-Waibel Agreement
        Mitsui Indigo Agreement
        Naphthol Agreement
Japanese Corporations

(2) Ammonium Sulfate—Vertical Type
Convention Internationale de l'Azote

        Domestic and Foreign Ammonium
        Sulfate Agreement
Japanese Corporations

(3) Soda—Vertical Type (+Horizontal Type)
ICI, Belgian Solvay, and ALKASSO

                (Accords relating to world market)
        Price Agreement on Soda Lime
Asahi Glass and Nippon Soda

(4) Synthetic Oil—Horizontal Type
I.G. Farben, Standard Oil of New Jersey, Royal Dutch Shell, and ICI

                International Patent and Technology Pool
                Accord on Licensing to Japan
        (Licensing)
Japanese Corporations

(5) Incandescent Electric Light Bulbs—Horizontal Type (+ Vertical Type)
European and American Corporations

                General Patent and Business Development
                Agreement
        British-Japanese Agreement
        Direct Investment (GE-Tokyo Denki)
Japanese Corporations

(6) Heavy Electrical Equipment—Horizontal Type
European and American Corporations

                International Notification and Compensation
                Agreement
        Direct Investment and/or Licensing (GE-Shibaura,
        Westinghouse-Mitsubishi, Siemens-Fuji)
Japanese Corporations

(7) Telephones—Horizontal Type
European and American Corporations

                Western—Siemens Agreement
        Direct Investment (Western-Nippon Denki, Siemens-Fuji, Fujitsu)
Japanese Corporations

Fig. 2   Seven Cases.

had exhibited a slowdown. Under these circumstances, Japanese dyestuff corporations were able to compete even more vigorously for a share of the market. As a result of this, the share of the three-party cartel fell. Thus it was made clear that in circumstances such as these, the ability of even an international cartel to cope was limited.[20]

At this time exports of European companies to Japan were showing a downward trend. This was caused by the fall of the yen following the re-imposition of a ban on the export of gold in December 1931. In addition, one after the other, Nihon Senryō Seizō (Japan Dyestuffs Manufacturing Co.) and Mitsui Mining Co. were successful in developing new products. Thus the international cartels and their member corporations were forced to find new ways to deal with the situation. One way was by intensifying efforts to form vertical-type relationships through the concluding of agreements with Japanese corporations. In March 1935, I.G. Farben concluded the Variamine Blue Agreement with Nihon Senryō Seizō. This was later ratified by three Swiss firms. By this agreement, Nihon Senryō Seizō recognized I.G. Farben's patent and agreed not to carry out exports of identical products. As vicarious compensation, an accord was obtained on sales quotas for the Japanese market; for Naphthol AS the share was I.G. Farben 32% and Nihon Senryō Seizō 68%, while for Variamine Blue-B the figures were reversed. At the same time, the sales price was to be equal. Thus a vertical-type agreement came into being. This agreement lasted until 1941.[21]

I.G. Farben also made the Astraphloxine Agreement with Nihon Senryō in February 1934. The main points of this ran parallel to those in the Variamine Blue Agreement. In return for relinquishing exports, Nihon Senryō Seizō got a 50% share of the Japanese market and I.G. Farben the remaining 50%. This agreement lasted until the end of 1939.[22]

A vertical-type relationship was formed also between I.G. Farben, the international dyestuffs cartel, and Mitsui Mining. First, with regard to sulfur black dye, in April 1931 the three-party cartel made an agreement with Mitsui Mining's representative, Mitsui & Co., Ltd., regarding the quantity and price of exports to China. The American corporation Nacco (National Aniline and Chemical Co.) and Du Pont de Nemours & Co. were also drawn into this agreement, which lapsed as early as the end of 1933.

In addition, in October 1931 I.G. Farben concluded an agreement with Mitsui & Co., which was henceforth to be the sole representative of Mitsui Mining with regard to alizarine blue. The agreement concerned the division of the Japanese market, and at first this was apportioned at a ratio of 60% to I.G. Farben and 40% to Mitsui & Co. This agreement was revised again and again, and, although it lasted until 1940, during its term the market ratio was in fact reversed to I.G. Farben 40%, Mitsui & Co. 60%.[23]

The biggest problem remained indigo. In April 1926, Mitsui Mining finally managed to achieve its aim of the industrialization of indigo production. Then, in October 1929, the company managed to obtain a subsidy for the promotion of dyestuffs manufacture. Thus construction of a factory was begun in February 1931. Its products were finally put on the market in the latter half of 1932. Meanwhile, Nacco and Du Pont, which had already succeeded in the development of indigo immediately after the First World War, now embarked in rapid succession on export ventures to the Far East. The four-party cartel concluded a six-party agreement with these two corporations concerning the sales ratio of the Japanese, Chinese, and Far Eastern markets.[24]

In addition to this, the six corporations concluded an agreement with Mitsui Mining in February 1934. This concerned cooperation over the sales price within the Japanese market and the sales ratio, which was to be 25% for the six corporations and 75% for Mitsui Mining. This was a temporary agreement valid until July 1934. Soon after, discussions for the conclusion of a formal agreement took place.[25] At last, in May 1935 a settlement was reached. The formal agreement held Japanese exports to China of indigo (20%) to a three-year total of 96,300 piculs. As vicarious compensation, the six corporations were limited in their exports to Japan.[26] This agreement was extended several times in favor of Mitsui Mining until the end of 1940, but war in Europe broke out before it had expired, and thus Imperial Chemical Industries (ICI) broke the agreement.[27]

Ammonium Sulfate.   In the first half of the 1920s, the first plant and equipment investment boom occurred in Japan, for which Nippon Chisso Hiryō (Japan Nitrogen Fertilizer Co.) and Denki Kagaku Kōgyō (Electrochemical Industries) were mainly responsible, and thus an ammonium sulfate industry was established in Japan. At the end of the decade, there was, on the one hand, a second plant and equipment investment boom, and on the other, an increasing aggressiveness in the export offensive by European and American companies. In August 1930, the Convention Internationale de l'Azote (CIA) was set up, and European firms began to revise their relationships with Japanese companies accordingly. As a result, in December 1930 a proposal for an agreement, known as the Fujiwara-Bosch Agreement Proposal, which mainly concerned sales, was drawn up, but this was not in fact put into effect. Later, in April 1931, a proposal for a Domestic and Foreign Ammonium Sulfate Agreement, with more or less the same contents as the previous agreement, was made, but this also was not put into effect.

In July 1932, the CIA was set up once more, and through this, in March 1934, an agreement regarding domestic and foreign ammonium sulfate was able to at last be made. In it limits were placed on exports to Japan by enterprises belonging to the CIA, while restrictions were also placed on exports by Japanese corporations in terms of quantity, price, and area. This was a vertical-type agreement. It was subsequently re-newed twice. However, I.G. Farben, which considered that exports to Japan would not increase any further, agreed to provide the technology for the Harber-Bosch method to Taki Seihisho (Taki Fertilizer Works) in May 1935. It subsequently agreed to do the same for Nippon Tāru Kōgyō (Nippon Tar Industries, now Mitsubishi Chemical Industries) and a number of other companies.[28]

Soda.   In 1920, an international alkali cartel was organized, mainly by Belgian Solvay, with the participation of Brunner, Mond & Co., and United Alkali Co. As a result of this, market-control rights over the European mainland were given to Solvay and over all other areas to the two British companies, which in December 1926 became Imperial Chemical Industries, ICI. However, in 1919, the ALKASSO Alkali Export Union was set up by American corporations, mainly those using the Solvay process, thereby forcing competition on the British com-panies in the world market. Both sides engaged in a desperate struggle to capture markets outside of Europe until a truce was finally called in February 1924.

The most important markets for Brunner, Mond–ICI were the Asian market centering on Japan and the South American market. Between 1921 and 1924 dumping of magadi soda and soda lime was carried out in competition on the Japanese market, from which Brunner, Mond came out successful. Therefore it made a truce with ALKASSO at about the same time, and they were thus able to face their other competitors in unity. In 1929 they came into confrontation over dumping with the Japanese companies Asahi Glass Co. and Nippon Soda Co.

Meanwhile, in 1929, sales quotas for the world market were decided on between ICI and ALKASSO, and interests were balanced with Belgian Solvay. In 1930, when the Japanese government was making preparations for the application of an antidumping law, ICI entered into a price agree-ment over soda lime with Asahi Glass and Nippon Soda. As a result, a vertical-type relationship was formed. However, this agreement collapsed almost immediately, and dumping began once more, finally ceasing some time after the re-imposition of a ban on the export of gold. Thus a vertical-type relationship was not in fact able to be re-established.

In 1936, ICI, ALKASSO, and Belgian Solvay came to an accord over regional distribution and sales quotas for the world market. Within this the Japanese soda lime market was divided between ICI and ALKASSO at a ratio of 65% and 35%, respectively, thereby establishing a horizontal-type agreement. However, it must be noted that in 1937 imports to Japan fell to zero and thus the quota agreement did not in fact have any substance.[29]

Synthetic Oil.   In 1927, I.G. Farben and Standard Oil of New Jersey made the first agreement over the exchange of hydrogenation processing technology, and the scope of this was considerably extended in November 1929. Later on, Royal Dutch Shell and ICI also entered into this agreement. Moreover, in the early 1930s Standard Oil and Royal Dutch Shell set up the International Hydrogenation Patents Co., Ltd. (IHP), thereby forming an international patents pool. I.G. Farben was eager to provide licenses to Japan, whereas the British and American companies, taking into account the political situation at the time, did not welcome this development. However, they did not express strong opposition in the period up until the summer of 1939. In fact, in July 1939 I.G. Farben and IHP came to an accord regarding licensing to Japan (fixing licensing fees and determining obligations regarding the exchange of know-how), thereby establishing a kind of horizontal relationship. Thus for a time it seemed as if I.G. Farben would succeed in its licensing plans. However, opposition was demonstrated to this by the Japanese Navy, which was developing its own production method. Starting with the failure of talks with South Manchurian Railways Co. in 1935, I.G. Farben faced many frustrations until it managed to hold negotiations with Ogura Oil Co. from 1938 to 1939. Furthermore, Standard Oil and Royal Dutch Shell took the chance given them by the outbreak of the war in Europe to harden their stance against Japan. Thus provision of licenses by I.G. Farben became an absolute impossibility.

For I.G. Farben, the directives of the German government to cooperate with Japan held more importance than I.G.'s consideration with regard to the British and American corporations. Thus at the end of the war, in January 1945, it finally managed to conclude some kind of contract for the provision of technology with the Imperial Japanese Army. But this contract proved to have very little basis in reality, and this was the end of this particular episode.[30]

Incandescent Electric Light Bulbs.　In 1924 an incandescent electric light bulb international cartel was formed through the General Patent and Business Development Agreement. During the Depression, four business groups in this industry were set up one after the other in Japan, thereby organizing most of the small-to-medium-sized companies in Japan into some kind of grouping. In October 1933, these joined to form the Japan Electric Light Bulb Industrial Association Federation. The largest corporation outside of this federation, Tokyo Denki (Tokyo Electric Co., General Electric Co.'s subsidiary), finally joined it in November 1934. Following this, the organization continued to grow.

From about 1931, Japanese exports began to grow rapidly, through the efforts of the smaller enterprises (Tokyo Denki was forbidden by an agreement made with General Electric in 1919 from exporting to countries other than China), and thus trade friction arose in various parts of the globe. In May 1934, an agreement was made with certain British companies, the main point of which was the restriction of exports to Britain to 33.8 million units for a one-year period starting in February 1934. In fact, the actual figures went far in excess of this limit. In February 1935, Phoebus, a syndicate set up in 1924, made an application to join the international cartel; in spite of negotiations, this never came to pass. Therefore, the vertical relationship formed within this industrial sector did not develop fully. Moreover, one of the characteristics of the relationship that developed here was that it had tried to limit Japanese exports more than in the other cases examined.[31]

Heavy Electrical Equipment.　The international arm of General Electric Co., namely, International General Electric Co. (IGE), made an agreement with its subsidiary company in Japan, Shibaura Seisakusho (Shibaura Manufacturing Co.) in 1919, thereby recognizing the latter's exclusive rights with regard to the Japanese market. Siemens and Westinghouse Electric & Manufacturing Co., on the other hand, concluded an agreement in 1924 over exchange of patents, technology, and division of markets. Through this agreement, Siemens took the markets of Germany, Austria, and the three Baltic states, while Westinghouse took America and Canada. All other areas were to be open to competition. Regarding the Japanese market, the exclusive rights of the various subsidiary companies, including Fuji Denki Seizō (Fuji Electric Manufacturing Co.), established in August 1923, and Mitsubishi Denki (Mitsubishi Electric Co.), which had made a patent agreement with Westinghouse in November 1923, were recognized. Thus the respective subsidiaries of General Electric, Siemens, and Westinghouse in Japan, Shibaura Seisakusho, Fuji Denki, and Mitsubishi Denki, were all able to obtain exclusive rights within the Japanese heavy industrial equipment market. However, on the other hand, Japanese subsidiaries were still limited to the Japanese market in the context of "export terms." Control over the Japanese market was thereby exercised mainly by direct investment.

During the period of the Depression, in December 1930, General Electric, Westinghouse, Allgemeine Elektrizitäts-Gesellschaft, Siemens, plus the British firm English Electric Co., Ltd., and the Swiss company Brown Boveri and Cie. entered into a global sales agreement, which went under the name of the International Notification and Compensation Agreement (INCA). Japan and Southern Manchuria were areas not covered by this agreement, and therefore it did not have any direct influence on Japanese companies. However, the markets into which Japanese enterprises had finally begun to advance, namely, China, India, Soviet Asia, and Southeast Asia, were put under the control of the European and American companies. By carrying out direct investment, certain European and American companies had managed to spread the web of control over the Japanese market through an ambiguous form of horizontal-type agreement.

Around this time, General Electric, Westinghouse, Siemens, etc. flinched from engaging in fierce competition within the Japanese market. They hoped that Japanese companies would cooperate by price agreements, corporate mergers, and holding companies. Particular attention was given to the examination of a proposal for a merger by the Special Bureau for Industrial Rationalization of the Ministry of Commerce and Industry. This was not in fact put into effect. Efforts towards cooperation, however, achieved success in May 1931 through the achievement of an agreement on sales quotas, prices, and market outlets between Shibaura Seisakusho, Mitsubishi Denki, Fuji Denki, and the wholly Japanese Hitachi Seisakusho (Hitachi Manufacturing Co.). This proved to be a great relief to the European and American companies.[32]

Telephones.   The Japanese telephone industry and telephone equipment market began to expand around the turn of the century. In response, the American company Western Electric Co. set up Nippon Electric Gōshi Kaisha (NEC) in 1898, and thus began production in Japan of telephone equipment, using the company's own technology. Nippon Electric was incorporated in the following year, with Western Electric having a stockholding ratio of 54%.[33] In contrast to this, the German company Siemens continued its response in the form of exports. This caution owed to the fact that the company occupied only second place in the telephone equipment field, as well as to the fact that it felt Japan to be in psychological terms as well as in actual distance, "the furthest place on earth."[34]

Before the First World War, Western Electric and Siemens had made an agreement regarding division of the Japanese market and technical cooperation. This was eventually renewed by the two companies after the war, in 1921. The main points of the revised agreement were, first, the division of the Japanese market at a ratio of 10% to Siemens and 90% to Western Electric, to be achieved by the end of 1925. The second point concerned technical cooperation including cross-licensing. The third point was that this agreement was treated as a link in the two companies' global cooperation strategy, and it was thus to run until the end of 1935.[35]

Although this agreement did not allow for diversified expansion, as would have been the case had an international cartel been formed by the two companies, it can be included within the definition of horizontal relationships as given here. Western Electric was in fact carrying out direct investment in Japanese companies, and Siemens upon tying up the agreement also plunged straight into a course of direct investment at the beginning of the 1930s. So direct investment took the place of exports as the way of entering into the Japanese market. Thus it can be assumed that it was hoped that a horizontal-type agreement would play a role in achieving direct investment.

Of the seven examples given here, the agreements within the dyestuffs, ammonium sulfate, and soda industries fall mainly into the vertical-relation category, whereas those in the incandescent electric bulb, heavy electrical equipment, telephone, and synthetic oil industries fall largely into the horizontal-relation category. Therefore, apart from the case of synthetic oil, the chemical industry was made up of vertical and the electrical equipment industry of horizontal relationships. The reasons that the relations in the synthetic oil industry were of the horizontal type are that in this case exports had virtually no significance and an international patents pool existed within the industry, as was the case in the electrical equipment industry.

IV. International Cartels and Direct Investment
The typology of horizontal and vertical relations was evolved through a perception of the features characterizing the Japanese market, namely, rapid growth and the rise of economic nationalism, and the industrial characteristics of the chemical and electrical industries. Taking a different perspective, this could be said to represent the two responses of the European and American companies to Japan's challenge through high growth

Table 3 Challenge and Response

Challenge \ Response	Vertical Type	Horizontal Type	Case
A High Growth Rate	Ineffective	Effective	Japan 1920s
B Economic Nationalism	Effective	Ineffective	
A + B	Ineffective	Ineffective	Japan 1930s
Case	Chemical Ind.	Electrical Ind.	

and nationalism. These responses were the vertical relationship as represented by international cartels and the horizontal relationship as represented by direct investment. If we judge the effectiveness of the responses from the above analysis, we can arrange the data as in Table 3. In the 1920s the Japanese challenge was intensified due to a high economic growth rate against which the horizontal response proved effective, whereas the vertical response was not. The vertical-type response of international cartels should have been effective against the challenge of economic nationalism, but the situation in Japan in the 1930s was a combination of high growth and economic nationalism, where both vertical and horizontal responses were rendered ineffective.

To paraphrase this, in order to deal with the breaking up of the control networks of the multinational companies, especially those of German origin, due to the cataclysmic movements of the world economy caused by the First World War, a need arose for the reformation of the international cartels based in the West, or rather Western Europe, in the 1920s. The high growth rate and rise of companies in the peripheral area, namely, the East, especially Eastern Europe and East Asia, posed a challenge to the old order of the international cartels. In response to this, the Western European companies tried to draw American corporations, on the one hand, and the companies of the Eastern European nations and Japan, on the other, into the international cartel net.

As a part of the "eastern world," the Japanese market was mainly treated as a freely competitive and cartel-free zone. Therefore, within the Japanese market competition with European and American companies was added to the competition between Japanese firms. The former practiced putting external pressure on and dumping against the Japanese heavy and chemical industry corporations, which had suddenly expanded during the First World War. However, these corporations had the power to survive such offensives.

The Western companies had two ways of dealing with this. In the case of the electric industry, in which there was direct investment in Japan, the response was for Western companies to establish agreements among themselves with regard to the Japanese market, thus creating a horizontal relationship. This was, in fact, successful. In the case of the chemical industry, in which there was virtually no direct investment, the response was for international cartels to make separate agreements with Japanese companies, in other words to seek to achieve cooperation through a vertical relation. However, this achieved no success in the 1920s. Within the dyestuffs industry, the Saitō-Waibel Agreement could be said to be an exception to this. But even in this case, when the international cartel raised its export prices in 1928, the Japanese corporations did not follow suit. Thus the cartel's share of the market fell. This clearly shows us that the power of control that international cartels could exercise over the Japanese corporations had its limitations.

In the 1930s economic nationalism, as well as a high growth rate, had a hand in the challenge posed by Japan. The Japanese market became restricted and systematized by economic nationalism. In response to this, the international cartels that had achieved steady success in the West tried to make or actually made individual agreements with Japanese corporations. However, these companies, using a high growth rate as their weapon, enlarged their share of the market and were not in fact drawn into the net of the international cartels. An illustration of this situation is shown in the dyestuff industry. Even in industries such as the electrical industry, which had been subject to direct investment, faced with the pressures of nationalism and the desire for independence of subsidiary companies in Japan, foreign companies were forced to make a gradual retreat.

We have examined the relationships that emerged between the Japanese corporations and international cartels as they were formed within the wider context of relations between Japan and European and American corporations. Moreover, we have divided these relationships into horizontal and vertical types. In view of our emphasis on this definition, we must first discuss why these two types came into being and how these caused differences to arise in the business performances of individual corporations. More detailed research is necessary to determine whether this is an appropriate perception of the facts and to determine the reasons for the emergence of differences. Finally, there is a need to examine the relations between multinationals and international cartels. More research still needs to be done on determining whether the two were complementary and whether they possess interchangeable elements or not.

NOTES

1. United Nations, Department of Economic Affairs, *International Cartels* (New York, 1947), p. 1.

2. Ibid., p. 1.

3. The following are some of the works on international cartels that concern our viewpoint. P. Kypriotis, *Les Cartels Internationaux* (Paris, 1936); Laurence Ballande, *Essai d'Etude Monographique et Statistique sur les Ententes Economiques Internationales* (Paris, 1937); E. Hexner, *The International Steel Cartel* (Chapel Hill, N.C., 1943); idem, "International Cartels in the Postwar World," *Southern Economic Journal* (October 1943); a study made for the Subcommittee on War Mobilization of the Committee on Military Affairs, United States Senate, *Economic and Political Aspects of International Cartels* (Washington, D.C., 1944); G.W. Stocking and M.W. Watkins, *Cartels in Action: Case Studies in International Business Diplomacy* (New York, 1946); International Chamber of Commerce, *Competition and Business Agreements*, brochure no. 162 (Paris, 1952); A. Teichova, *An Economic Background to Munich: International Business and Czechoslovakia, 1918–1938* (Cambridge, 1974); E.S. Mason, *Controlling World Trade: Cartels and Commodity Agreements* (Cambridge, Mass., 1946), which was translated into Japanese by Hiraoka Kinnosuke, Kanagawa Tōru, and Motomura Teruo (1977); A. Teichova, M. Lévy-Leboyer, and H. Nussbaum (eds.), *Multinational Enterprises in Historical Perspective* (Cambridge, 1986); A. Teichova, M. Lévy-Leboyer, and H. Nussbaum (eds.), *Historical Studies in International Corporate Business* (Cambridge, 1989); and C.A. Wurm, *International Cartels and Foreign Policy* (Stuttgart, 1989).

4. Frederick Haussmann and Daniel Ahearn, "International Cartels and World Trade: An Explanatory Estimate," *Thought, Fordham University Quarterly*, series no. 1, vol. 19, no. 74 (September 1944): 429, 434, cited by the United Nations, op. cit., p. 2.

5. Ervin Hexner, "International Cartels in the Postwar World," *Southern Economic Journal* (October 1943): 124, cited by the United Nations, op. cit., p. 2.

6. According to the account given in the United Nations, op. cit., pp. 2–3.

7. Ballande, op. cit., pp. 312–13.

8. Kypriotis, op. cit., pp. 39–40.

9. This explanation is according to Ballande, op. cit., chapter 13 (pp. 324–31) and chapter 14 (pp. 332–41).

10. International Chamber of Commerce, op. cit., p. 22.

11. United Nations, op. cit., pp. 10–13.

12. This classification into three types is according to the United Nations, ibid., pp. 12–22.

13. Ibid., pp. 12–22.

14. Nakamura Takafusa, *Senkanki Nihon Keizai Seichō no Bunseki* (An Analysis of the Japanese Economy in the Interwar Period) (Tokyo, 1971), p. 3.

15. Miwa Ryōichi, "1926 Nen Kanzei Kaisei no Rekishiteki Ichi" (The 1926 Revision of Tariffs in a Historical Perspective), in Sakai Takahito et al. (eds.), *Nihon Shihon Shugi: Tenkai to Ronri* (Capitalism in Japan: Development and Reason)

(Tokyo, 1978); Masaru Udagawa, "Business Management and Foreign-Affiliated Companies in Japan before World War II," in Takeshi Yuzawa and Masaru Udagawa (eds.), *Foreign Business in Japan before World War II* (Tokyo, 1990).

16. Hoshimi Uchida, "Western Big Business and the Adoption of New Technology in Japan: The Electrical and Chemical Industries 1890–1920," in Akio Okochi and Hoshimi Uchida (eds.), *Development and Diffusion of Technology* (Tokyo, 1980).

17. Within the steel industry, we have an actual example of this type of agreement: namely, the extraordinary agreement concerning exports to Japan of the international wire rod cartel, which was under the jurisdiction of the international crude steel cartel. See the historical data in the possession of Haniel-Archiv, 400 003/4 Walzdraht Japan-Export, 1928–33.

18. Kudō Akira, "I.G. Farben no Tainichi Senryaku: Senryō no Keesu" (I.G. Farben's Japan Strategy: The Case of Dyestuffs), Tokyo Daigaku, *Shakai Kagaku Kiyō*, no. 36 (1987): 14–93. The original historical data is in the Hoechst Archives.

19. Harm G. Schröter, "Cartels as a Form of Concentration in Industry: The Example of the International Dyestuffs Cartel from 1927 to 1939," *German Yearbook on Business History 1988* (1990): 123–28.

20. Kudō, op. cit., p. 166.

21. I.G. Farben an Geigy und CMC vom 4. Juli 1931, Firmenarchiv der CIBA-Geigy; FAG VE/IGK 15; I.G. Farben Control Office of the Decartelization Branch, Economics Division, of the Office of Military Government for Germany (U.S.), *Activities of I.G. Farbenindustrie AG in the Dyestuffs Industry* (1946): 90–91.

22. Ibid., pp. 88–89.

23. I.G. Farben an Schweizer, Französische und Englische Gruppe vom 18./20. Juni 1936, Firmenarchiv der CIBA-Geigy; FAG VE/IGK 15/1; Suzuki Kunio, "Senji Keizai Tōseika no Mitsui Bussan, III" (Mitsui & Co. under the Control of the Wartime Economy, III), *Mitsui Bunko Ronsō*, no. 20 (1986): 211–12, 221. The original material is contained in historical data in the possession of the Mitsui Library.

24. I.G. Farben Control Office, op. cit., pp. 77–85.

25. Suzuki, op. cit., pp. 216–17, 239.

26. Agreement of May 14th, 1935, Firmenarchiv der CIBA-Geigy; FAG VE/ IGK 15/1.

27. I.G. Farben Control Office, op. cit., pp. 86–87.

28. Ōshio Takeshi, "Fujiwara-Bosch Kyōteian to Nihon no Ryūan Kōgyō" (The Fujiwara-Bosch Agreement Proposal and the Japanese Ammonium Sulfate Industry), Meiji Gakuin Daigaku *Keizai Kenkyū*, nos. 49–50 (1978); Hashimoto Jurō, "Ryūan Dokusentai no Seiritsu" (The Establishment of the Ammonium Sulfate Monopolistic System), Tokyo Daigaku *Keizaigaku Ronshū*, vol. 45, no. 4 (1980); Kudō Akira, "I.G. Farben no Tainichi Senryaku: Chisso no Keesu" (I.G. Farben's Japan Strategy: The Case of Nitrogen), Tokyo Daigaku *Shakai Kagaku Kenkyū*, vol. 39, no. 2 (1987); Suzuki Tsuneo, "The Foundation and Amalgamation of Miike Nitrogen Industries Inc. and Toyo Koatsu Industries Inc.," in *Japanese Yearbook on Business History 1987* (1987).

29. Suzuki Tsuneo, "Senkanki Waga Kuni ni Okeru Sōda Kōgyō no Hatten: Asahi Garasu o Chushin ni" (The Development of the Japanese Soda Industry in the Interwar Period: Asahi Glass Co., Ltd.), *Fukuoka Kenshi Kindai Kenkyū Hen Kakuron* (1), 1989.

30. Kudō Akira, "I.G. Farben's Japan Strategy: The Case of Synthetic Oil," in *Japanese Yearbook on Business History 1988* (1989); I.G. Farben Control Office, op. cit., pp. 135–36.

31. Nihon Denkyū Kōgyōkai (ed.), *Nihon Denkyū Kōgyōshi* (A History of Japanese Electric Lamp Industry) (Tokyo, 1963).

32. Hasegawa Shin, "Satsukikai (Jūdenki Karuteru)" (Satsuki Association, the Heavy Electric Equipment Cartel), Hashimoto Jurō and Takeda Haruhito (eds.), *Ryōtaisen Kanki Nihon no Karuteru* (Japanese Cartels in the Interwar Period) (Tokyo, 1985); Yoshida Masaki, "Senzen ni okeru Waga Kuni Denki Sangyō no Kigyōsha Kōdō" (Activities of Japanese Entrepreneurs in the Electrical Equipment Industry in the Prewar Period), *Mita Shōgaku Kenkyū*, vol. 22, no. 5 (1979); Wilfried Feldenkirchen, "Zur Unternehmenspolitik des Hauses Siemens in der Zwischenkriegzeit," in *Zeitschrift für Unternehmensgeschichte*, vol. 33, no. 1 (1988).

33. *Nippon Denki Kabushiki Kaisha Nanajūnenshi* (A Seventy-Year History of NEC Corporation) (Tokyo, 1962), pp. 45–50.

34. Takenaka Tōru, "Siemens-sha no Tokyo Dentō e no Yūshi Keikaku" (Siemens' Plans for Investment in the Tokyo Electric Lighting Co.), *Shirin*, vol. 71, no. 2 (1988): 108. See also idem, "Die Tätigkei der Firma Siemens in Japan vor dem Ersten Weltkrieg," in *Vierteljahrschrift für Sozial- und Wirtschaftsgeschichte*, vol. 76, no. 3 (1989).

35. Aussprache am 22. November 1924 über die künftige Behandlung des Telephongeschäftes in Japan, Siemens Archiv-Akte 20/La 216; *Nihon Denki Kabushiki Kaisha Nanajūnenshi*, op. cit., pp. 174–75.

Comment

Hiroaki Yamazaki

The joint paper by Professors Hara and Kudō surveys the research history of international cartels during the interwar period and raises six points to be discussed in this conference. The paper also examines empirically seven industries in Japan and concludes as follows.

(1) There were two types of international cartels in terms of the relationship with competitors in Japan: horizontal type and vertical type.

(2) Horizontal type means those that consisted of European and American companies and that Japanese companies did not join. Instead, direct investments were made in Japanese companies. We can find this type in electrical equipment industries.

(3) Vertical type means those that consisted of European and American companies, and Japanese companies as well. We can find this type in chemical industries.

(4) As for effectiveness of international cartels, only those of the horizontal type in the 1920s were effective. Those of the vertical type in the 1920s and those of both horizontal type and vertical type in the 1930s were ineffective.

This paper was very stimulating for me because it ventures to raise a hypothesis about the typology of international cartels. I value the paper because it establishes a basis for the discussions in this conference. I would like to express my own view about the typology of international cartels in relation to this paper.

First, Hara and Kudō classify the international cartel in the soda industry as the vertical type, but there were no cases where the international cartel contracted with Japanese companies. According to their manner of classification of international cartels, this should be classified as a horizontal type.

Second, they classify the international cartel in the incandescent electric bulb industry as the horizontal type, but Tokyo Denki, the largest company in this industry, joined the international cartel. We should classify it as the vertical type based on their manner of typology.

                    H. Yamazaki

Third, the rayon industry is excluded from the empirical study in this paper, but this industry has the characteristics of the chemical industry, its scale was much larger than that of any industries examined here, and there was a large international cartel in this industry during the interwar period. The fact to be noted about this industry was that the international cartel did not concern itself with the Japanese market. There was a clear difference in the attitude of international cartels toward Japan between the case of the rayon industry and the cases classified as horizontal type in this paper. In the former, the international cartel did not concern itself with Japan, whereas in the latter, the international cartels invited Japanese companies to join but did not succeed in this. If we take this difference into consideration, there may well have been three types of international cartel: horizontal type 1, which showed no interest in Japan; horizontal type 2, which showed considerable interest in Japan and often invited Japanese companies to join but did not succeed in this; and the vertical type, whose definition is the same as that of Hara and Kudō.

The fourth point of my comments concerns the relationship between international cartels and direct investments in their definition of the horizontal type of international cartel. They say that "these responses were the vertical relationship as represented by international cartels and the horizontal relationship as represented by direct investment." This statement gives the impression that they regarded horizontal-type international cartels in the same light as direct investments. But, needless to say, international cartels and direct investments are different things in themselves. We had better classify cases according to the combination of the type of international cartels and existence or nonexistence of direct investments. When we bear these questions in mind and reclassify eight industries, including the rayon industry, we can construct Table 1. What do you think about these questions and how do you evaluate this table?

Furthermore, I would like to add two comments about the table. First, as for the cases where direct investments were made, we can distinguish between the case of the rayon industry and the other cases. The latter were industries in which the international cartels showed much interest in Japan, and in the rayon industry the international cartel did not show any interest in Japan. In most horizontal-type industries, established *zaibatsu*, such as Mitsui, Mitsubishi, Sumitomo, and Furukawa, set up joint ventures with foreign corporations. In contrast to this, in the rayon industry, a newly developing industrial group, such as Nitchitsu, contracted with a foreign corporation. International cartels showed much interest in Japanese industries led by established *zaibatsu*, but they were not interested in industries led only by a newly developing industrial group.

TABLE 1 Typology of International Cartels

	Direct Investments Dominant	Direct Investments Partial	Direct Investments None
Horizontal 1		Rayon	
Horizontal 2	Heavy Electrical Equipment Telephone Equipment		Soda, Synthetic Oil
Vertical		Incandescent Electric Light Bulbs	Dyestuffs, Ammonium Sulphate

Zaibatsu relationships were, then, an important factor that affected the behavior of international cartels toward the Japanese market.

As for the cases where international cartels showed much interest in Japan, we can further distinguish between the case of the incandescent electric light bulb industry and the cases of the heavy electrical equipment industry and the telephone equipment industry. In the former case, an international cartel could let a Japanese company join because one company that was affiliated with a leading foreign company occupied a dominant position in the Japanese market. In contrast to this, in the latter cases, there were many large companies affiliated with foreign corporations that were leading members of the international cartel. There was sharp competition among Japanese companies and competition between Japanese companies and foreign companies. It was not so easy for the international cartel to let Japanese companies join.

Second, as for the cases where direct investment was not made, which is the case of the chemical industries, we can distinguish between the soda industry on one hand and the ammonium sulfate and dyestuffs industries on the other. When we think about the factor that caused the difference, it is important for us to note the position of general trading companies in the marketing channel of the goods. In the former case (soda), a foreign company sold most of its products directly in Japan, whereas in the latter case (ammonium sulfate and dyestuffs), Japanese general trading companies, such as Mitsui & Co. and Mitsubishi Shōji, occupied an important position in the marketing channel. The general trading companies dealt with a large quantity of imported goods, on the one hand, and became a sole agent for the domestic manufacturers that were affiliated with the same industrial group, on the other. Thus, when they judged it more advantageous to join the international cartel than to be independent of it, they persuaded the domestic manufacturers to do so. In the soda industry, domestic manufacturers competed severely with international cartels in the Japanese market, whereas in the ammonium sulfate and dyestuffs industries, Japanese general trading companies played a role as a coordinator of interests between international cartels and domestic manufacturers.

Response

Terushi Hara and Akira Kudō

The typology that we proposed at this conference was a simple one, and we are well aware of the fact that other important factors need to be taken into consideration and that many points are in need of revision and improvement. In spite of this, we offered our hypothesis as a way of stimulating debate on the subject of international cartels. In this sense, we must express our gratitude to Professor Yamazaki for undertaking to face the questions raised by the typology proposed.

The first point that Yamazaki made was that there was no case within the soda industry of an international cartel that reached an agreement with a Japanese company. With regard to this, however, we drew attention in our paper to the fact that in 1930, ICI made a price agreement with Asahi Glass Co. and Nippon Soda Co. regarding soda lime. This we took as indicating the formation of a vertical-type relationship. Moreover, in 1929 ICI came to an agreement with ALKASSO over sales quotas for the world market, and, in addition, the company managed to achieve a balance of interests with Belgian Solvay. In other words, we saw the existence of an international cartel, in the broad sense, in the industry. Our interpretation was that ICI confronted the Japanese corporations in its capacity as representative of the international cartel. However, there is still room for investigation to find actual proof for the accuracy of this interpretation.

Concerning Yamazaki's second point, that Tokyo Denki Co. joined the international cartel Phoebus, we have explained that this was because the company was a subsidiary of General Electric. If we take this fact into consideration, we can say that the most important type of relationship within the incandescent electric light bulb industry would thus seem to be horizontal rather than vertical.

The third point he raised was that we did not include rayon in the chemical industry. As he pointed out, this case is in fact unique and should, if anything, be therefore included among the individual case studies. In connection with this, Yamazaki's division of the horizontal-type cartels into "horizontal type 1" and "horizontal type 2" comes closer to the truth in comparison with our own typology, and thus gives an indication as to how the typology can be made all the more dynamic and realistic.

In response to the fourth point Yamazaki made, we would state that we did not consider horizontal-type cartels and direct investment in the same light, but rather as the obverse and reverse of one another. In other words, in the cases where European and American companies carried out a fair amount of direct investment in Japan, e.g., the incandescent electric light bulb, heavy electrical, and telephone industries, they had the possibility of exercising control over the Japanese market through direct investment, or to put it another way, their Japanese subsidiaries. Therefore, they had no need to form a vertical-type relationship with Japanese companies, a horizontal relationship alone being sufficient. We do, however, fully recognize that synthetic oil, being classified under a horizontal-type relationship, although direct investment did not take place, must be taken as representing an exception to this. Therefore, this indicates that there may indeed be a need to give a classification combining the type of international cartel with the presence or otherwise of direct investment in the way that Yamazaki has done.

I. The Chemical Industry

The International Dyestuffs Cartel, 1927–39, with Special Reference to the Developing Areas of Europe and Japan

Harm G. Schröter

Before and after the First World War, the chemical industry was in the forefront of international cartelization.[1] The international dyestuffs cartel was one of the most influential cartels. This was partly because of its turnover; only the steel cartels (Entente Intenationale d'Acier, EIA, in 1926–31, and renewed but restricted to exports in 1933–39) had a significantly bigger turnover, but the nitrogen cartels (Convention Internationale de l'Azote, CIA, 1930–31, 1932–39) or the potassium cartel were quite the same size in turnover. Furthermore, the dyestuffs cartel was a key cartel in a key industry.[2] The development of organic chemistry was to a great extent based on processes that were applied first in the production of dyestuffs, and within the chemical industry the dyestuffs cartel pioneered a new type of international convention. This new type of cartel was much more comprehensive and for its members much safer than its forerunners. The latter were based on one dye or one group of dyes only, which meant that there was always the possibility of circumventing the contract by the development of other types of dyes not subject to the clauses. The new type of cartel included all artificial dyes whatsoever, including possible new ones in the future. The only exceptions were the old natural dyes like natural indigo, logwood, madder, etc., that played only an insignificant and declining role. All calculations within the dyestuffs cartel were very much simplified, e.g., 750 chrome-black dyestuffs were converted into five different types.[3] Of extreme importance was the fact that the cartel was to last for the entire foreseeable future—40 years, from 1927/29 to 1968! And last but not least, all the economic torture instruments[4] that were developed during 50 years' experience with the build-up and breakdown of cartels were applied. For these reasons we can take the international dyestuffs cartel as one of the most advanced organizations within the movement of cartelization. Therefore, we will go into detail with this cartel. Our contribution will concentrate on the problem of outside competition. This problem has several aspects, such as the building of the cartel and its relations to the industrialization of third countries, to competition in export markets, to competition in home markets, and to state bureaucracies of member states and to foreign governments.

I. The Building of the International Dyestuffs Cartel: Its Organization and Internal Structure

The core of the international dyestuffs cartel was the chemical industry in certain European countries. Before international cartelization took place, there was extreme concentration on a national basis. This was a sine qua non. Other cartels, such as the international coal cartel, could not be formed[5] because of the lack of national concentration or because a certain nation was not admitted to the cartel for the same reason.[6] In the interwar period market concentration in Germany often took the form of a cartel, but the chemical industry was special. One-half of all capital invested in the whole chemical industry of Germany was with I.G. Farben,[7] which made the enterprise the biggest one of this country. Dyestuffs were produced by I.G. Farben only, putting this firm into a monopoly position. On the other hand, dyestuffs production was only one of several branches of I.G. Farben. Its technical potential, its size, and its ambition made I.G. Farben one of the major players in the international chemical industry: "There was no operation of chemical industry which it could not undertake and no industrial combine in the world which it could not face or outface."[8] I.G. Farben was formed in a merger in 1925 in order to regain the international position the German chemical industry enjoyed before the First World War. For the same reasons the Swiss dyestuffs producers formed a national cartel, the so-called Swiss I.G.,[9] as early as 1918. Apart from the direct investments of I.G. Farben in Switzerland, the Swiss I.G. had assumed the entire dyestuffs production in that country.[10]

French dyestuff production was based to a great extent on former German direct investment, sequestered during the First World War. It was not concentrated in just a single cartel, C.M.C. (Centrale des Matières Colorantes, Paris);[11] the biggest partner, Ets. Kuhlmann,[12] participated in nearly all other firms. Only the British industry was less concentrated. ICI (Imperial Chemical Industries, Ltd., London) stood for 58.0% of British dyestuffs sales in 1938.[13] With the exception of the USSR—of which virtually almost nothing is known of its dyestuff production—the industry was not concentrated to the same degree (e.g., the U.S. industry) or it was rather small. Though there are no well-founded statistics on world production, Table 1, combined from various sources, can give a rough overview of the development.

The table may well give an impression, but even the percentages are not to be compared directly, as in 1926 some nations are missing.[14] The eco-

TABLE 1 World Production of Dyestuffs, 1926 and 1938

Country[d]	1926 Production[a] (in 1000 t)	1926 Quantities[a] (%)	1926 Values[b] (%)	1938 Production[c] (in 1000 t)	1938 Quantities[c] (%)	1938 Values[b] (%)
Germany	68.0	41.6	49.9	57.0	25.9	46.0
U.S.A.	39.9	24.4	22.3	37.0	16.8	17.2
Switzerland	9.0	5.5	9.1	8.0	3.6	10.6
France	17.1	10.5	6.2	12.0	5.5	4.2
Great Britain	13.5	8.3	10.7	21.0	9.5	5.5
Italy	7.0	4.3	–	11.0	5.0	1.6
Japan	7.5	4.6	–	28.0	12.7	3.2
USSR	–	0.0	–	35.0	15.9	8.7
Others	1.5	0.9	1.8	11.0	5.0	3.0
Total	163.5	100.0	100.0	220.0	100.0	100.0

Sources: [a] Internal calculation of I.G. Farben (Hö, p. 1094)
[b] Calculated from Hans Kugler, "Activities of I.G. Farbenindustrie AG in the Dyestuffs Industry," Economics Division, Decartelization Branch Control Office, 5.6.1946, unpublished manuscript in Archives of Hoechst AG, Frankfurt, no number: 1926, production; 1938 sales.
[c] Svennilson, *Growth and Stagnation in the European Economy* (Geneva, 1954), p. 290.
[d] Including foreign direct investment.

nomic background for the dyestuffs cartel can be inferred from these figures. The major old industrial nations and Switzerland dominated production, with Germany at the head. But while these countries stagnated in terms of quantity, newcomers like Italy expanded rapidly. The most important change was to be found in Japan. In 1926 it already produced dyestuffs in a considerable amount, and it was successful to the extent that it quadrupled its output by 1938.

So we get a sense of the stagnating and dynamic elements in the field of dyestuffs production. The idea of any cartel is basically defensive. The status quo is to be preserved. The question of whether the dyestuffs cartel was successful will be dealt with below. All the major dyestuffs producers in Europe perceived the dynamic industrialization of other countries as a threat to their business. Because of this common conviction, all of them were basically willing to join a cartel. The question was not whether to form a cartel, but to what extent their individual interests could be advanced inside such a cartel.

It was not possible for any important international cartel to be formed right after the First World War. The economic and political turmoil in Europe made even the very near future uncertain. In Germany and Great Britain concentration or, in the words of the actors, the national gathering of forces, was not yet carried out. Under these circumstances there was little possibility to test each others' strength, which has to be done in every case before a cartel is formed. But in the case of dyestuffs, even before this was done there had been contacts, suggestions, negotiations, and even some limited agreements concluded, of which a German-French convention, signed only one year after the Versailles Treaty was signed, was the most outstanding.[15]

The comprehensive international cartelization of dyestuffs started in 1926. Though when the dyestuffs cartel is mentioned, the focus naturally is on I.G. Farben, it is to be stressed here that there was another major player: the Swiss I.G. It was this Swiss I.G. which on June 11, 1926, signed a contract with the French Ets. Kuhlmann to last for 30 years.[16] By this the Swiss I.G. showed the much bigger I.G. Farben that it was not ready to stand back and wait until it would be approached. The contract itself was quite favorable for Kuhlmann, which by this step was in a much better position to go on with its negotiations with I.G. Farben. The German-French proceedings ended with a very comprehensive agreement only ten months later. This contract fixed all dyestuff sales on a quota 88.5 (I.G. Farben):11.5 (C.M.C.). Furthermore, it intended to form a joint-stock company for dyestuff production of which 88.9% of voting rights would have been with I.G. Farben. Though actually this company never was founded, the cartel promoted the intense entanglement of I.G. Farben and Ets. Kuhlmann.[17]

The Swiss and the Germans were by far the most experienced in the field of dyestuffs techniques. An agreement between these two was seen as the core of any international cartel on dyes. So they started negotiations. Overall they had a very good relationship, e.g., the Swiss boycott of Soviet Russia was circumvented via I.G. Farben: in all German dye deliveries to the Soviet Union the Swiss I.G. had a certain contingent that officially was of I.G. Farben's production.[18] But for the less diversified Swiss chemical firms, the cartel was a question of vitality. Therefore, one of the first Swiss steps was to put pressure upon I.G. Farben by negotiations with the British ICI. I.G. Farben as well had had talks with ICI even before, but they had broken down at a very early stage. So I.G. Farben, in spite of its size, was relieved when the Swiss-British negotiations were halted, since ICI got information on the German-Swiss proceedings.[19] The latter ran into a period of intense negotiations that took three-quarters of a year, and both sides had to make important concessions.[20] The French side was kept informed but had little to say. On April 27, 1929, the Three-Party Cartel[21] was formed. Its validity was backdated to start on January 1, 1929. As before, home and other markets were allocated and the overall quotas set on a sales ratio of 71.67%:19.00%:9.33% (I.G. Farben: Swiss I.G.: C.M.C.).[22] On the same day, a German-Swiss agreement was signed,[23] and all agreements of all sides were renewed. The construction was that all contracts remained in power separately, which was possible only because both Two-Party Cartels were already designed to be incorporated into a bigger one, while the Three-Party Cartel was ruling over all others. With this construction the members enjoyed the best security, even if one of the contracts became obsolete in the future for any reason. Though the agreements went into small details,[24] more important was their common spirit.

This was not exceptional; it is a common trait of all international cartels. The international steel cartel EIA broke down when the Germans wanted it to do so.[25] In the electrotechnical industry, the Swedish ASEA had formed a cartel with AEG and Siemens of Germany concerning the Swedish market. As a result, a "friendly relationship" was formed. Its nature is illustrated in a letter from ASEA to Siemens in which ASEA complained that the Germans did not intervene against the proceedings of a Swiss firm (Brown Boveri & Co., BBC) in the Finnish market.[26] Neither BBC nor Finland were mentioned in the agreement, but a friendly relationship was to cover much more than a number of paragraphs written down. Likewise, if the potassium cartel had worked just to the

TABLE 2 Shares of British Dye Producers, 1925 (%)

ICI	44
Clayton	21
Brotherton	10
Brit. Alizarine	9
Holliday	7
Others	9
Total	100

Source: Archives of Hoechst AG (Frankfurt), no. 310.

letter, the French Société Commerciale de Potasse d'Alsace would have left it, which would have caused the cartel to go bust. Therefore, its main partner, the German Deutsches Kali-Syndikat, gradually handed over additional percentages. The same thing happened in the dyestuffs cartel during the 1930s. C.M.C. was not able to fill its quota. Therefore, its Swiss and German partners repeatedly had to open new outlets for C.M.C. products in markets they dominated, and they did so.

The incorporation of ICI into the cartel was different. The formation of the cartels up to 1929 took place through talks, threats, counterthreats, and intense negotiations, but without real fighting. In 1927 already ICI and I.G. Farben had agreed basically to form a cartel for dyestuffs,[27] but both sides asked for too much. I.G. Farben was not prepared to take ICI as a partner on equal terms. In its eyes ICI should be restricted in its dyestuff production to certain groups, which meant restriction in potential development. ICI asked for the entire British Empire as its exclusive home market and for the takeover of Clayton. Clayton was a direct investment in Britain by the Swiss CIBA that was carried out before the First World War. Before CIBA acquired Clayton it was a thoroughly rotten firm—at least in German and Swiss eyes[28]— but CIBA had turned it into the most advanced dyemaker in Britain. In 1925 the small Clayton produced half as many dyes as the mighty ICI (Table 2).

There clearly was no possibility to meet the demands of ICI, and the Three-Party Cartel and the test of strength began. ICI embarked on a policy of attacking I.G. Farben's patent rights in Britain, while the Three-Party Cartel dumped its dyes on the British market. Both sides were successful: German patent rights were restricted, and ICI's dyestuffs division had to write red figures. This made both sides ready for negotiations, which ended with the formation of the Four-Party Cartel on February 26, 1932. Two other steps had helped in this course: the foundation of the nitrogen cartel CIA in 1929, in which ICI and I.G. Farben were the main

TABLE 3 Quotas of the Four-Party Cartel (%)

I.G. Farben	65.602
Swiss I.G.	17.391
C.M.C.	8.540
ICI	8.467

Source: Kugler, op. cit., p. 33.

partners, and the contract for mutual technical aid between ICI and Du Pont of the United States.[29] Within the Four-Party Cartel ICI got a share similar to that of C.M.C., but the internal cartel organization stood very much as before (Table 3).

Within the Four-Party Cartel, ICI was on one side, the other being the Three-Party Cartel. The Three-Party Cartel acted as one bloc. For internal talks this cartel met beforehand to establish a common line, and only after that was done did they face the ICI managers. Official letters to ICI from the Three-Party Cartel were signed by all three partners. Different forms were printed for internal letters inside the Four- and Three-Party Cartels.[30] Inside the Three-Party Cartel, the partners had equal rights and decisions were made in scheduled meetings that took place in the headquarters of all three in a revolving turn. But below this official level there were many and important contacts between I.G. Farben and Swiss I.G. These two valued each other more highly than C.M.C. This fact was not so much based on their bigger shares or on their common mother tongue, but on their technical excellence. Up to the Second World War only these two were a match in advanced dyestuffs. But still I.G. Farben was the much bigger partner with a much bigger organization. Therefore, with various cartel negotiations to come after 1929 with smaller dyestuff firms, I.G. Farben alone negotiated for the whole cartel, sometimes even signing alone for the whole cartel. This meant that the other partners just were informed by I.G. Farben about their share of the common burden, as each new partner to the cartel naturally decreased the quotas of all other members and very often sales too. Clearly, I.G. Farben was as much the cartel leader in the dyestuffs cartel as was DSS[31] in the nitrogen cartel or Climax[32] in the molybdenum cartel.

II. The Dyestuffs Cartel and International Competition

The dyestuffs cartel favored a general industrialization of third countries. In most cases this development meant a considerable build-up of textile industries, which in their turn were the best customers for dyes. But the cartel tried to prevent the production of dyestuffs wherever possible. The means that were employed to achieve these ends were not only the means of the cartel itself; but other cartels were applied as well and even concentrated diplomatic pressure of major nations, especially Great Britain and Germany, in a combined action.[33]

In the following, the policy of the cartel will be illustrated with four different case studies in which it can be seen how the cartel tackled its problems on various levels. Our first case is Norway, where an indigenous production was going to be implemented. The second is Poland, where foreign direct investment of cartel members and imports held the majority of the market against production in Polish hands. The third is Italy, where competition from indigenous and independent firms was much stronger, and the fourth case is Japan. Japan caused the biggest problems as in this country there was no production by European firms, but the Japanese themselves were in the midst of a vigorous industrialization of chemical production.

1. The Case of Norway: Shut Down Against Compensation

The biggest Norwegian enterprise in the interwar period was Norsk Hydro (NH), which produced mainly artificial nitrogen. NH was tied to I.G. Farben directly and indirectly: I.G. Farben had by exchange of stocks a stake of 25% in NH (while NH held 1–2% of I.G. Farben's). Nearly all products of NH were channeled through the German sales organization. Important stockholders of NH were Kuhlmann of France and the Swedish Stockholms Enskilda Bank, both with a well-established and reliable, friendly relationship with I.G. Farben.[34] In 1934 a subsidiary of NH started to manufacture simple dyes.[35] As the business turned out to be successful, I.G. Farben intervened at NH. For stopping the whole production, NH was compensated with US\$35,500.[36] This agreement was only an oral understanding that was never signed.[37]

2. The Case of Poland: Government Protection and the Cartel

The situation in Poland was more difficult for the cartel than in Norway. The Polish government favored national production. Furthermore, it was in economic confrontation with Germany. I.G. Farben had no open production there. The breakdown of sales in 1938 was as shown in Table 4.

Of these enterprises Boruta and Wola were Polish. Winnica was an investment carried out by the French cartel member Kuhlmann in 1929. Secretly I.G. Farben had a participation of 50%, but this was well hidden. Only French management dealt with Winnica and even in internal cartel balances Winnica counted into Kuhlmann's account. Pabianice was a direct investment of CIBA, dated 1899.[38] With Winnica and Pabianice

TABLE 4 Polish Sales of Dyes, 1938 (%)

Boruta	40
Winnica	30
Pabianice	21
Wola	6
Others	3

Source: Kugler, op. cit., p. 16.

the cartel represented about 50% of indigenous production, but as Poland had to import dyes the dye cartel's share of sales was much bigger. The cartel's aims were twofold: first, to curb Polish production and second, but even more important, to contain and direct Polish exports. These exports were quite small, but they could disturb markets. The cartel and I.G. Farben were very much concerned with the export market. As the following example shows, this concern was not restricted to third countries only: in Britain there was a single aggressive exporting firm, Holliday.[39] Though this was but a medium-sized enterprise with a work force of about 750 employees, it was constantly a point of discussion in I.G. Farben's Farben-Ausschuß (dye-committee).[40] For the cartel, any export mattered, the small amounts from Poland included.

It was clear that the Polish producers would expand in their home market, relying on government protection, and in export markets, because of the low external value of the Polish currency. This had already been exercised in the coalmining industry: during the fight preceding the British-Polish coal cartel, the Poles had demonstrated how vigorously they could compete even against the biggest producers in Europe and the world market leader Great Britain.[41] Therefore, it was wise to exercise a certain conciliatory attitude. In 1932 the Three-Party Cartel signed a preliminary contract with the Polish group consisting of Boruta and Wola, which in 1934 was followed by a formal agreement. Export sales were restricted to 1 million zloty (US$0.19 million).[42] Sales inside Poland were allocated in a ratio between 29.5:70.5 (1935) and 33.3:66.7 (1942). The Polish group got the smaller but annually by 0.5% rising share. All firms connected with the Three-Party Cartel counted into that share, e.g., ICI, etc. If one side had not fulfilled its quota at the end of the year, it was to receive a compensation of 20% of the turnover it did not sell. This was the case in later years as the Polish group could not fulfill its quota because of its limited range of dyestuffs.[43] Though there was, according to Section 7, "intimate cooperation" for techniques of rational production, there was no transfer of knowledge. It is possible that the Polish group slackened its drive for better products after its security was guaranteed by the contract. The difficulties the group faced in fulfilling its quota points in that direction, but there is no evidence.

3. The Case of Italy: The Limitation of the Cartel's Influence

The situation in Italy was different. First of all, Italy was much more industrialized than Poland. Secondly, the policy to protect and promote Italian production was extremely strong. In Italy well-known chemical enterprises such as Montecatini were existent. During the interwar period, Italy was a partner in the international sulfur cartel and a main supplier of Europe with this raw material for chemical production. The Three-Party Cartel held direct investments in Italy (Bianchi, Bergamasca) that accounted for less than 20% of the country's output (Table 5). Therefore in various aspects the cartel's situation in Italy was less favorable than in Poland.

In 1930–31 the biggest producer in Italy, ACNA, went bankrupt. For the sake of national industrialization, the Italian state intervened and asked Montecatini and I.G. Farben to reorganize ACNA. In the process Montecatini received 51.0% of all ACNA shares and additionally 48.99% of Bianchi's that I.G. Farben was to hand over. In return I.G. Farben received 49.0% of ACNA's, while keeping 51.01% of Bianchi's shares. After that, Bianchi's sales still counted into the quota of I.G. Farben, while ACNA was bound into the cartel for the first time. I.G. Farben had agreed to help reorganize ACNA in order to draw this enterprise into the cartel's network and to curb ACNA's exports. ACNA was restricted to an export amount of 10 million lire (US$0.5 million) in 1931,[44] which was to be gradually raised up to 15.65 million lire (US$0.8 million) in 1939. Again there was no formal contract signed. The agreement was based on minutes, an exchange of letters, and a spirit of common interests. In most cases I.G. Farben again negotiated for the whole Three-Party Cartel. But all in all, ACNA remained a difficult partner. While all others were loyal to the letter and spirit of any understanding, ACNA was not. The firm

TABLE 5 Italian Sales of Dyestuffs, 1938 (%)

ACNA	51.6
Bianchi	15.1
Melegnano	13.1
IPCA	5.1
Others	15.1

Source: Kugler, op. cit., p. 15.

preferred to go its own way, accepting economic "punishment" rather than direction by the cartel. With that policy, "ACNA repeatedly cut the cartel prices with consequent retaliation by I.G. Farben and the other parties to the Three-Party Cartel. . . . On the whole, the agreement did not operate satisfactorily because of the unreliability and aggressiveness of ACNA."[45] Though ACNA was included in the sphere of the cartel, its policy placed it on the very margin of the cartel network. While, on the whole, the competition of ACNA was curbed, this enterprise showed signs of opposition to the cartel.

ACNA illustrates the limits of the cartel's power to enforce its policy. The case of ACNA shows that there was no clear-drawn dividing line between cartel members and outsiders, but that there existed a "grey-zone" between these blocs. This is not a singularity but a common feature of nearly all cartels. Within the history of cartelization, the Three-Party Cartel with its little internal frictions was rather an exception, while the majority of cartels had to face quite a lot of internal struggle. It was the new type of cartel that the Three-Party Cartel stood for that to a great extent successfully prevented such differences.

4. The Case of Japan: Beyond the Cartel's Influence?

In the interwar period Japanese industrialization was well under way. The export of cotton textiles surpassed that of Britain. But British industrialists were unwilling to answer this threat by cartelization inside their country as well as together with Japan.[46] Japanese manufacturers of dyestuffs were not so advanced but were developing with considerable speed. As early as 1926, they turned out 4.6% of world production.[47] This was more than Italy and nearly as much as Switzerland produced. But these figures are quantities. In values the Japanese and the Italian share would have been reduced by half, while the Swiss one would have doubled. In 1930 the home market consumed dyestuffs for ¥27 million, of which ¥9 million were from indigenous production.[48] Within the cartel there was no accurate information of the different producers' shares inside Japan. For 1930 two assessments were made (Table 6).

These assessments, made by the same expert within eleven months, vary considerably. For the various European and American enterprises the cartel had much better figures. Though I.G. Farben, compared with all other non-Japanese firms, had the best knowledge of the indigenous enterprises, it still had to rely on assessments. This seems to be an expression of the cultural differences that were stressed internally on various occasions. The cartel's assessment for 1938 (Table 7)—which in other words was that of I.G. Farben, as this firm had by far the best overall

TABLE 6 Sales of Japanese Dyes, 1930 (%)

Firm	Assessment I[a]	Assessment II[b]
Nihon Senryō Seizō Kabushiki Kaisha, Osaka (N.S.K.)	50	60
Mitsui Bussan Kaisha Ltd., Tokyo[c]	10	15
Daidō Ai K.K.	15[d]	–
Daikoku	–	10
37 small firms	25	–
Others	–	15
	100	100

Sources: [a]Internal assessment of the Three-Party Cartel by Waibel (I.G. Farben), Minutes of January 5, 1931 (HA CIBA-Geigy, Geigy VE/IGK 15).
[b]Internal assessment of the Three-Party Cartel by Waibel (I.G. Farben), Minutes of November 12, 1931.
[c]Mitsui Bussan acted as a sales organization of Mitsui Kōzan Kabushiki Kaisha, Tokyo/Miike.
[d]Obvious typing error (50%) corrected. It is presumed that Daidō and Daikoku are the same firm.

TABLE 7 Sales of Japanese Dyes, 1938 (%)

N.S.K.	60
Mitsui	20
Mitsubishi Dye Co., Tokyo	10
Others	10
Total	100

Source: Kugler, op. cit., p. 15.

knowledge, keeping a big economic department in Berlin ("NW 7")—was quite similar to the second of 1930.

The Japanese state heavily intervened in the dyestuffs business, especially with its "Dyestuffs Encouragement Law."[49] High tariffs protected the industry, and heavy subsidies promoted it. Nihon Senryō Seizō Kabushiki Kaisha (N.S.K.), the biggest producer, received ¥0.6–0.7 million annually, which in 1931 amounted to about ¥18 million.[50] During negotiations with I.G. Farben, N.S.K. admitted not only accepting these subsidies, but also that it needed at least ¥0.25 million annually in order to pay a dividend of 5%.[51] Mitsui also received heavy subsidies for the development of artificial indigo. The House of Peers agreed to pay ¥3,414,500 to Mitsui within five years at its meeting of March 12, 1929.

Mitsui was required to raise its production from 50 tons to 1,000 t during that period.[52] While 50 t was very little, 1,000 t was much more than the Japanese home market could consume.

The third strategic point for the Three-Party Cartel was that no party had any direct foreign investment in Japan. Various difficulties militated against it, and they were enhanced further: N.S.K. mentioned to I.G. Farben in 1930 that any direct investment could be nationalized as had been done before in the cases of the French Air Liquide, the German Siemens, and the British Lever Brothers.[53] The situation of the Three-Party Cartel is well illustrated in an internal letter of the Swiss I.G.

> The Japanese dyestuffs industry is already grown up and has had a certain success. The ambition, the patriotism and the energetic support of the government will ensure the wished place in the sun for the Japanese dyestuffs industry. We should not miss the moment, not waiting too long, but at least take up the opportunity to negotiate, when the occasion comes.[54]

The occasion to negotiate was soon to come. In Japan both government and industry had expressed their willingness to cooperate with the cartel or I.G. Farben, who served as its representative.[55] But about 1930 both sides considered the time not to be ripe for negotiations. The Japanese asked for high quotas that the cartel was not ready to give freely. Therefore they wanted some more years to build up. On the other hand, for I.G. Farben the Japanese industry was not organized well enough[56] for a comprehensive agreement compared to the Three-Party Cartel. Furthermore, technical standards were not as good as I.G. Farben's (or the even better Swiss firms).[57] Therefore, both sides made agreements only for a limited amount of products.

The Japanese knew that their techniques were not as good as some European ones. They tried to recover by various means. Some leading chemists were hired in Europe for a very good salary: a Swiss, Dr. Ryser, received from 1925 to 1931 about 190,000 French francs annually (US$7,500) as the main chemist for N.S.K.,[58] but applying for a job at Kuhlmann's he asked only for 96,000 francs ($3,700).[59] Several times Japanese managers very cautiously and often indirectly asked for technical aid. In this approach, established relationships were used, and the most outstanding European firms never were asked. In 1929 Inabata Jirō (of N.S.K.) approached the French St. Denis,[60] with which it had a special relationship.[61] In 1936 Uyeno Yoshio of Mitsubishi approached another French enterprise,[62] but these overtures were unsuccessful. All members of the cartel network, that is, not only the Three-Party Cartel, had agreed not to assist any firm without the cartel's consent. There was even a very cautious boycott for "chemical" intermediates not to be exported to Japan.[63] These intermediates were carefully chosen and restricted to those goods outsiders could not supply.

In organizational matters, for the whole industry I.G. Farben clearly had an advantage over the Japanese dyestuffs sector based on its long experience of cartelization. This was acknowledged by the Japanese side when Doitsu,[64] I.G. Farben's sales organization in Japan, was invited to help with the reorganization of the home market. This was quite remarkable as, first, Doitsu was not Japanese and, second, it was the only foreign organization selling directly, while all other foreign firms needed the help of a Japanese wholesale trading house for their sales. In 1929 Doitsu was asked to help in building up Aisen Kai (Association of Friends of Dyestuffs), an organization of dyestuff trading houses. On the whole, I.G. Farben preferred to sell directly, but it was flexible enough to adopt to the special conditions of Japan. The aim of Aisen Kai was to reduce competition and to raise prices. N.S.K. and Doitsu, being the main suppliers of the market, were to guarantee the support needed by Aisen Kai, according to the suggestions of the promoters of Aisen Kai.[65] In various meetings, some inside the offices of Doitsu, I.G. Farben was able to change several crucial points, e.g., the mechanism of how and when Aisen Kai could boycott a trading house. More important was that Doitsu was able to convince N.S.K. that Mitsui should be invited to join as well as all major foreign firms that were present in the market.[66] When Aisen Kai was founded on September 12, 1929, all the aims I.G. Farben had set out for were achieved, including the election of desired persons onto the board.

During the following years, more and more agreements concerning certain dyes or groups of dyes were concluded. The first one, in 1931, was quite limited.[67] The Astraphloxine Agreement of 1934 between I.G. Farben and N.S.K. was limited as well. More important were the agreements that included exports. These were later ones, as the Japanese export of dyes was insignificant in the beginning. In 1935 I.G. Farben (quota: 68%) and N.S.K. (quota: 32%) prolonged and enlarged their understanding of 1931 to cover the whole world.[68] Most important was the Mitsui Indigo Agreement of January 1, 1935 (effective date), in which Mitsui exports were restricted to China and to a limited amount.[69] In return it was guaranteed 85% of the Japanese home market for indigo by the Four-Party Cartel plus Nacco and Du Pont, both of the United States.[70] Later Mitsui's export rights were enlarged. All cartels were prolonged up to the war. The impression of the Europeans was that the Japanese and Mitsui especially were very loyal partners. With these cartels, a considerable part of the Japanese home and export markets could be influenced by the dyestuffs cartel.

III. Conclusion: The Relevance of the International Dyestuffs Cartel

In 1938 62.2% of worldwide dyestuff sales were made by members of the European dye cartels.[71] Parts of American and Japanese sales are to be added to that figure as these sales were bound into the cartel's network by separate agreements. Altogether more than 70% of world production was influenced by the cartel. In absolute figures the sales of the Three-Party Cartel remained quite stable (Table 8).

In exports the cartel was even more important. Small firms, not bound into the network, used to restrict themselves to their home market. The Soviet Union did not export dyestuffs. Altogether the cartel was able to exert its influence on well over 90% of all world exports in 1938.[72]

During the 1930s dyestuff imports in Europe as well as to a certain extent in the United States were restricted by various means of state and private intervention. In that period the most important free markets for dyes were those in Asia—except for the Japanese one—and in Latin America. In Asia, China and India were most important of these. The Asian export markets consumed dyes for $49.4 million in 1937 and for $41.8 million in 1938.[73] The situation is illustrated in Table 9.

The table shows that while the Japanese expanded, the Americans were the ones who lost market shares. The cartel managed to safeguard its share and even to expand a little. We can presume that without agreements the European share would have been smaller.

TABLE 8 Sales of the Three-Party Cartel (in million "gold marks")[a]

1929	482.7	1934	412.2
1930	441.8	1935	418.5
1931	430.5	1936	423.4
1932	389.0	1937	434.7
1933	409.6	1938	398.3

Source: Kugler, op. cit., p. 36.

[a]It was reckoned in a fictional currency "gold marks," that is, German reichsmarks were converted into a nonexistent gold currency. This was done to correct the cartel's internal balance differences between existing currencies, which were caused by devaluations, deflations, different foreign exchange rates, etc.

TABLE 9 Exports to the Asian Market (%)

Country	1933	1937	1938
Germany	58.27	63.66	57.30
Switzerland and France	13.17	8.96	12.83
Great Britain	7.43	11.64	12.47
Other Europeans affiliated with the cartel	1.32	0.75	0.80
Total, Europeans within cartel	80.19	85.01	83.41
U.S.A.	15.59	9.09	6.13
Japan	4.22	5.90	10.46
	100.00	100.00	100.00

Source: Kugler, op. cit.

In some cases the build-up of dyestuffs production may have been hampered by the cartel. Compensation for renunciation was paid not only to Norway but to Poland and other countries too. The cartel's policy of moderate pricing did not invite very many newcomers to start production. In such cases experts from cartel firms were often asked for technical and commercial advice. Their recommendations used to be negative. Existing firms that were not bound to the cartel were to be fought back when they expanded their market share or undercut prices. It was an outspoken policy of I.G. Farben not to give away *any* sales for reasons of prices. But the cartel pursued no aggressive competition against big outsiders and only moderate or little competition against small ones. Access to knowledge was denied in nearly all cases, and the supply of raw material for outsiders was also denied even when there was no alternative source. In cases of heavy state intervention, as in Italy and Japan, the cartel was not able to prevent the emergence of dyestuff capacities. In those cases it tried to cooperate and in this way to draw the newcomers into its network.

Compared with other international cartels, the dyestuffs cartel was very successful. One group of cartels, like the Alliance Aluminium Company, broke down.[74] Another group, like the European steel cartel, faced heavy difficulties that forced a renegotiation of quotas. A third group of international cartels, like that for nitrogen, had not so many difficulties with internal problems but was not able to incorporate all the important countries they wanted for members. The dyestuffs cartel belonged to a fourth group of eminently successful cartels. Of the more important cartels—in terms of turnover—only the international potassium cartel, into which virtually all producers of the whole world were incorporated, had a better performance than the international network of dyestuff cartels that was directed by the German-Swiss-French Three-Party Cartel.

Notes

1. See the overview on international cartelization of E. Hexner, *International Cartels* (Chapel Hill, N.C., 1946). But Hexner had only limited access to sources. Though his overview is right, his book is packed with errors in the details and in the interpretation of the intentions. More recent contributions are to be found in H. Pohl (ed.), *Kartelle und Kartellgesetzgebung in Praxis und Rechtsprechung von 19. Jahrhundert bis zur Gegenwart* (Stuttgart, 1985); H. Pohl (ed.), *Wettbewerbsbeschränkungen auf internationalen Märkten* (Stuttgart, 1988); C. Wurm, "Politik und Wirtschaft in den internationalen Beziehungen. Internationale Kartelle, Außenpolitik und weltwirtschaftliche Beziehungen 1919–1939," in C. Wurm (ed.), *Internationale Kartelle und Außenpolitik* (Stuttgart, 1988), pp. 1–32.

2. For the role of dyestuffs in the development of the chemical industry, see S. Kaku, "The Development and Structure of the German Coal-Tar Dyestuff Firms," in A. Okochi and H. Uchida (ed.), *Development and Diffusion of Technology* (Tokyo, 1980), pp. 77–94; J. Beer, *The Emergence of the German Dye Industry* (Urbana, Ill., 1959).

3. Hans Kugler, "Activities of IG Farbenindustrie AG in the Dyestuffs Industry," Economics Division, Decartelization Branch Control Office, 5.6.1946, unpublished manuscript in archives of Hoechst AG, Frankfurt (hereafter Hö), no number.

4. Such as compensations, fines, common funds, internal cartel justice, etc.

5. E.g., the international coal export cartel because of the lack of a British coal cartel. When this was achieved finally, the international agreement was signed in 1939. But it did not come into power because of the war. For details, see H. Schröter, *Außenpolitik und Wirtschaftsinteresse* (Frankfurt, Bern, New York, 1983), pp. 237–44.

6. Because of its poor organization, Britain could not join the first international steel cartel.

7. Its full name was I.G. Farbenindustrie Aktien-Gesellschaft, Frankfurt (M.).

8. W.J. Reader, *Imperial Chemical Industries, A History*, vol. I: *The Forerunners, 1870–1926* (London, New York, Toronto, 1970), p. 412.

9. The Swiss I.G. was referred to as "Basler I.G." as well. But Basler I.G. was totally different from "I.G. Basel," which was a holding company for the international investments of I.G. Farben.

10. Swiss sales in 1938 in %:

Swiss I.G.: CIBA 45; Sandoz 20.5; Geigy 20.5

I.G. Farben: Durand & Huguenin 12; Rohner 2

For details, see H. Schröter, "Cartels as a Form of Concentration in Industry: The Example of the International Dyestuffs Cartel from 1927 to 1939," in *German Yearbook on Business History 1988* (Berlin/Heidelberg, 1990), pp. 113–44.

11. The C.M.C. was formed in 1929. Its forerunner was C.I.F., Communauté des Intérêt Français, Paris. Both cartels had the same members (Kuhlmann, St. Denis, St. Clair, Mulhouse, Steiner, Durand & Huguenin/Huningue, Mulhouse/Dornach).

12. Its whole long name was: Compagnie Nationale des Matières Colorantes et Manufactures de Produits Chimiques du Nord Réunies, Etablissements Kuhlmann, Paris.

13. Schröter, op. cit. (1990), Table 5.

14. More detailed figures in ibid.

15. The Versailles Treaty came into effect on January 10, 1920, the convention on January 31, 1921 (BWA 19, Farbstoffe 15). Another example is the convention for chrome black (Chromschwarzkonvention), signed June 17, 1924 between the Swiss I.G. and the German firms that later formed I.G. Farben (Bayer AG, Historical Archives, BWA, 19.1).

16. Historical Archives (HA) Sandoz, file: Kartellbeziehungen No. 1.

17. A figure of this is to be found in Schröter, op. cit. (1990).

18. HA Sandoz, Kartellbeziehungen No. 2, 27.11.1929.

19. Internal letter of I.G. Farben (Meyer to Krekeler) 19.10.1928 (Hö, RV A/F 25).

20. I.G. Farben put it as a sine qua non that the Swiss I.G. should be merged into one single enterprise, which the Swiss wanted to avoid above all (A. Bürgin, *Geschichte des Geigy-Unternehmens von 1758 bis 1939* (Basel, 1958), p. 253f.).

21. The Two-Party Cartel had a twofold meaning, inside the Swiss I.G.: Swiss-French cartel; inside I.G. Farben: German-French cartel.

22. Kugler, op. cit., p. 52.

23. Sales ratio 79:21 (I.G. Farben: Swiss I.G.).

24. E.g., the rules for accounting included the geographical point of account: quotas were based on sales, which still leaves a wide field for arguments. Therefore, exports had to be accounted as c.i.f. up to the border where the goods actually passed it. This, of course, gave the Swiss I.G. a small advantage as it had almost no freight and insurance because the country is small. This clause worked to the end that the Swiss I.G. could fill their quota nearly up to 100% with dyestuffs, while the others had to incorporate the freight and insurance into theirs. The contract went down to these details.

25. A. Teichova, *An Economic Background to Munich: International Business and Czechoslovakia 1918–1938* (Cambridge, 1974), p. 152f.

26. Letter S. Edström (ASEA) to Köttgen (Siemens), December 2, 1925, quoted in Schröter, op. cit. (1983), p. 342.

27. Notes on the talks dated 5.7.1927 Bundesarchiv Koblenz (BA), NL Silverberg 236.

28. German enterprises in search for a British firm to buy had ended talks after having been shown around at Clayton's. CIBA, being in desperate need for a secure source of raw materials, took it though it had found out that according to Swiss (and German) standards of calculation Clayton produced nothing but losses (HA CIBA, VR 1, KG 2.071.01, Kons. 103).

29. See M. Fox, *Dyemakers of Great Britain* (Manchester, 1987), p. 182.

30. Printed forms for the Three-Party Cartel had a "3" inside a triangle; forms for the Four-Party Cartel had a "4" inside a circle. Messages between the Swiss and the Germans had "D-S" inside a square.

31. Deutsches Stickstoff-Sydikat (which in its turn was dominated by I.G. Farben). See H. Schröter, "Privatwirtschaftliche Marktregulierung und staatliche Interessenpolitik: Das internationale Stickstoffkartell 1929–1939," in H. Schröter and C. Wurm (eds.), *Politik, Wirtschaft und internationale Beziehungen. Studien zu ihrem Verhältnis in der Zeit zwischen den beiden Weltkriegen* (Stuttgart, 1990), pp. 117–38.

32. Climax Molybdenum Company, New York; for the cartel, see Hexner, op. cit., p. 233.

33. Case studies in H. Schröter, "Risk and Control in Multinational Enterprise: German Businesses in Scandinavia, 1918–1939," *Business History Review*, vol. 62 (Autumn 1988): 420–43.

34. For this relationship with a neutral Swedish bank, see G. Aalders and C. Wiebes, "Stockholms Enskila Banken, German Bosch and IG Farben: A Short History of Cloaking," *Scandinavian Economic History Review* 1985, No. 1, 25–50.

35. Its name was Norsk Tjaereprodukter (for details, see Schröter, op. cit. (1983), p. 290f).

36. Exactly 140,000 Norwegian crowns (ibid.).

37. Ilgner's (senior manager of I.G. Farben) overview on Norway of October 14, 1941 (Bayer Works Archives, 84).

38. HA CIBA-Geigy, CIBA KG 2.15.04.

39. See Fox, op. cit., p. 147.

40. See minutes in Hö 110.

41. See Patrick Salmon, "Polish-British Competition in the Coal Markets of Northern Europe 1927–1934," in *Studia Historiae Oeconomicae*, VAM vol. 16 (Poznan, 1983), pp. 217–43.

42. Contract, §2 (HA Sandoz, Kartellbeziehungen No. 1).

43. Kugler, op. cit., p. 65f.

44. Extracts of the contract in ibid., pp. 106–9.

45. Ibid., p. 108.

46. Government-backed attempts for a British-Japanese textile agreement failed. See C. Wurm, "Handelsdiplomatie in der Weltwirtschaftskrise. Internationale Kartelle, Stahl und Baumwolltextilien in der Außenpolitik Großbritanniens 1924–1939," in Wurm, op. cit. (1989), pp. 103–50; C. Wurm, *Industrielle Interssenpolitik und Staat. Internationale Kartelle in der britischen Außen- und Wirtschaftspolitik während der Zwischenkriegszeit* (Berlin, 1988).

47. See Table 1.

48. Internal assessment of the Three-Party Cartel by Waibel (I.G. Farben), Minutes of January 5, 1931 (HA CIBA-Geigy, Geigy VE/IGK 15).

49. Mentioned in the confidential letter of the I.G. Farben representative to the headquarters, April 12, 1929, confidentially passed on to the Three-Party Cartel (May 6, 1929, ibid.)

50. Note of Jan. 5, 1931, ibid.

51. The share capital of N.S.K. was ¥7 million; the missing amount for the dividend could be earned (discussion of Nov. 12, 1931, ibid.).

52. Extract from the stenographic records, Special Committee, ibid.

53. "Mr. Inabata told me that he could take no responsibility in the event that the subsidiary is 'japanized' . . ." ("Report on the Chemical Industry of Japan," ibid.).

54. CIBA's letter to Geigy and Sandoz, May 8, 1929 (ibid.).

55. To Mr. Voigt of I.G. Farben on his trip to Japan (Letter of I.G. Farben for the Three-Party cartel, May 2, 1929).

56. This was a standard demand of I.G. Farben, which, however, did not prevent the I.G. from forming a cartel with ICI!

57. I.G. Farben constantly monitored the technical standards of all its competitors. On May 6, 1929, for instance, it informed the members of the Three-Party Cartel that the latest indigo of Mitsui consisted of 91.1% indigotin and

1.06% water, which made it 8–10% less rich than I.G. Farben's type sold in Japan (ibid.).

58. His letter to C.M.C. February 29, 1932 (ibid).

59. In the end he stayed at N.S.K.

60. Information for the Swiss I.G. May 27, 1929 (ibid.).

61. Inabata Jirō was managing director of N.S.K. and son of Inabata Katsutarō, who was (1) president of N.S.K., (2) owner of Inabata & Co., one of Japan's most distinguished dyestuff trading firms, which served as an agent for St. Denis as well, (3) owner of a big dye-house in Osaka, (4) president of Osaka's Chamber of Commerce, and (5) a member of the Japanese House of Peers (Letter of I.G. Farben to the Three-Party Cartel, May 2, 1929).

62. Letter of I.G. Farben to the Three-Party Cartel, March 4, 1936, ibid.

63. Letter of I.G. Farben to the Four-Party Cartel, February 21, 1938, ibid.

64. Doitsu Senryō Gōmei Kaisha, Kobe.

65. In this group, again, Inabata played a leading role. Letter of April 25, 1929, and drafts sent to I.G. Farben (ibid.).

66. The Italians and their Japanese trading house (Chūgai Bōeki) were not invited to join in order to give no information. Representative of Geigy in Osaka, Mr. Rordorf, to Geigy, August 14, 1929 (ibid.); I.G. Farben to Geigy, Sept. 16, 1929 (ibid.).

67. N.S.K. and I.G. Farben concerning one dye (Variamine Blue Salt B) and one group (Naphthol AS) on the Japanese market for three years (I.G. Farben's letter to the Three-Party Cartel, April 22, 1931, ibid.); Mitsui-I.G. Farben for one dye (Alizarine Blue S) on the Japanese market for three years (I.G. Farben's letter to the Three-Party Cartel, Dec. 5, 1931, ibid.). The Japanese market always included Korea and Formosa.

68. Kugler, op. cit., p. 90f.

69. Ibid. p. 86f.

70. These formed the China-Six-Party Cartel, which from 1930 onwards covered China for the most important dyes.

71. For details, see Schröter, op. cit. (1990).

72. Ibid.

73. Calculated from Kugler, op. cit., p. 19.

74. Yet this was a carefully built cartel, based on the experience of several international aluminum cartels from 1901 onwards. But a heavy demand for armaments, which from 1934 onwards started in different countries with different intensities and in different years, made the influence of the cartel dwindle, though it remained in force on paper up to 1939.

Comment

Jun Sakudō

In the domain of organic chemistry, international agreements or conventions were largely developed from the late 19th century. As regards dyestuffs and pharmaceuticals, a great number of staple products were integrated into an international network of agreements. But these agreements did not last long, nor did there exist an international cartel covering the whole industry. In this sense, the international dyestuffs cartel, with which Dr. Schröter deals in his paper, was really the first one in organic chemistry. We cannot stress too much the significance of this intensive study. But I would like to raise some questions, especially from the point of view of the French fine chemicals industry.

The first question refers to the origin of the German-French treaty in 1927. In this respect, Schröter very properly insists: "All the major dyestuffs producers in Europe perceived the dynamic industrialization of other countries as a threat to their business. Because of this common conviction, all of them were basically willing to join a cartel." But the immediate cause of this treaty lay in the fierceness of the competition between the two countries. As far as French industry is concerned, this competition was so stiff that it might have undermined the foundation of the French dye industry.[1] In my view, this was more or less true of the German industry also. According to the statistical data, dyestuffs production in France expanded very rapidly in the 1920s, and its exports grew favorably in this period. Regarding the Asian market, Etablissements Kuhlmann sold a quantity of its products (especially synthetic indigo) in China.[2] S.A. Saint Denis held long and stable relationships with Inabata Katsutarō, a Japanese leader in the dye industry.[3] That must have been a threat to German companies. In fact, just after the German-French treaty of 1927 the volume of French exports went down sharply because of the reduction of its exports to Asian countries. But the rise of prices would have well compensated for it.

My second question concerns the impact of the development of the American fine chemicals and pharmaceuticals industries on the European cartel. In this respect, the case of European Plate Glass Convention (1904–39) will give us some suggestions. This international cartel was formed in 1904 because the rapid development of American industry was considered as a threat to European countries. This cartel played a major role in associating the European producers, and it formed a real community of European interests, just like the European Coal and Steel Community (ECSC) in 1952.[4] So can we regard the international cartels in the interwar period as one of the prototypes of the EC?

Third, I would like to inquire into the governmental attitudes toward the international dyestuffs cartel. In France, the government promoted very actively the conclusion of the German-French treaty, according to the annual reports of Ets. Kuhlmann.[5] In this way, the French government often interfered in the dye industry in order to control the primary materials for explosives, just as they did in the nitrogen industry. Regarding the French dye industry before World War I, Schröter slightly underestimates its potentialities and writes: "French dyestuff production was based to a great extent on former German direct investment, sequestered during the First World War." But in reality there had already existed several important companies in organic chemistry, such as S.A. Saint Denis and Usines du Rhône (the predecessor of the present Rhône-Poulenc).[6] Neverthless, during World War I, far from promoting the development of these companies, the government took the initiative in establishing a new company by Kuhlmann, which had no experience in organic chemistry. Under these conditions, it was quite natural that the French dye industry should be at the mercy of governmental will. I guess, therefore, that the conclusion of the 1927 treaty was influenced by the pessimistic view of the French government regarding its industry. I would like to know whether this was the case in other countries.

Finally, we have to make clear the effect of an international cartel on technology transfers. This problem is related to the effectiveness of international cartels. In the case of the Japanese dye industry in the 1920s, the technology transfers from French companies made a great contribution to its development.[7] But the German-French treaty stopped these transfers. In spite of this, the Japanese industry succeeded in commercializing some staple products. That illustrates the limits of the effectiveness of international cartels in impeding the progress of newly developing countries. On the other hand, the German-French treaty is supposed to have contained stipulations for exchange of patents and processes. Was the international dyestuffs cartel to promote technology transfers within the European countries, particularly between these two countries? What was the relation of this international cartel to individual agreements, for example, the

1929 patents and processes agreement between ICI and Du Pont? Answering these questions, we would be able to analyze some concrete aspects of the international cartels between the wars.

NOTES

1. Cf. M. Fauque, "L'Evolution économique de la grande industrie chimique en France," Ph.D. thesis, Strasbourg, 1932, section IV; J.H. Lucas (Secrétaire général du Bureau EIA), "L'industrie française des matières colorantes," *Chimie et Industrie* (June 1928): 1151–54.

2. Minutes of ordinary general assemblies of Etablissements Kuhlmann, 1921–28.

3. Inabata Sangyō Kabushiki Kaisha (ed.), *Inabata Sangyō Hachijūhachi Nenshi* (The 88-Year History of Inabata Industrial Corporation), 1978.

4. Cf. J.-P. Daviet, *Un destin international, La Compagnie de Saint-Gobain de 1830 à 1939* (Paris, 1988), chap. VII.

5. Minutes of Etablissements Kuhlmann, June 7, 1928; May 30, 1929.

6. The Minutes of the Meetings of the Board of Directors of La Société chimique des Usines du Rhône, 1914–19; Sakudō Jun, "Jūkyū Seiki Kōhan kara Daiichiji Taisenki no Furansu Yūkikagaku Kōgyō (France's Organic Chemical Industry from the Second Half of the 19th Century to the First World War)," *Japan Business History Review*, vol. 24, no. 2 (July 1989): 1–32.

7. Nihon Senryō Seizō Kabushiki Kaisha (ed.), *Nissen Nijū Nenshi* (The 20-Year History of Nihon Dye Manufacturing Company), 1936, pp. 65–67.

Response

Harm G. Schröter

In the field of pharmaceuticals there was strong international competition indeed. This threatened the French dyestuffs industry as it threatened all others except the old established ones of Germany and Switzerland, which both relied on their superiority in research and development. But even these two were vulnerable to competition in prices, as Professor Sakudō mentioned in his first point. Therefore, one of the major ideas of the international dyestuffs cartel was to restrict the smaller producers to their home countries, which included their colonies, etc. The French industry was mainly restricted to the markets of France and the French empire. This is why French exports fell sharply after the signature of the treaty.

The second point I take issue with. I see no parallel between cartelization and the European Community. While the first is mainly an economic entity, the second is mainly a political one. While the first is to safeguard and/or enrich its members, the second one is focused on politics. The integration of Europe, of course, will be good for the European economy, but it is not directed against and will, I hope, not be detrimental to the economy of other nations.

Concerning the French potential in dyes, I keep up my view, but I would like to clarify it: up to 1914 there was only one indigenous French enterprise producing dyes; all others were foreign direct investments by German and Swiss firms. But I concede that for production know-how is needed. Many French chemists and engineers were employed in all these firms, which meant that there was indeed a substantial potential for the development of the French dye industry. But how much it lagged behind is exemplified in the French-Swiss cartel agreement: all dyes listed on the French list by name because of their value were licensed from Germany, while the Swiss had their own patents. The figures Sakudō referred to are not convincing, because they are based on weight. Dyes are small, light, and expensive. Any assessment here should be based on values. Concerning the pessimistic view of the French government towards its dye industry, this was shared by nearly all other governments as well, because it was obvious that without any protection the situation of 1914 would have re-emerged: about 97% of all dye exports coming either from Germany or Switzerland.

Sakudō's question concerning technology transfer is an extremely important one. Inside the dyestuffs cartel, there was very little of such transfer. The points he mentioned of the French-German treaty were not carried out. On the contrary, we can find in the letters exchanged between the two leaders in advanced techniques, I.G. Farben and the Swiss I.G., that no one was to give any help to anyone. There was little exchange between these two as well. The patent agreements between Du Pont and ICI or between Standard Oil and I.G. Farben or between I.G. Farben and the American rubber industry and their development are too complicated to be answered in a few sentences.

The Management of High Technology: The Use of Information in the German Chemical Industry, 1890–1930

Jonathan Liebenau

That "information is a resource" has become a truism of modern organizational theory. Although the words used in this term are ambiguous, we should be able to test the concept that information is used in the way that other resources are for managerial functions, especially decision making and production control.[1] In this paper I present an analysis of the German chemical industry from the late nineteenth century through the interwar period in relation to its use of cartels. This analysis focuses on the differences in decision-making processes in German companies and considers them in relation to their foreign competitors.

The argument is built on first an analysis of the structure of the chemical industry followed by a more detailed description of the organizational and administrative conditions in Bayer, Hoechst, and Schering. Then the key controlling elements of the management of technology at the time, especially patents, are considered, with a view of the information use by managers concerned with technology and what that might mean for cartelization. Finally, I consider the general theme of decision making and the use of information in relation to information about technology in the industry's move to cartelization.

I. Structure of the German Chemical Industry

The modern German chemicals and pharmaceutical industry emerged in the late nineteenth century from two distinct routes. On the one side there had long been a traditional industry based on standard products which supplied manufacturers and pharmacies as well as the general public with common preparations. The second route was from the newly emerging dyestuffs industry, which by the 1870s had overtaken the previously dominant British and French industry. During the period 1880–1914 this growth was consolidated and the industry built the foundations for further expansion, internationalization, and modern corporate structure. In sum, we can say that the German chemicals and pharmaceuticals industry grew from humble origins in the mid-nineteenth century into a world-dominating position in the early twentieth century. This has previously been explained in terms of the role of scientists and the institutionalization of industrial research and development. In this paper the perspective of the company is taken to show the decision-making processes within firms and the roles they played in international corporate development.[2]

The chemical industry grew out of a variety of businesses based on providing general materials, such as cleaning products for consumers, plus intermediates and catalysts for manufacturers. Paints, dyes, wood treatments, fertilizers, and other such bulk products dominated. The basic products of the chemical industry included acidic and alkaline products for industrial intermediaries, dyes for the textile industry, minor petroleum products, and a wide range of soaps.

The modern pharmaceutical industry grew out of the traditional business of processing and distributing basic medicinal products and drugs. Some of the major firms operating today emerged from the apothecary business, for instance the famous Engel Apotheke, which became Merck A.G., and the business of Meister, Lucius und Brüning (later Hoechst), which left the medicines business to specialize in fine chemicals and dyes before re-entering the industry with synthetic organic pharmaceuticals in the late 1880s. Then, as today, the best-selling medicines were for the relief of dyspepsia, headache, sore throat, constipation, cough, and anaemia. Most large firms also sold popular tonics, antipyretics, antiseptics, and aphrodisiacs.

The pharmaceutical industry during the late nineteenth century was growing and restructuring, and in Germany and the United States, at least, it was following a pattern similar to that which Alfred Chandler, Jr., described for the restructuring of the manufacturing industries.[3] A professional management was taking over a large proportion of the functions, companies were adopting hierarchical structures, and decisions were made in a more systematic manner. Of special importance was the growth of the chemical and pharmaceutical firms as science-based companies, for which the growth of laboratories was especially important.

This changed in the 1880s when the new dyestuffs manufacturers began to produce synthetic medicines. Although England and France held the dominant positions in coal-tar dye production in the 1860s, by the mid-1870s German production accounted for six times the value of English production and overshadowed French output by over seven times. The German industry was also becoming composed mainly of big firms.

In the mid-1880s two problems coincided to throw the dye industry into crisis. The price and marketing convention governing the crucial red dyes broke up in 1885, forcing prices down to half their previous level within a year. At the same time the price of coal tar rose. Laboratories helped to resolve the crisis with new dyestuffs and later by opening up the new field of synthetic medicines. Rapid development continued throughout the 1880s and 1890s and yielded high profits. Not that industrial research can be used as a full explanation for these profits; it was rather a contributing factor, and of course there was a need for sufficient funds to finance R&D staff and facilities.

The place of industrial research and development within corporate structures affected the opportunities companies had to forge strong links with academics. Differences among national contexts, as they affected the use companies could make of academic scientists, are essential to these opportunities.

It was as companies were establishing their scientific laboratories that their range of options was confronted and sometimes discussed. Subsequent practices were often based on the precedents set during those formative periods. They are also revealing of prevailing attitudes, some of which are generalizable over the range of science-based industry, others particular to the pharmaceutical industry, some even more local, applying to conditions in Frankfurt, the Ruhr, or Berlin. These factors caution us about the necessity of limiting our generalizations.

Before the late nineteenth century there had been no commitment to organized research at companies such as Bayer and Hoechst. The conditions of the 1880s, however, made research and development much more attractive. It offered a strategy that might reduce dependence on the ups and downs of the business cycle. For chemists, too, the depressed economy stimulated change. Their numbers had been growing steadily due to expanded opportunities for training in the 1870s. When that expansion slowed in the 1880s academic careers were blocked, and as mobility reduced, chemists more readily accepted industrial employment.

The change in structure of the businesses led to the need to change the use of information about business and about the technology which it employed. In modern terms we might consider this an issue of providing "strategic information." The data which was necessary to understanding trends, and the assessments which had to be made, for example, to determine the extent to which in-house facilities should be used, as opposed to relying on universities and other outsiders, were the kinds of issues which were of utmost importance. Research results were important, as were patent data, but the construction of organizational structures to analyze such results was the real innovation.

The move to IR&D, then, was a result both of a crisis in the dye industry which forced producers to look to different markets and the pull from opportunities offered by new scientific developments. The move to pharmaceuticals, in particular, grew out of this drive to diversify and to become more flexible. For firms such as Bayer and Hoechst, which had previously been in the pharmaceutical industry, the route for such a move seemed clear. However, the stress on pharmaceutical research was new and had major implications for the organization of their research efforts.

At the same time there was increasing interest in sponsored R&D. Universities increasingly organized research laboratories along with their teaching seminars, and government laboratories, largely within the military or public health structure, increasingly became active in R&D which was to prove of commercial value.[4] The value of research results for commercial development was then clear, and the means to use the resulting information was becoming systematic.

Bayer

Bayer established a pattern of hiring Ph.D. chemists for one year and then sending them to a university or Technische Hochschule laboratory, where they worked on research problems related to the company production program. Not until 1886 did they build their own laboratory for academic-style research, but even then they kept it a safe distance from the manufacturing site.

The critical change at Bayer came as the result of the influence of Carl Duisberg. Duisberg had joined the company in 1884 after having done research for Bayer at the University of Strassburg. As his work on artificial organic colors expanded he gathered a large team of chemists which performed many functions. Its members had to make rapid shifts among research, development, production, and sales and began to have increasing influence in the company. The company responded in 1890 by recognizing the research chemist as a distinctive full-time role, and in 1891 opened a new, centralized, integrated laboratory. As the laboratory grew, its functions became more clearly defined, and the general purpose of transforming findings into profitable products was clarified. Testing and process improvements became a separate area, as did the patent bureau. Chemical engineering was the concern for the technical room, where laboratory procedures were scaled up into manufacturing processes. Duisberg joined the Bayer Board of Directors in 1900, championed his laboratories, and was assured that they received due attention from the management. The success of Aspirin provided him with enough backing to support his strong claims. By 1913, 10 of 17 members of the Bayer Board of Directors were chemists, and 25 of 43 Prokuristen.[5] Their ability to understand scientific information and to influence decision making by the top management had become recognized as a valuable resource.

Hoechst

The growth in the number of chemists employed at Hoechst resembled that at Bayer. Between 1888 and 1912, the number of chemists rose from 57 to over 300 in total, while those classified as "Techniker" rose from 9 to 74 during that period, when the total number of employees rose from just over 2,000 to over 9,000. This rise, impressive as it was, did not quite keep up with the proportion of sales people in the company.[6]

A high proportion of the scientists associated with Hoechst research and development from the late nineteenth century through the interwar period acted primarily as consultants. They were either kept on retainer while they maintained their university positions, or, in some cases, brought their work to the company laboratories. This role of consultant is especially interesting in relation to the ability of companies to use technical information for commercial purposes. It is also an indication of the seriousness with which companies took such sources.

Many of the major universities and a few Technische Hochschule were represented among the consultants brought in to work at Hoechst. Especially good contact was maintained with Munich and Berlin through such chemists as Konrad Fromherz, who established a working relationship with the company while still a student. He was brought in by Dr. E. von Gerichten, a Hoechst laboratory leader who had worked in Munich as assistant to Adolf Baeyer, Emil Fischer, and Otto Fischer in the early 1880s. Von Gerichten brought Fromherz to the company part time in 1913, but Fromherz maintained his position as assistant in Munich through the war, moving to Hoechst as a full-time research scientist only in 1920. Four years later he returned to Munich, where he resumed his academic career.

Fromherz's relationship with the company and the university was exemplary in some ways, but there was no "typical" status. Some simply maintained active correspondence with leading scientists in the company, while others used the laboratories for major research projects. Most had at least some form of financial tie, usually through the assignment of patents to the company, for which they were paid well, often by royalties as well as fees. Professor Einhorn, a chemist at the University of Munich, was one such collaborator who worked on Novocain, Holocain, Nirvanin, and other anaesthetics. He received around 1,200 reichsmarks annually between about 1900 and 1912, ostensibly for chemicals, glassware, and other laboratory necessities, in addition to royalties on patents he assigned to Hoechst. Apparently, however, his pay acted as a retainer.

The network of personal contacts and institutional associations was extensive but not complex. For the 38 influential Hoechst scientists of the early 20th century whom we studied, the universities or Technische Hochschule in Berlin, Bonn, Breslau, Erlangen, and Munich were strongly represented, with extensive contacts also at Giessen, Halle, and Jena. Surprisingly, only a small number of people can be identified as key outsiders supporting that network, but not suprisingly three of the most important individuals were Robert Koch, Wilhelm Filehne, and Emil Fischer, among the leading professors of the day.

The careers of some company scientists were also highly productive in academic terms. Johannes Bieberfeld began his association with Hoechst through the first manager of the company pharmaceutical laboratory, Dr. Friedrich Stolz. Stolz had developed Hoechst's first major pharmaceutical success, "Pyramidon," in 1893 in association with Wilhelm Filehne while Filehne was professor in Erlangen. In 1906 Stolz worked with Takamine Jōkichi to synthesize adrenaline at Hoechst, and throughout the period worked on neurotropic medicines. Stolz brought Bieberfeld into the development side of the work in 1901 while Bieberfeld was still an assistant at the Pharmacological Institute at Breslau under Filehne, who was at that time the Institute's director. With both affiliations, Bieberfeld maintained an active career which earned him professorial status in 1909 while working on such major products as Anaesthesin, Novocain, Suprarenin, and, during wartime, advanced anaesthetics. He died in 1922 after over 20 years of active association with the company but was remembered with mixed feelings: "Maybe Bieberfeld was just a little too cautious in the judgement of some new promising preparations. As a consequence, further collaboration and consultation could not be exploited entirely."[7] Although meant as criticism, perhaps these are the characteristics which contributed positively to the balanced career development of company scientists.

Attitudes toward sponsorships and collaborations changed slightly after the war, perhaps to take advantage of the successes resulting from prewar associations with Paul Ehrlich's research institutes in Frankfurt a.M. When the director of the Eppendorf-Hamburg hospital approached Hoechst with a plan to found a pathological-pharmacological institute in his hospital to test new and old medicines through his clinic, he received serious consideration. He proposed a systematic testing procedure in collaboration with pharmacological theorists which would make best use of hospital facilities. Hoechst agreed to initial support of 50,000 reichsmarks for the first five years, in partnership with some state and eleemosynary funding.[8]

Attitudes toward company scientists also changed somewhat faster after the war. There was a greater emphasis on internal training, with a new enthusiasm for preparing pharmaceutical staff for apothecary certification. Fourteen scientists, including eight who already held doctorates, passed their state exams in 1920 and were duly recognized and rewarded by the company. This marks the next major change in attitudes toward company scientists. By the interwar period a stable relationship with academics had taken on the form of regular recruiting, commissioning, collaborating, and sponsored in-house training. Already before the war the scale of these first two operations was large enough to necessitate some standard operating procedures, and after the war the latter two came into their own, largely as a consequence of the confidence which came from over 25 years of experience, but also because of the availability of responsible in-house intellectual resources.

Hoechst's use of scientists for commercial purposes is a model for how to build up the resources to assess the kind of technical information necessary to assess the business advantages of cartels. Most of the leading firms in cartels had deep-rooted scientific resources.

Schering

Schering's gradual internalization of research functions followed better than that of Bayer or Hoechst a logic of minimizing transaction costs. After a few years of growing relations with the Berlin academic community, it became evident to the Schering managers that they would make better use of their equipment and have more stable links outside the firm if they built up their permanent staff.

Located in Berlin, Schering had first choice among a number of the leading medical scientists and close ties with the University of Berlin and with the Charite Hospital complex. As a pharmaceutical firm, they were somewhat older than the young dyestuffs manufacturers and had a more traditional line of remedies on which to base the business. For this reason they were less pressed to innovate for the sake of opening new product lines. They did, however, wish to take advantage of the local talent and so were willing to build laboratories at the firm in which university scientists and their students could extend their academic work toward product development.[9]

Schering produced some of the new medicines of the 1890s but lost its position to Hoechst by 1900 because of the move of Ehrlich's ministry of health laboratory from Berlin to Frankfurt and Hoechst's ability to capitalize on that. Schering's approach was to base as much as possible on outsiders working within the company, but they regularly hired for periods of two to five years the students of leading Berlin manufacturers.[10]

The industry, then, began with company-sponsored R&D in a haphazard, reactive way. No strategy for corporate laboratory development was discussed, and even the notion that there should be an adequate return on investment was missing. The people brought in or consulted were for the most part either academic chemists or general medical scientists, and rarely specialists. By the period immediately before the First World War this had changed as it became apparent that laboratories capable of conducting academic-style research were necessary. For competitive advantage and to be able to keep up with the raised technical standards of both the industry and its consumers, laboratories had to be integrated into the newly expanded corporate structures of large fine chemical companies. Already at the end of the nineteenth century strategies for exploiting this technological lead in a systematic way were being developed to strengthen what had become a strongly export-oriented industry, with close to 70% of German production exported by the turn of the century. In this context the importance of cartels was paramount, and competitive advantage was seen largely in terms of scientific skill.

Ervin Hexner gives a few examples of this vagueness when he describes a set of hypothetical agreements which might be regarded as cartels, but for which there is no documentation and perhaps even an opportunity for the participants to claim that they were not aware that they were making any sort of illegal agreement, to say nothing of a binding cartel-type contract.[11] Such tacit and secret understanding certainly did exist, sometimes leading to documented cartels.

Archives of companies contain a wide range of types of documents. Often we find market reports, laboratory reports, cost estimates, and data on staff. We as historians use them in a variety of ways, but too little have we considered what use the decision makers in the companies made of that material. How important was it in helping them decide what to do next? How were they used in conjunction? This problem is aggravated by what Hexner describes as the aversion of cartel members to formulate and record the cartel's plans, policies, and procedures. They were frequently formulated "in brief, rather fragmentary documents and founded on hazy records and oral conventions. . . . One of the great cartel practicians,

Aloys Meyer, wrote that the 'ideal entente' would have no written regulations at all."[12]

II. Patents and Cartels

Patents

Patents were among the most important sources of strategic information. In 1902 the number of German-held American patents exceeded British and continued to rise at a spectacular rate. Patents for the chemical industry accounted for a large proportion of that rise. By the decade after the turn of the century, Germans had taken out 1,754 patents in the 10 largest classes of chemical patents, as opposed to only 212 British and around 1,550 acquired by Americans. By far the most patents in any one area of chemical patenting between 1900 and 1910 was in pharmaceuticals and organic colors. Of 862 U.S. patents, 701 were held by Germans, as opposed to only 11 held by Britons and 19 by Americans. Swiss inventors held a further 115, making the German and Swiss holdings account for well over 90% of all American organic color patents. Other areas of significant patenting included inorganic salts, dyeing agents, mineral acids, and internal medicines. In total, Germany held 43% of American chemical patents, compared with Britain's 5%.

This spectacular rise was not just the consequence of a highly successful chemical industry; these statistics do not reflect the size of the industry accurately, and they are evidence of a concerted strategy to use patents as a tool of business. In outline, the strategy involved patenting as many potentially interesting products of industrial R&D as possible. By potentially interesting I mean that there was no effort first to ascertain the utility of the chemicals, and the results went beyond the need to protect single entities. Patents were taken out to build walls around whole research areas. It became a bar to a competitor that every potential product, intermediary product, or spin-off was going to be held by a rival's patent, then it would serve as a powerful disincentive to explore territory already eliminated by the company first in the field. This strategy was certainly already recognized by the three leading German firms by the end of the 19th century. From that time, the big three, Bayer, BASF, and Hoechst owned between them 66% of all German-held U.S. chemical patents.

Those firms which acquired a large number of American patents had begun to use the patent system as a major weapon in their attempt to secure markets by blocking domestic competition from American manufacturers. Along with this strategy they used their powerful market position to compel foreign firms to join them in international control or cartel agreements in which patents played a major part.

By 1913 Germany was producing 85% of the world dyestuffs output and providing 95% of Britain's imports. The German dyestuffs industry was 25 times as large as its British counterpart, a position it had stabilized before the war by its intricate network of cartels based on the strength of its patents.

The German chemical and pharmaceuticals industry was by the turn of the century very strongly export oriented. Based on its well-coordinated product development strategy and efficient large-scale production techniques, these large firms constructed a system of international commercial domination which only the war could undermine. As the later history of I.G. Farben shows, the structures formed at this time were relatively easy to reconstruct, contributing to the further domination of the world chemicals market in the interwar period.

From the point of view of the companies, at least three factors need to be considered. The most important is the conception of senior managers of what scientists could best do within their business. A second is the size and structure of the firms themselves. Third, and related to the other two, is the notion of common and accepted practice in the countries of origin.

As for the conception of managers, the difference between the view of a person like Carl Duisberg of what a scientific staff might do for Bayer is quite different from the view held by managers in a leading British firm such as Allen & Hanbury's, where there was no drive for new product development and the low level of science necessary for quality control was more important than grand scientific enquiry. These differences meant that both the size and the relative influence of the scientific staff was different. It also made the difference between scientists who had incentives and opportunities to cultivate academic links and those whose routine work left them in relative isolation.

Where firms were large, as were the German manufacturers, the investment in scientists was marginal to the total cost of running the business. Where the firms were divisionalized and made use of middle managers, the scientific staff could more easily fit into the structure without undue threat to the existing professionals. Finally, whether having corporate scientists was a common and accepted practice was influenced as much by the attitude of scientists as of managers. That German scientists were forced to look to industry for careers was partly a result of the overproduction of researchers trained for academic careers. That German managers were willing to consider them as fruitful contributors to company ambitions is related to the attitude of many of those managers who saw themselves also as professionals, and in some cases as scientific managers.

From both sides the concept of a career as corporate scientist was acceptable in Germany.

Overall, the German pharmaceutical industry was remarkably successful in product development, from even before the growth of corporate scientific staff. Its effective use of them is directly related to its especial achievements in the 20th century. That use cannot be simplified as one limited to the activities of single-minded researchers working competitively to develop new medical products. Corporate scientists proved their value in a much broader range of activities, ensuring an enduring relationship between companies and researchers which was the cornerstone for cartelization. Their role in the control of patents and processes, at least as much as the value of trademark agreements, formed the basis of cartels in pharmaceuticals.[13]

Cartels

It was in the German chemical industry in the late 19th century that techniques for building cartels and strategies for using them became highly developed. First, in association with each other, later extending internationally, these cartels, selling agreements, and pricing conventions did more than manipulate national markets for single products; they strongly influenced the rate and direction of the industry's growth.

Based on the strength of the dye industry and the expansion of Germany's economic sphere of influence, German companies began to compete on a variety of fronts. To reduce that competition, German chemical makers began to use marketing agreements among themselves and soon to include their foreign competitors. Examples of agreements entered into between 1887 and 1910 include those covering iodine, camphor, salicin, bromine, strychnine, caffeine, and codeine. For the most part these agreements specified prices and markets, defined geographically. Sometimes they specified further what proportion of raw material available generally could be allocated among signatories.[14] Hexner is correct when he points out that cartel growth was not usually the result of conscious planning but rather from following the line of least resistance. Their organizational structure tended to be appropriate for the tasks they were expected to perform, and the chemical cartels, since they were based on patents and the exchange of technological experience, had a different structure from those based on other products.[15]

An indication of the background to cartelization in the pharmaceuticals industry is apparent in the correspondence between Thomas Morson and the Boehringer company in the 1870s.[16] The frustration is apparent in the inability of the British seller to know how much his competitors are selling their German imports for until market control has already been affected. Morson pleads with Boehringer to help control the prices of all of the British sellers of their products. The next step, which took another 15 years to take on its formal structure, was that of cartels.

From the point of view of the British industry especially, the arrangements they entered into became a major aspect of their business. Regarded as "remedial" and "defensive," rather than monopolistic, these agreements were initially only oriented toward raising prices in the aftermath of price wars. Combinations also allowed temporary alliances without requiring significant rationalization, increased productivity, or expanded marketing. Particularly good examples are the caffeine, iodine, and camphor cartels. The first two are illustrations of the reaction of firms to the need for combinations, and the third is an example of the fragility of these agreements due to their inability to address the cause and not just the symptoms of market share problems.

The caffeine combination was initiated in 1894. The signatories were the German firm Boehringer & Söhne and the English companies Howard & Sons and Thomas Whiffen. The agreement established an accord for the mutual purchase of tea sweepings which were needed in the production of caffeine. After joint purchase, the sweepings were divided up with one half going to the Germans and the other half being split 20/30. A ceiling was placed on the purchase price to guard against price inflation. Prices for the finished product were to be agreed on and could be reduced only under special circumstances in particular markets, as was the case for the United States in the mid-1890s. The agreement had three purposes. These were to guarantee access to tea sweepings at a competitive price, to divide market shares, and to obtain a higher price for caffeine. A fourth purpose was to be able to maintain control over information about trade, so that no nasty shocks would disrupt business.[17]

The first was relatively simple to achieve. Since sweepings were purchased mutually and divided according to contract, there was little risk in obtaining supplies. At the same time it barred signatories from disproportionately increasing production, reducing their ability to grow quickly. Although the agreement specified three-year renewal, indicating their assumption that this would be a short-term tool, it was so successful in controlling German and American competition that it was repeatedly renewed.

The iodine combination involved 18 companies. All signatories agreed to purchase iodine exclusively from one German supplier. They agreed to cease transferring iodine to firms outside the combination, but could exchange supplies among themselves. To secure the agreement they were each required to deposit a £1,000 promissory note from which fines could be deducted. Its size and the stringency of threatened sanctions distinguished the iodine from the caffeine combination. Again, its success can be measured by its repeated renewal through to the outbreak of war and then into the interwar period.[18]

The camphor cartel was radically different in structure from the other two, though it sought to address the same internal factors. Unlike the other two, this combination encountered external factors which easily destroyed it. The arrangement was between fifteen firms, four British, six German, two French, two Italian, and one Czech, and was based on an informal, secret agreement. Goodwill was casually assured by the understanding that since most of the members were formally involved in other combinations, gentlemanly behavior could be expected.[19]

They quickly ran into trouble. One German and the major Japanese suppliers were unwilling to join the combination. Since the Japanese government controlled the production in all the regions where crude camphor grew, Taiwan and the Philippines, they were able to undercut agreed prices and offer divisive terms to opportunistic members through the Suzuki trading company. In 1909 the agreement completely collapsed, after much secretive acrimony.[20] A further effort was made in 1918 by the Japan Camphor Company, Ltd., of Kobe, a state monopoly. But synthetic camphor affected prices, and marketing agreements could not be reestablished and enforced.[21] The case of the camphor cartel and its dissolution on account of the encroachment of synthetic camphor is an interesting example of the threat of technical development on a product which is not well protected by patents. In 1927 the extent of this encroachment was made clear by the British consul at Tamsui who wrote that "the inroads made by synthetic camphor into the markets of Formosan natural camphor in foreign countries have . . . attracted much attention [and have created a] serious problem [which] threatens the existence of one of the most important Formosan industries."[22]

In 1905 a salicin agreement was established (or reinforced) by C.F. Boehringer & Söhne (Mannheim), as head agents, and E. Merck (Darmstadt), J.F. MacFarlan, T.&H. Smith, and Thomas Whiffen (all of London). The intention was "to hold the same price and terms for the sale of salicine in Europe and the United States of America, and all other markets."[23] Details of the terms are then spelled out in documents which specify prices in local European currencies.

A more clear example of the use of information in the conduct of cartels is specified in the strychnine convention involving Boehringer, Hoffman La

Roche, E. Merck, Schaefer Alkaloid Works (Maywood, New Jersey), and Thomas Whiffen.[24] In addition to the normal clauses, there is provision for an umpire and controller, Dr. Paul Rottenburg, who will "inform members of their respective quotas, but will not divulge the share of one party to any other." Furthermore, "all data [are] to be reported to Rottenburg showing quantities of strychnine pure and respective salts, as delivered."

These cartels were typical of the arrangements used by German companies to try to stabilize trade, but they served national interests differently.[25] To the Germans it opened markets overseas and took advantage of superior British supply routes. This facilitated their growth especially by opening up new areas. For the British, however, the agreements were usually drawn up with the intention of covering products which were already being imported, processed, and sold or exported. Their advantage was primarily in price-fixing, and it was a defensive strategy which staved off competition. British interests were directed at imperial territories and the United States, the first to postpone German commercial encroachment and the second in the naive hope that they could regain their early-nineteenth-century position as major suppliers. What they failed to understand was that by emulating the German industry, American manufacturers, with effective governmental aid, were being transformed fundamentally.[26]

The quinine cartel is of particular interest because it shows how the operation of a complete cartel could be controlled by using key information about the product from its production as a bark grown on tropical plantations (largely in Java), its shipment, and the production of the final product. Quinine is a general antipyretic and a prophylactic for and remedy against malaria. Since the late nineteenth century the government of the Dutch East Indies controlled the plantations and established a license system whereby exports were regulated.

In terms of marketing controls two cartel organizations were active: the Association of Cinchona Producers, which controlled the production and export, and the producers of quinine salts, who cooperated with the association. At the end of the nineteenth century German and Dutch manufacturers organized a buying cartel to press down the prices of raw materials.[27] This affected price movements from 1884 to 1904 and led in 1907 to the colonial government's establishment of a comprehensive organization of producers, leading in 1913 to the Kina Bureau in Amsterdam. The bureau fixed prices for sulfate of quinine, and governments and welfare institutions were permitted to take large discounts. Retail prices were also fixed by the cartel, and the cartel is said to have bought up cinchona bark supplies of Latin America to prevent these supplies from becoming available to the United States.[28]

Perceptions of the functions of cartels differed. The British view was largely defensive, to protect established areas of trade and to avoid having to alter company structure to introduce new products. The Swiss were involved reluctantly. They needed to become involved in order to acquire initial market share, but they entered into relatively few arrangements and withdrew as soon as their short-term goals were met. Among the French companies, only the leading manufacturers participated. Most were not involved with large-scale exports, so wished only to secure their own domestic market, and otherwise they competed directly with for-eigners.

III. Conclusion: Decision Making and the Use of Information

In the use of information, the use of quantitative data is one of the most easily assessed indicators. Most cartels, and almost all of the ones in the fine chemicals industry, had statistical services informing members about market situations, stocks, actual business transactions, and so forth.[29] Managers were of course interested in costs and in investments in technology, but there were few guidelines about how to measure what might be reasonable levels of expenditure. Investments in technology differed from other business expenditures in that they were different from marketing new products, or even in product development activities where relatively short-term calculations could, and sometimes were, made.

The key question we must try to answer is: what differences did different management make for these company's decisions to cooperate in cartels? We can begin to answer that by looking at what kinds of concerns they each had. Most were interested in the enforcement of cartels and would base their decision on whether to join more on their perception of the enforceability of the agreement than on the details of the original offer. That is because the selling prices could always be renegotiated, but if the structure of the cartel was weak then there was no point in trying to main-tain control.

In recent years it has become increasingly evident that the quality of information which businesses have to use and the skill with which decision makers use it is crucial to the businesses' success. We can analyze the use of information by businesses by a careful analysis of decision-making proc-esses. This will give us a clearer idea of not only the ability of managers to gather and analyze data which is available to them, but also of their ability and interest in turning it into usable information for the purpose at hand. Where the goal was the arrangement of a cartel, the kind of information needed was various and extensive.

Furthermore, since there was an extremely wide range of types of cartel arrangements, especially in the pharmaceutical industry, the varying interpretations of appropriate information meant that different managers had vastly different criteria of appropriateness. For example, where arrangements were made to limit involvement in certain markets, there was an implicit assumption that the agent restricted would otherwise have wished to have moved into that market, and that it had the capability to do so. The information which was presumed in such a situation would go well beyond what was actually happening and would be the result of a complex set of inferences.

NOTES

1. Jonathan Liebenau and James Backhouse, *Understanding Information* (London, 1990), pp. 2–3.

2. Jonathan Liebenau, "Industrial R&D in Pharmaceutical Firms in the Early Twentieth Century," *Business History*, vol. 26 (1984): 329–46; Sachio Kaku, "The Development and Structure of the German Coal-Tar Dyestuffs Firms," in Akio Okochi and Hoshimi Uchida (eds.), *Development and Diffusion of Technology: Electrical and Chemical Industries* (Tokyo, 1980).

3. Alfred D. Chandler, Jr., *The Visible Hand: The Managerial Revolution in American Business* (Cambridge, 1977).

4. Wilhelm Vershofen, *Wirtschaftsgeschichte der Chemisch-Pharmazeutischen Industrie, 1870–1914*, vol. III (Wuerttenburg, 1958), pp. 110–24.

5. G. Meyer-Thurow, "The Industrialization of Invention: A Case Study from the German Chemical Industry." *Isis*, vol. 73 (1982): 361–381; Gottfried Plumpe, "Chemische Industrie und Hilfsdienstgesetz am Beispiel der Farbenfabriken, vorm. Bayer & Co." (1984): 179–209.

6. "Chronik der Pharmazeutischen Abteilung Hoechst" (anonymous typescript, circa 1934), Hoechst Firmenarchiv.

7. Ibid., pp. 341–42.

8. Jonathan Liebenau, "Paul Ehrlich as a Commercial Scientist and Research Administrator," *Medical History* (1989).

9. Schering A.G. archive, XB 1.11.3.3; Paul Hirschfeld, "Mittheilungen über die Entwickelung der Chemische Fabrik auf Actien (vorm. E. Schering)," in R. Jannasch (ed.), *Berlins Grossindustrie*, vol. II (Berlin, n.d. circa 1900); P. Korn, "Geschichte der Bakteriolog. Abteilung der Schering A.G. 1893–1942" (unpublished ms, Schering archive, 1942).

10. Hans Hollaender, *Geschichte der Schering Aktiengesellschaft* (Berlin, 1955), pp. 25–43.

11. Ervin Hexner, *International Cartels* (London, 1946), p. 65.

12. Ibid., p. 64.

13. Ibid., pp. 331ff.

14. Jonathan Liebenau, "Ethical Business: The Formation of the Pharmaceutical Industry in Britain, Germany and the United States before 1914," *Business History*, vol. 30, no. 1 (1988): 116–29.

15. Hexner, op. cit., p. 69.

16. Morson Papers, private collection of the Morson family, Letterbook, pp. 155ff.

17. "Caffeine" files, Whiffen Company Papers, Greater London Record Office, B/WHF/25.

18. "Iodine Preparations Combination" Whiffen Company Papers, Greater London Record Office, B/WHF/25; B/WHF/160.

19. "Crude Camphor" Whiffen Company Papers, Greater London Record Office, B/WHF/161.

20. Ibid., correspondence regarding Mr. S. Takemura, Mitsui & Co. and Mr. Suzuki, between Julius Grossmann and Thomas J. Whiffen, November 1908 to February 1909.

21. Hexner, op. cit., pp. 306–7.

22. Letter of 14 December 1927, H.M. Consul, Tamsui, "Crude Camphor," Whiffen & Son papers, Greater London Record Office, B/WHF/161.

23. Whiffen papers, Greater London Record Office, "Conventions" B/WHF/25.

24. Ibid., "Strychnine Combination, 1 Jan 1907."

25. Jerome Arthur Eddy, *The New Competition* (Chicago, 1917); John Hilton, *Combines and Trade Organizations* (London, 1919).

26. G.R. Carter, *The Tendency Towards Industrial Combination in Some Spheres of British Industry* (London, 1913); J. Morgan Ress, *Trusts in British Industry* (London, 1922).

27. Hexner, op. cit. p. 337.

28. Ibid., p. 337.

29. Ibid., p. 109.

Comment

Nobuo Kawabe

In his paper on the development of German chemical and pharmaceutical industries and the formation of cartels, Dr. Liebenau emphasizes the role of business information in the decision-making processes. The use of such business information as market reports, laboratory reports, cost estimates, and data on staff by business managers has not received sufficient attention, and Liebenau analyzes the decision-making processes through which German companies participated in the formation of cartels. Although the subject of this paper is very challenging, not all the objectives have been successfully attained.

Liebenau's paper addresses three aspects: the development of close relations between science and business; patents; and cartels in the chemical and pharmaceutical industries. The relations among these three aspects are not clear and in terms of information and the decision-making process, many questions come to mind.

First, the German companies Bayer, Hoechst, and Schering established their own laboratories and developed close relations between science and business, which contributed to their competitive advantage. Was this unique only to German companies? When we consider the nature of products manufactured by pharmaceutical companies, this approach should be applicable to foreign companies in the same industry. What was the situation of such companies in the United States, England, and Switzerland, for example?

Second, regarding cartels, Liebenau suggests that German companies used their powerful market position to compel foreign firms to join the international control or cartel agreements in which patents played a major role. Company scientists were valuable assets as interpreters of scientific information who could influence the decision making of the top management. But how could these scientists use their ability or influence over the formation of cartels to prevent the entrance of foreign companies into the market?

Third, in the section on patents Liebenau stresses the importance of patents as strategic information. Although the competitive advantages of German companies are explained in terms of the number of their patents, there are no concrete examples of cartels in which technological or scientific advantages played important roles.

The examples cited of cartels for caffeine, iodine, camphor, and quinine do not seem to be based on scientific advantages, i.e., patents. Concrete examples of cartel formation in which companies such as Bayer, BASF, and Schering took leadership based upon their patents would have been instructive.

Fourth, even if there had been advantages in the formation of cartels, foreign competitors were supposed to protect their positions. Sometimes governments and other interest groups were involved in the negotiation process. The negotiation and decision-making processes in the formation of the cartels could have been addressed: How were differences among countries brought out? How were they coordinated?

Finally, the conclusion of the paper is very general. As Liebenau concludes, "The key question we must try to answer is: what difference did different management make for these company's decisions to cooperate in cartels?" The case studies and discussions in the main text of the paper do not seem to support his conclusion. I look forward to future studies that will fit historical evidence into a general theory or model of decision making and information usage in the formation of cartels.

Conflict and Cooperation between the International Nitrogen Cartel and Japan's Ammonium Sulfate Industry

Takeshi Ōshio

I. Introduction

The discovery of the Haber process, which first made the synthesis of ammonia possible, was an epoch-making event in the history of the nitrogen-fixing industry. Moreover, it can be counted as one of the most important advances in the chemical industry as a whole. Given this impetus, a number of other synthetic processes were developed in the 1920s, but the corporations using these processes had to provide huge amounts of capital. Moreover, when it came to sales, these methods proved to have other difficulties. In other words, it was envisaged that the factories producing the ammonia would be operated continuously. However, actual demand for the ammonia was seasonal, as it was mainly consigned for use in chemical fertilizers. Therefore, preparations of large-scale storage facilities had to be made, and capital had to be raised to pay for the large amount of stock necessary. Thus participation in the synthetic ammonia industry was limited to big corporations with abundant capital reserves. Moreover, in view of the existence of the danger of overproduction, agreements regarding the control of markets were made not only domestically but internationally too.[1]

At the end of the 1920s, the threat of overproduction became a reality, and this led to the formation of an international cartel. Needless to say, Japan too was affected by these developments. Japanese corporations were competing with each other to introduce the various types of technology derived from the Haber process, developed in the technologically advanced nations of Europe and America, and their relationship with the international nitrogen cartel changed in a short time from one of competition to one of cooperation. This paper sets out to explain how this took place, while at the same time singling out the various factors causing the change.

Incidentally, before undertaking this, I feel it would be expedient to give, in as far as is necessary, a general view of the development of the Japanese ammonium sulfate industry.

The man who was able to comprehend most precisely the trends in the global nitrogen industry and who led the development of this industry in Japan, was one Noguchi Jun. He was not only a technical expert, but also possessed superb skills as an administrator. Noguchi, in fact, made a contribution to the development of the Japanese chemical industry as a whole. He purchased the patent license to the cyanamide process and set up Nippon Chisso Hiryō Co. (Japan Nitrogen Fertilizer Co.) in 1908. This was only ten years after the invention of this process by A. Frank and N. Caro. Noguchi Jun succeeded in combining sulfuric acid with ammonia, obtained from calcium cyanamide separated in steam, to produce ammonium sulfate. Production of this was begun in 1914 and progressed smoothly. In 1921, he acquired the patent license to the synthetic ammonia method originated by Luigi Casale and planned to carry out production using this method. In 1923, operation of the synthesis equipment was begun, and in 1924 a commercial production system was set up. Following the success of this, Noguchi began large-scale development of electric power resources in the Korean peninsula and started to develop a sizable synthetic ammonia enterprise there. Nippon Chisso Hiryō's subsidiary, Chōsen Chisso Hiryō Co. (Korea Nitrogen Fertilizer Co.), began production in 1930. Production figures for Chōsen Chisso Hiryō were 193,000 tons in 1931, and by 1937 they had reached 405,000 tons. During this time the average prime manufacturing cost for ammonium sulfate was only ¥17.[2] It is probable that the German I.G. Farbenindustrie AG (I.G. Farben), which was in the same field, showed a performance that was by no means inferior to that of Noguchi's enterprise.

A number of corporations, goaded by the success of Nippon Chisso Hiryō, introduced synthetic ammonia technology and began production of ammonium sulfate. Representative examples of such enterprises include Dai Nippon Jinzō Hiryō Co. (Japan Artificial Fertilizer Co.) with the Fauser process, Miike Chisso Co. (Miike Nitrogen Co.) with the Claude process, Sumitomo Kagaku Co. (Sumitomo Chemical Co.) with the N.E.C. (Nitrogen Engineering Corp.) process, and Shōwa Hiryō Co. (Showa Fertilizer Co.) with the Tokyo Industrial Experimental Laboratory process. In short, most of the variants of the Haber process that had been developed in Europe and America in the 1920s were in fact utilized by the various Japanese ammonium sulfate corporations. This willingness to introduce technology and make investment in plant and equipment supported the steep growth that these Japanese companies managed to achieve in the 1930s. In the case of the introduction of synthetic ammonia technology, the time lapse between the initial technological development in the advanced nations of Europe and America and the introduction of this technology by the Japanese corporations was minimal. However, a slight gap did exist in the time it took the Japanese corporations to introduce the new technology, and its existence was emphasized by the fact that overproduction using these synthetic ammonia processes in Europe occurred just at the time when their introduction was beginning to take off in Japan. This helped to complicate relations between the international nitrogen cartel and the Japanese ammonium sulfate companies.

II. The Competition between the International Nitrogen Cartel and Japan's Ammonium Sulfate Industry

In the mid-1920s, nitrogen produced by synthetic ammonia held a 41.4% share in the world nitrogen production of 1,090,000 tons. Synthetic ammonia thus exceeded Chile saltpeter, ammonia as a by-product, and calcium cyanamide as the main material for nitrogen manufacture. When I.G. Farben was set up in 1925, its production capacity was 350,000 tons. It was in the latter half of the 1920s that leaders in terms of productive capacity in the various countries began to actually emerge. Production of synthetic ammonia by the predecessors of Britain's ICI (Imperial Chemical Industries), Brunner, Mond & Co., Ltd., and Du Pont de Nemours & Co., E.I., began in 1925. In 1928–29, synthesis production plants, including those of the aforementioned companies, were put into actual operation in Europe and America, and production of ammonium sulfate increased. Moreover, production of Chile saltpeter expanded after 1927, and its exports also rose.[3] Thus the signs of a trend towards overproduction and overproduction capacity began to appear, and this influenced the decision to form a cartel. Especially after 1929, with the fall in demand owing to the worsening of the agricultural depression on the one hand, and the increase in each country's productive capacity on the other, there was a sudden increase in stock due to worldwide overproduction. Therefore, at the end of 1929, moves towards the actual setting up of an international cartel began. In February 1930, a ten-year agreement between I.G. Farben and ICI was signed. This concerned production limits, sales quotas, and provision of sales facilities worldwide excluding the North American continent. At this point Germany, Britain, and Norway formed the DEN group, which from then on took the initiative in negotiations. The focal point for discussions at the following three International Nitrogen Conferences became the confrontation between the European producer nations and Chile. Moreover, within Europe itself, confrontation arose between the DEN group, which was trying to protect existing export markets through the imposition of uniform general production limits, and the later group formed by France, Belgium, and Holland, which sought to expand the productive capacity of its domestic industries through protection of domestic markets. Eventually a compromise was reached by which the DEN group acknowledged the right of protection of their own markets by France and others. The European countries and Chile also came to an understanding. Therefore, in August 1930, a total of ten countries beginning with Germany, Britain, and Norway concluded the international nitrogen agreement, the Convention Internationale de l'Azote (known as the CIA), which was to run initially until 1931. The main points of this were: the restriction of increases in productive capacity, demand in the markets of the countries that were party to the agreement and their subject states being met by production from the said country, and the division by fixed quota of exports to those countries outside the agreement. Moreover, the administration of exports was to be given over to a nitrogen syndicate and ICI. This international nitrogen agreement (CIA) was due to be renewed in June 1931, but this was not done owing to opposition by Chile. However, in 1932, Chile was granted membership and the second CIA was drafted. This agreement was revised repeatedly and lasted until the outbreak of the Second World War.[4]

Following this, from 1929, the international nitrogen cartel began a dumping offensive against Japan. The price of ammonium sulfate, which had been above ¥130 per ton in 1929, dropped to ¥100 in March 1930 and ¥70 by November. This was because the international cartel forced German and British companies to export to Japan. As is shown in Table 1, up until 1931 domestic production in Japan did not exceed imports. Therefore the price on the ammonium sulfate market was decided by imports. According to Figure 1, by 1929 the price gap between imports and domestic products had suddenly narrowed, and moreover both had fallen drastically. In other words, we can ascertain that the price-controlling effect of imports on the Japanese market had become stronger. If we look at which countries demonstrated this type of market price control capacity, we can see that according to Table 2, these were Germany, England, and America, and the relative importance of Germany in this was overwhelming.

In reaction to this offensive by the international nitrogen cartel, the Japanese ammonium sulfate industry tried to break out of the situation by negotiations. These continued from 1930 through to the spring of 1931, and after a break of about a year recommenced in 1933. Incidentally, as the contents of the discussions differed in the two periods, I will consider

TABLE 1 Supply and Demand of Ammonium Sulfate in Japan (unit: 1000 tons)

Year	Production	Imports	Exports	Imports[a]	Exports[b]	Consumption
1926	147	296	4	—	39	400
1927	176	250	1	—	40	385
1928	232	284	2	—	58	456
1929	235	381	2	—	93	521
1930	266	303	15	18	84	488
1931	393	224	12	53	41	617
1932	460	119	18	125	67	619
1933	471	108	50	84	62	551
1934	494	161	2	85	88	650
1935	612	239	6	72	103	814
1936	880	314	18	56	182	1050
1937	932	224	8	17	181	984

Source: Ministry of Agriculture and Forestry, *Hiryō Yōran* (Statistics of Fertilizers)
[a] Import from Japan's colonies
[b] Export to Japan's colonies

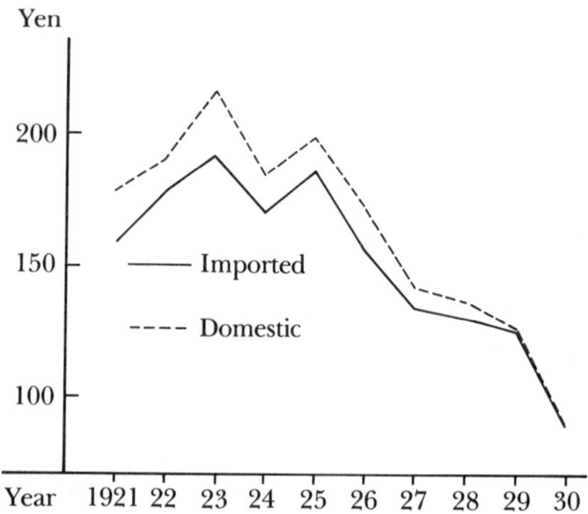

FIG. 1 Trade Price of Ammonium Sulfate in Japan (per ton).
Source: Ministry of Agriculture and Forestry, *Hiryō Yōran* (Statistics of Fertilizers)

them separately. The conclusion, which I will give in advance, is that the period up until 1931 was one in which the competitive aspects between the Japanese ammonium sulfate industries and the international nitrogen cartel came to the fore, whereas from 1933 it was the cooperative aspects

TABLE 2 Nations from Which Japan Imported Ammonium Sulfate (unit: 1000
tons)

Year	U.K.	Germany	U.S.A.
1926	40	175	69
1927	61	137	41
1928	98	149	28
1929	139	183	54
1930	84	173	41
1931	53	155	4
1932	36	75	2
1933	21	80	—
1934	22	136	0
1935	4	152	3
1936	0	137	62
1937	2	73	—

Source: Hashimoto Jurō, "Senkanki no Kagaku Kōgyō" (The Chemical Industry
in the Interwar Period), in *Kanagawa Kenshi, Kakuron Hen 2, Sangyō Keizai*
(1983), p. 309.

that did so. As well as showing the various aspects of the strategies employed by Japan's ammonium sulfate industry and the international nitrogen cartel, I will also discuss the reasons why the conflicting strategies converged into competition or cooperation.

The Japanese ammonium sulfate industry, which due to the lack of any kind of protectionist measures by the government, had dealt with the dumping offensive not by a concerted effort but in isolation, now faced an even more aggressive onslaught owing to the rise in the yen exchange rate following the lifting of the gold embargo. Thus in March 1930, attempts at forming some kind of union began. This was achieved through the formation of the Nitrogen Council. In order to protect the Japanese ammonium sulfate industry against the fierce price offensive being carried out by the members of the international nitrogen cartel, the council made a request to the Japanese government for application of the antidumping law. However, this was not possible in view of the serious depression being faced by agricultural communities at this time. At this point, the Nitrogen Council requested negotiations with the international nitrogen cartel as a way out of the situation. In mid-October discussions were begun between representatives of the members of the Nitrogen Council, namely Nippon Chisso Hiryō and Dai Nippon Jinzō Hiryō, and Brunner, Mond & Co. (ICI), Ltd. Noguchi Jun, of Nippon Chisso Hiryō, expressed indignation at the clause which stated that indemnity should be paid to British and

German companies with regard to the Chinese and South Pacific markets for the three years that the agreement was to run. Therefore, the talks ended in failure. For this reason market conditions suddenly worsened, and the international nitrogen cartel, in order to strengthen its ploy of cheap sales, slashed the market quotation price by ¥10. Therefore, the price of nitrogen, which had been over ¥130 a ton in 1929, suddenly fell to nearly ¥60. Thus in November, negotiations working towards an agreement began once more. The president of Denki Kagaku Kōgyō Co. (Electrochemical Industries), Fujiwara Ginjirō, held secret discussions with Hermann Bosch of H. Ahrens & Co. Nachf. As a result of these, a provisional signing of an agreement took place at the end of 1930.[5] This agreement is known as the Fujiwara-Bosch Agreement.[6]

The Fujiwara-Bosch Agreement[7]

(1) The Japanese Group promised expressly not to carry out exports of ammonium sulfate.

(2) The Japanese Group was to form a cartel, and purchase 200,000 tons of ammonium sulfate a year from abroad. (However, the amount could be reduced by a maximum of 50,000 tons per year.)

(3) The market price was to be ¥85 per ton.

(4) The Japanese Group was to make every effort to ensure that no new nitrogen industries were set up in Japan.

(5) All imported ammonium sulfate was to be sold through Mitsui & Co., Ltd. and Mitsubishi Corp.

(6) The length of the agreement was to be five years.

The First Clause. According to Akira Kudō's "I.G. Farben's Japan Strategy,"[8] the corporations included in the CIA aimed to draw Japanese companies, as outsiders, into the sphere of influence of the cartel by individual agreements, and this is why they began negotiations with these companies. Within the report on the meeting of the members of the nitrogen department of I.G. Farben with responsibility for these affairs, it is recorded that "we have no intention in the slightest to threaten production by Japan aimed for the domestic market. The reason being that should we do so, the Japanese side will try all the harder to disrupt the export market." I.G. Farben foresaw that Japan would become self-sufficient in the near future, and it saw the problem in hand as being how to control Japan's exports. Therefore, the strategy of the CIA group, among whose members I.G. Farben had the closest relations with the Japanese ammonium sulfate industry, can be considered as being the restriction of Japanese exports. The first clause, therefore, encapsulates the wishes of the CIA. On the other hand, according to Table 1, in 1930, the year in which the Fujiwara-Bosch Agreement was made, domestic production of ammonium sulfate was 266,000 tons and the volume of imports was 303,000 tons. Domestic consumption at this time was 488,000 tons, and thus domestic self-sufficiency was not above 55%. As domestically produced supplies could not satisfy more than half of demand, there was in fact no reserve capacity for export in existence at the time. Therefore, the first clause, by which a ban on exports was imposed, did not have a direct effect on the profits of the Japanese ammonium sulfate industry. Although it could be foreseen that this clause would become an impediment to Japanese corporations in the future, for the present they did not express their opposition to it, in order to thereby obtain a balance of interests by being able to check imports in return. This should thus be considered as just a way of putting off finding a definite solution to the problem.

The Second Clause. For the Japanese side, this was to be the collateral they obtained for the concessions made in the first clause. In 1929 the amount of imports was 381,000 tons, whereas by 1930 it had fallen to 303,000. Moreover, the amount of ammonium sulfate that had to be imported from abroad as fixed in the agreement was 200,000 tons in 1931, the first year of the agreement, and this represented a large-scale restriction of imports. If, in accordance with the agreement, imports to Japan were reduced by 50,000 tons a year, by 1935 they would completely cease. This second clause represents the wishes of the Japanese ammonium sulfate corporations, which at this time had virtually no power to control import prices. On the other hand, from the point of view of the CIA, this concession was quite predictable because the CIA was in any case preparing to withdraw from the Japanese market, owing to the appraisal it had made of the investment in plant and equipment that was being carried out within the Japanese ammonium sulfate industry.[9]

The Third Clause. In December, when the discussions concerning the agreement were being held, the price per ton of ammonium sulfate had been cut to ¥70. The price of ¥85 per ton was designed to guarantee, on the Japanese side, the profits of Denki Kagaku Kōgyō, which was the company having the lowest productivity, using the cyanamide production process. Therefore, this price was considered adequate by the Japanese side.

The Fourth Clause. It is impossible to believe that the Japanese ammonium sulfate industry of the time would have been endowed with the means necessary for the execution of this clause. It seems that CIA asked for this clause to be put in writing in order to try to curb any export capacity that might be created in Japan.

The Fifth Clause. With regard to ammonium sulfate sales in Japan, the direct sales system was adopted by ICI in 1933, and by I.G. Farben in 1930. Therefore, in that sense, the CIA was making a concession in this clause. However, this was subject to the ban on Japanese exports, and as the CIA was preparing anyway to withdraw from the Japanese market, the abandonment of the direct sales system can be seen as being within the consequences of this.

The CIA tried to achieve its strategy of stopping Japanese exports through the Fujiwara-Bosch Agreement. The second, third, and fifth clauses represented nothing but mere formalities that were gone through in order to bring about the realization of the first clause. The Japanese side sought, through this agreement, to bring about the reduction and finally the total end of imports by the time of the completion of the construction of the factories of Shōwa Hiryō, Sumitomo Hiryō, and Miike Chisso.

The agreement was planned to be formally signed on January 20, 1931, but this did not in fact take place. According to a newspaper article of the time, the government, acting on behalf of the farmers who were dissatisfied with the price of ¥85 and the ammonium sulfate corporations who felt insecure about the clause banning exports, intervened to render the signature impossible. In place of this, the government decided to set up an antidumping committee. This committee did not in fact take any action in particular, but this new development did force the CIA to make concessions. In February, Bosch made a presentation to the Ministry of Commerce and Industry to the effect that he wanted mediation in order to solve the problems between the parties concerned. At this point the said ministry reported the main purpose of the presentation to the president of Nippon Chisso Hiryō, Noguchi Jun.[10] Thus negotiations were held between Bosch and Noguchi, and a definite accord was thus obtained.

The Noguchi-Bosch Accord[11]

(1) The Foreign Group was to be composed of H. Ahrens & Co. Nachf. and Brunner, Mond & Co. (ICI), and the Japanese Group of Mitsui & Co. and Mitsubishi Corp.

(2) The amount of imports (only to be made from Britain and Germany; imports of ammonium sulfate were not to be made from the United States):

1 year from July 1931—at least 110,000 tons,
1 year from July 1932—at least 80,000 tons,
1 year from July 1933—at least 60,000 tons.
(3) The amount of exports:
From July 1931 to June 1935—7,500 tons per year.
(4) The above exports were to be handled jointly by Mitsui and Mitsubishi. Apart from these two companies, no other domestic ammonium sulfate companies were to handle exports.
(5) According to domestic production and demand, taking the aforementioned import and export amounts into consideration, if there were any danger of oversupply, adjustments were to be made by the reduction of Nippon Chisso Hiryō or Chōsen Chisso Hiryō's production.

The Second Clause. Within the Fujiwara-Bosch Agreement, although the possibility of changing the import amount existed, it had been fairly rigidly fixed. However, this new accord went no further than specifying the lowest limits for imports. It left the option open for increasing imports according to circumstances in the Japanese ammonium sulfate market. We can infer from this that in fact Japanese ammonium sulfate corporations were facing difficulties in meeting domestic demand. Therefore, there was no choice but to make use of imported ammonium sulfate as a safety net within the Japanese market. It can be said that the later strategy of the Japanese ammonium sulfate corporations, of treating CIA as a kind of "limited supplier for the Japanese market,"[12] had begun to take shape at this point.

The Third Clause. A few months after the failure of the Fujiwara-Bosch Agreement, the CIA had hereby abandoned its attempts to include a clause banning exports. This proved a great concession to the Japanese ammonium sulfate corporations.

The Fifth Clause. According to the second clause, the lowest limit on imports was 110,000 tons for the first year of the agreement, 80,000 for the second, and 60,000 for the third. I can thus say that compared to the figures for imports to Japan in 1930 of 303,000, these figures rendered oversupply completely impossible. Therefore, there was no possibility that adjustment would have to be made by the reduction of Nippon Chisso Hiryō or Chōsen Chisso Hiryō's production. Thus this fifth clause should be considered as being put in only for effect. It may have been that the threat of oversupply was the card played in order to get the CIA to set aside the clause banning exports, or to stress its dangers to the Ministry of

Agriculture and Forestry in order to get the ministry to advocate the proper restriction of imports. However, there is no historical data to back up this assumption.

Following the reaching of an understanding on revisions to be added to the Noguchi-Bosch Accord in February 1931, the signing of the interim agreement took place in April 1931.

The Interim Agreement[13]

(1) Both Britain and Germany were to cease direct sales, and instead sole agency was to be granted to Mitsui & Co. and Mitsubishi Corp. The decision was to be reserved on Mitsubishi's import rights for American ammonium sulfate. The ratio of British and German ammonium sulfate handled by Mitsui and Mitsubishi was to be determined by discussions between both companies.

(2) The agreement was to run for three years from July 1st.

(3) The total amount of imports from Britain and Germany was to be 100,000 tons in the first year of the agreement, 80,000 in the second, and 50,000 in the third. Apart from this, whenever there were shortages of domestic ammonium sulfate, deficiencies were to be made up by imports.

(4) The agreement did not specify export terms. As a kind of gentleman's agreement taking the place of the actual sanctioning of exports, accord regarding export prices was to be reached with England and Germany.

The Second Clause.   The length of the agreement in this case, being only three years, was shorter than that of the Fujiwara-Bosch Agreement (five years), and of the Noguchi-Bosch Accord (four years). This shortening of the period of the agreement should be thought of as a concession by the CIA.

The Third Clause.   Compared with the Noguchi-Bosch Accord, the lowest limits for import amounts were lower by 10,000 tons for the first and third years respectively. Thus the Japanese side had once more managed to win concessions from the CIA. Moreover, the phrase stating that whenever there were shortages in domestic ammonium sulfate the deficiencies were to be met by imports meant that the Japanese side had succeeded in its aim to treat the CIA as a limited supplier to the Japanese market. The fact that it was the Japanese side that was to take the initiative in freely deciding the amount of imports, should this go in excess of the agreed amount, was made even clearer here than in the Noguchi-Bosch Accord.

The Fourth Clause. In comparison with the Noguchi-Bosch Accord, the CIA made even more concessions, and thus the limits on the amount of exports were removed. Therefore, only five months after the discussions between Fujiwara and Bosch, the CIA's strategy of trying to prevent Japanese exports had failed.

This interim agreement was initially signed, but as talks within the CIA on its renewal broke down, as an agreement it had no binding powers.

From 1929, the international nitrogen cartel tried to use dumping offensives in order to restrict Japanese exports. However, this attempt was hampered by the sudden rise of the Japanese synthetic ammonium industry due to the start of production by Nippon Chisso Hiryō and Chōsen Chisso Hiryō as well as to the building of factories by Mitsui and Sumitomo, and the attempt eventually failed completely. CIA's strategy of banning Japanese exports and the Japanese ammonium sulfate industry's strategy of limiting imports were based on the premise that the Japanese ammonium sulfate industry did not have the capacity to meet the rapidly increasing demand in the Japanese market. It was inevitable that a change in circumstances would have an effect on the respective strategies. Therefore, the sudden rise of the Japanese synthetic ammonium sulfate industry had the effect of hindering the realization of the CIA's plans regarding Japan as well as of making the Japanese corporations' aims easier to accomplish. These corporations took the opportunity hereby given in order to turn their relationship with the CIA into a cooperative one.

III. Cooperation between the Japanese Ammonium Sulfate Industry and the International Nitrogen Cartel

The collapse of the CIA in June 1931 had the effect of causing competition in Europe to become more fierce and causing European nations to close their markets against foreign penetration. This made competition in the free market more intense. Naturally, this situation affected Japan as well. The price of German ammonium sulfate fell sharply after July. It reached ¥60 a ton in August. Then with the suspension of the gold standard in September the pound fell, and this caused an improvement in the profitability of British ammonium sulfate. This also pushed the ammonium sulfate price down. However, in December 1931, the Japanese reimposition of the ban on gold exports had the effect of greatly lowering the yen exchange rate, and this low exchange rate in fact ended up functioning as a nontariff barrier. The Japanese ammonium sulfate corporations, which had been excluded from exercising control over the price of imported ammonium sulfate, cleared out their excess stock by August 1932 and in October set up a cartel organization called the Ammonium Sulfate Distribution Union. Against the background of the Japanese government's policy of stabilizing a low exchange rate, the Japanese ammonium sulfate companies were able to become competitive against European ammonium sulfate. They were thus able to impose organized control on ammonium sulfate imports through the aforementioned union.[14] It is only here that cooperative aspects can be considered as existing in the relationship between the Japanese ammonium sulfate industry and the CIA.

The relevant Japanese companies were not able to capture the Japanese ammonium sulfate market, which expanded suddenly after 1933. The Ammonium Sulfate Distribution Union followed the wishes of the government, which advised allowing imports to stop a sudden rise in prices in order to protect the farmers. Thus on their own initiative they decided to effectuate ammonium sulfate imports, as long as these did not cause a drastic fall in prices. The union began discussions again for the first time in two years with the restructured CIA. In other words, it made the following proposal to H. Ahrens in July 1933.

The Proposal from the Distribution Union to H. Ahrens[15]

Regarding Imports

(1) Foreign companies were not to export ammonium sulfate to Japan unless a request was made by the Japanese side to make up deficiencies in domestic supply.

(2) In the case of the said imports, the price was to be agreed upon with the Japanese side.

(3) Sales of the above imports were to be handled by Mitsui Co. and Mitsubishi Corp.

Regarding Exports

(1) The foreign ammonium sulfate industry was to allow exports of ammonium sulfate by Japan in the case of domestic overproduction. However, the amount and the destination of the exports were not to be specified in advance.

(2) The price of the above exports was to be agreed upon with the foreign ammonium sulfate industry.

(3) The above exports were to be handled by Mitsui and Mitsubishi.

As the Japanese side had made a demand that no imports be carried out unless requested by them, this meant that they wanted complete control as regards any initiative on ammonium sulfate imports. They had also made a demand for the price of the imports to be decided through agreement with the Japanese side. Therefore, the CIA was literally made "a limited supplier for the Japanese market." The aim was to formulate the agreement on the basis of this proposal, and thus the first, second, and third Domestic and Foreign Ammonium Sulfate Agreements were concluded in March 1934, February 1935, and November 1936, respectively.

Let us take a look at the first agreement as far as is necessary within the context of this paper. The agreement[16] contained ten clauses: 1–4 concerning the imports to and 5–10 the exports from Japan. The first clause was as follows:

> Subject to the exceptions hereinafter indicated the Foreign Group will undertake to cease independent import of sulphate of ammonia into the Empire of Japan including Formosa, Korea, and Saghalien (hereinafter referred to as Japanese territory) unless permitted by the Japanese Group in each case.
>
> The Foreign Group will keep its agents or customers in Japan and/or abroad from importing Sulphate of Ammonia into Japanese territory so as to make the quantity of import amount to not more than the quantity permitted by the Japanese Group.

The previously mentioned demand that, if there were no shortages in supply in Japan and until there was a request from the Japanese side, the international nitrogen cartel was not to export ammonium sulfate to Japan, was thus included in the text of the document. Through this the Japanese were able to seize the initiative concerning imports into Japan. Actual figures for imports were given in clause four:

> In order to safeguard sufficient supplies for the Japanese market during the current fertilizer year, the Foreign Group binds itself to ship to Japan further quantities of sulphate of ammonia such as may be required by the Japanese Group. The Foreign Group promises to offer and/or sell its goods without reservation, up to a maximum of 100,000 tons (in which the quantities already sold for delivery or arrival in January/July 1934, that is 25,300 tons and 20,250 tons respectively, are to be included) at prices not higher than the prices at which the Japanese Group is selling at the time of sale. The present price of the Japanese Group, however, is to be accepted as a minimum price, i.e., ¥3.50 per kwamme in "kamasu" at any free inland station (changed selling conditions to be accounted for as usual).

The import amount was changed halfway through this clause from 100,000 to 150,000 tons. The price of ammonium sulfate imports was laid down in clause four as: "at prices not higher than the prices at which the Japanese Group is selling at the time of sale."

This represents the putting into effect of the demand by the Japanese side that the prices of imports should be agreed upon with them. Thus through this first agreement, decisions regarding the amount and price of imports were put under the jurisdiction of the Ammonium Sulfate Distribution Union. Meanwhile the amount of exports as laid down in clause five was: "For the period from July 1st until December 31st, the Japanese Group agrees not to sell more than 50,000 tons." The price of exports was stipulated in clause six: "The Japanese Group is entitled to sell its agreed export quota directly, but is bound not to sell cheaper than 4% below the price at which the Foreign Group is selling in the respective markets."

The export area was laid down in clause seven, and was as follows: South America (excluding Brazil), the United States (including Hawaii), South Sea Islands, China including Hong Kong, the Philippine Islands, Dutch East Indies, French Indo-China (Tonkin), and Siam. Thus after the first negotiations in two years between the CIA and Japan's ammonium sulfate industry, and following the proposal made by the Ammonium Sulfate Distribution Union to H. Ahrens, the first Domestic and Foreign Ammonium Sulfate Agreement was concluded. Therefore, as previously mentioned, the Ammonium Sulfate Distribution Union was able to take the initiative regarding determination of the amount and price of imports. In other words, they gained systematic control over ammonium sulfate imports. Looking at this from another angle, however, it could be said that by allowing exports by the Japanese ammonium sulfate industry, which in fact had virtually no export capacity, the CIA was acting superficially in respecting their wishes. Whereas in fact what it had actually done was to succeed in confining the Japanese ammonium sulfate industry to the Japanese market and thereby preserving its profits at their current levels. The essence of what cooperation existed between the Japanese ammonium sulfate industry and the CIA is contained in this first agreement. A number of changes can be seen in the second and third agreements, but fundamentally they were made in the same spirit of cooperation as the first.

IV. Conclusion

Japanese ammonium sulfate demand is shown in Table 1. Comparing the ratio of imports and domestic ammonium sulfate production, we find that in 1930, if we take the figure for the latter as being 100, the former equaled 114, making it the larger figure. However, in 1933 this figure (ratio of imports to production) fell to 24, while in 1934–36 it rose again to the 30s. In 1937, it again fell to the 20s. If we look a little more closely at these changes, we can see that regardless of the sudden drop in the existing levels of ammonium sulfate imports, or to put it another way, regardless of the increase in domestic self-sufficiency, the amount of imports in the 1920s and 1930s remained almost unchanged. Production of ammonium sulfate rose by 3.5 times in the period 1930–37, an average increase of 20% p.a., but even in the face of such a steep rise, imports remained at the same levels as before. The reasons for this must be examined.

In this context, I would like to draw attention to the following two points. One is the fact that consumption of ammonia was growing steadily. More important than this, though, is the fact that the changes in the rate of consumption grew increasingly complex. During the period 1931–33, consumption remained sluggish for a time and finally fell. After this period of stagnation, consumption grew explosively in 1933–36 to double in only three years. If we separate the two periods according to the changes in consumption and look at the connection between this and production, we can see that during the period of sluggish consumption, 1930–33, imports were restrained and production was increased. After 1934, although production continued to rise rapidly, it was unable to meet the explosion in demand, and imports were at more or less the same levels as in the latter half of the 1920s. This shows that import levels were adjusted to supply and demand in Japan. In other words, imported ammonium sulfate had become a limited supply source for the Japanese market. The second point is that the countries carrying out exports to Japan changed. This is shown clearly in Table 2. Comparing the late 1920s with the mid-1930s, we can see that imports from Britain and the United States continued to fall, while those from Germany recovered. In the 1930s Germany became the main supplier of ammonium sulfate to Japan.[17]

As has been explained, the ratio of imports to ammonium sulfate production, which in the 1920s was over 100, in the 1930s fell to under 100 and in fact dropped as low as from 20 to 30. Thus we can see that the Japanese ammonium sulfate industry was at a completely different stage of development in the 1930s as compared with the 1920s. The rapidity of growth of the Japanese ammonium sulfate industry in the 1930s is remarkable. The production rate rose by an average of 20% per annum to increase by 3.5 times during this period. It is at this point that it is necessary to remember the discord between the CIA and the Japanese ammonium sulfate industry regarding the Japanese and foreign markets. However, it so happened that in the 1930s demand in the Japanese ammonium sulfate market exceeded supplies from the domestic industry, and thus imports became necessary. To contribute to an understanding of these movements in the ammonium sulfate market, I would like to discuss and give my conclusions about competition and cooperation as they existed between the Japanese ammonium sulfate corporations and the CIA.

From 1929, the international nitrogen cartel began a dumping offensive against Japan. The Japanese ammonium sulfate corporations, which were at a stage in their development where they were unable to meet more than half of the demand in the Japanese market, were unable to control prices, and therefore they were anxious to find countermeasures to help them deal with this situation. The relative strength of the international nitrogen cartel compared to the Japanese ammonium sulfate corporations was thus made very clear. The cartel sought to make use of its strength to accomplish its strategy of stopping Japanese exports. The Japanese companies, although always being forced into a defensive position, still managed to put up resistance in order to check imports. However, the sudden growth of the Japanese ammonium sulfate industry from 1930 to 1931 placed definite limitations on the CIA's strategy of stopping Japanese exports. In other words, although this strategy did not begin directly to have an adverse effect on the profits of the Japanese ammonium sulfate industry, it nevertheless met with resistance, and the rapid expansion of the industry served to support this resistance. Moreover, this was enough to make the CIA think twice. With the expiration in June 1931 of the agreement with the CIA, negotiations were suspended until 1933. However, during this period, the production capacity of the Japanese ammonium sulfate industry rose still further. With the suspension of the gold standard, the yen exchange rate fell drastically, and this had the effect of acting as a nontariff barrier to ammonium sulfate imports. The fall of the yen caused an easing of the pressure that the CIA was able to apply to the Japanese ammonium sulfate corporations, and it became an additional hindrance to the CIA's strategy.

In response to the changing situation, the CIA considered altering its position to one based on cooperation in its negotiations with the Japanese corporations. In brief, by allowing exports by the Japanese ammonium sulfate corporations, which in fact had virtually no export capacity, the CIA could help these companies to keep up good appearances, while what it was in fact doing was preserving its export markets. In compensation, the CIA was to allow its exports to Japan to be controlled by the Ammonium Sulfate Distribution Union.[18] Looking at this from another angle, right from the beginning, the Japanese ammonium sulfate industry had adopted the control of imports as its strategy. The CIA, while having to adjust its Japan strategy, was still trying to achieve its ultimate aims and in the process made a number of concessions to the Japanese ammonium sulfate industry. The result of this was in fact to enable the Japanese side to succeed in its own strategies. However, the industry, which was unable to satisfy demand in the rapidly growing Japanese ammonium sulfate market, did not have the least desire for a total ban on ammonium sulfate imports. Rather it recognized that it was necessary to allow imports, while at the same time exercising systematic control over them. In other words, there had to be cooperation with the CIA.

NOTES

1. L.F. Harber, *The Chemical Industry 1900–1930* (Oxford, 1971), pp. 90–91. In addition to this book, the following works were also referred to in the writing of this paper: L.F. Harber, *The Chemical Industry During the Nineteenth Century* (Oxford, 1958); W.J. Reader, *Imperial Chemical Industries*, vols. I and II (Oxford, 1970, 1975).

2. Production figures and manufacturing costs for Chōsen Chisso Hiryō are according to the "Monthly Product Report" and the "Table of Manufacturing Costs by Product," appended to the company's "Minutes of the Board Meeting" (1932–37). For details on Nippon Chisso Hiryō, refer to my previous work *Nitchitsu Konzern no Kenkyū* (A Study of Nippon Chisso Hiryō) (Tokyo, 1989).

3. Kudō Akira, "I.G. Farben no Seiritsu to Tenkai (2)" (The Foundation and Development of I.G. Farben, 2), Tokyo Daigaku *Shakai Kagaku Kenkyū*, vol. 29, no. 6 (1978): 89–90.

4. Ibid., 136–137; Suzuki Tsuneo, "Nihon Ryūan Kōgyō Shiron" (Historical Essays on the Japanese Ammonium Sulfate Industry), *Kurume Daigaku Shōgakubu Fuzoku Shōgyō Keizai Kenkyūjo Kiyō*, vol. 14 (1985): 54–55.

5. The description of the negotiations follows a report in the *Tōkyō Asahi Shimbun* (January 27, 1931).

6. Ōshio Takeshi, "Fujiwara-Bosch Kyōteian to Nihon no Ryūan Kōgyō" (The Proposed Fujiwara-Bosch Agreement and the Ammonium Sulfate Industry), Meiji Gakuin Daigaku, *Keizai Kenkyū*, nos. 49–50 (1978). Within this work the popular opinion that the agreement was a humiliation for the Japanese side is criticized. It shows that their aims, according to the level-headed calculations that the Japanese side had made, were achieved. Following this, beginning with the Fujiwara-Bosch Agreement, it examines the agreements formed between the CIA and the Japanese ammonium sulfate industry. However, this has also been done in Suzuki, op. cit., and in Hashimoto Jurō, "Ryūan Dokusentai no Seiritsu" (The Establishment of the Monopolistic Structure within the Ammonium Sulfate Industry), Tokyo Daigaku *Keizaigaku Ronshū*, vol. 45, no. 48 (1980). However, Suzuki, due to his interpretation at face value, shows a tendency to miss the hidden intentions of the Japanese ammonium sulfate industry, as contained in the clauses. In the case of Hashimoto, his analysis of the interests of the ammonium sulfate industries is complicated by the fact that he overemphasizes the role of *zaibatsu*. Due to the limitations of space, I have restricted myself to an analysis based on the

interests of the Japanese ammonium sulfate industries, and an evaluation of the analyses used in these two papers will be presented elsewhere.

7. Terada Shōichi, "Hiryō no Tōsei oyobi Haikyū (Fertilizer Regulation and Distribution), Shōgyō Keizai Gakkai, 1941, p. 71.

8. Kudō Akira, "I.G. Farben no Tainichi Senryaku" (I.G. Farben's Japan Strategy), Tōkyō Daigaku, *Shakai Kagaku Kenkyū*, vol. 39, no. 2: 46–47.

9. Ibid., 46.

10. Suzuki, op. cit., p. 110; and Hashimoto, op. cit., p. 60, according to which actual examples are given, as has already been indicated. Hashimoto has made a systematic analysis starting with the Japanese ammonium sulfate industry in the 1930s, and his research has produced some excellent results.

11. The Mitsubishi Corp., *Ritsugyō Bōeki Roku* (History of the Mitsubishi Trading Co.) (Tokyo, 1958), p. 473.

12. Hashimoto, op. cit., p. 62.

13. Terada, op. cit., according to which the total amount of imports for the third year of the agreement was 30,000 tons. However, Suzuki's figure (op. cit., p. 17) of 50,000 tons is correct, and the former is in fact a typographical error. Accurate figures can be confirmed by looking at the figures contained in the Fujiwara-Bosch Agreement and the Noguchi-Bosch Accord.

14. The fact that the Japanese ammonium sulfate corporations managed to gain systematic control over imported ammonium sulfate is presented in Hashimoto, op. cit., p. 63ff.

15. Mitsubishi Corp., op. cit., p. 474.

16. H. Ahrens and Co. Nachf., 29 März 1934 mit 2 Anlagen: Agreement; M. Kobayashi and H. Bosch, March 23, 1934, T74/11 CIA Internationale Konventionsverträge 1932–34, BASF Archives. Copies of this material was made available by Kudō Akira of Tokyo University, to whom I wish to express my thanks.

17. Hashimoto Jurō, "Senkanki no Kagaku Kōgyō" (The Chemical Industry in the Interwar Period), in *Kanagawa Kenshi Kakuron Hen*, vol. 2: *Sangyō-Keizai* (A History of Kanagawa Prefecture, Section 2, Industrial Economy) (Kanagawa-ken Kenminbu Kenshi Henshūshitsu, 1982), p. 322.

18. As I.G. Farben, which handled most of the exports to Japan, was limited in its exports of manufactured products, it changed its Japan strategy to one of providing licenses and plant exports. In Kudō Akira's excellent study, op. cit., he arrives at a number of thoroughly substantiated and enlightening conclusions, using data in the possession of Japanese and German companies. In this the situation is presented as follows: "One of the reasons why the company undertook provision of licenses and export of plants to Japan was because they recognized the fact that exports of manufactured products to Japan could not develop further. Moreover, as by making agreements regarding the provision of licenses and plant exports they aimed to impose limits on Japan's export capacity, it can be said that a transition from a strategy of export of manufactured products to license provision was a highly attractive proposition" (p. 48).

Comment

Tsuneo Suzuki

Professor Ōshio's paper provides us with a full analysis of the fact that European cartel members, especially I.G. Farben and ICI, altered their strategies for the Japanese market around 1931–33: before 1931, they had dumped the ammonium sulfate in order to flood the Japanese market and also to force newly established companies out of the field, but after 1933 they cooperated with them.

I would like to comment on this paper from three perspectives: first, the state of the world market in nitrogen fertilizer during the late 1920s and early 1930s; second, the character of the Japanese market; and third, the attitude of the Japanese government towards the agreement between the European cartel and Japanese corporations, and the evaluation of the agreement not only from the viewpoint of the Japanese corporations, but also from that of the European cartel.

First, the estimate of the future of the nitrogen industry had dramatically changed from optimistic forecasts to pessimistic ones after 1928, when the European cartel members, especially the DEN group, studied the conditions of the world nitrogen industry and made plans to develop their world trade. Although I.G. Farben and ICI would prevent the establishment of the nitrogen industry in other European countries, the European market, with the exception of Spain and the Canaries, shrank after 1928. As the Great Depression reduced the demand for fertilizers and the problem of overproduction and even overcapacity was getting more serious, the Japanese market was important for the European cartel. It intended to maintain its hold on the Japanese market by dumping and by cutting prices, so the competition between the cartel and Japanese companies was very keen.

Second, the character of the Japanese market enhanced its importance. In Japan, while many kinds of fertilizers, such as fish meal or soybean meal, Chilean sodium nitrate, calcium cyanamide, and ammonium sulfate, were used for the nitrogenous fertilizers, Chilean sodium nitrate was not popular, and from the late 1920s the consumption of ammonium sulfate increased more than that of any other fertilizer. By the early 1930s, however, many Japanese ammonium sulfate companies had their own operations, and there were also plans to establish new ammonium sulfate plants in the near future. So cutthroat competition was more evident in the Japanese market than in any other market.

Third, why did the cartel change its competitive strategy to a cooperative one in the Japanese market? The Ministry of Commerce and Industry (MCI) as well as the Japanese producers did not favor a fall in price of ammonium sulfate. On the other hand, farmers welcomed it, but the Ministry of Agriculture and Forestry (MAF) thought that a fall in price was not necessarily good for Japanese agriculture. MAF welcomed it because cheap fertilizers and stable distribution by the Japanese producers were desirable, but it intended to prevent the Japanese producers from being destroyed.

As a result, price stabilization, which satisfied producers as well as farmers, was effected by controlling imports. On the other hand, MCI, which had promoted and protected the nitrogen industry, objected to the agreement proposed between the cartel and the Japanese because it would restrict the Japanese market as well as the Southeast Asian market. As the cartel had faced similar conditions earlier in Europe, it gave up the Japanese market and re-inforced other Asian, especially Chinese, markets.

I.G. Farben and ICI changed their export markets from Japan to China in the early 1930s. Regarding ammonium sulfate exported from England, its destinations also changed in the 1930s. In the early 1920s, it was mainly being shipped to France, Spain, and the Dutch East Indies. But in the late 1920s, it was being exported to Spain and Japan. In 1929, out of £5,620,000 of ammonium sulfate exported, exports to Japan and Spain were about £1,694,000 and £1,448,000 respectively.[1] While British exports to China increased gradually after 1928, those to Japan decreased rapidly after 1930. And in the early 1930s the exports of ammonium sulfate decreased totally on the whole and were shipped mainly to Spain, the Canaries, and China. In 1933, out of £1,933,000 of ammonium sulfate exported, exports to Spain/Canaries and China were £430,000 and £310,000, respectively, and those to Japan were only £138,000.[2]

In the 1930s, the Chinese market—as well as the markets in Spain and the Canaries, which had already been captive markets for England—was very important. Therefore, the agreement between the European cartel and the Japanese cartel realized both requirements: Japan was given control over its prices and imports, but a strict limit was imposed on its exports to China. As a result of the latter, the European cartel could control the Southeast Asian as well as the Chinese markets.

But since the price rose after the agreement had been signed, MAF and the farmers favored a decrease in prices and an increase in supply. An act that would regulate the price and distribution of fertilizers, entitled Jūyō Hiryōgyō Tōsei Hō (Act for Controlling Important Fertilizer Industries), was brought up for discussion and enacted in November 1936. Under the act, the prices of some nitrogenous fertilizers required, after 1937, the approval of the government.

So even though the Japanese cartel could control the domestic market, its pricing was restricted by the government. On the other hand, in the rest of Asia, especially in China, nitrogenous fertilizers were controlled by the European cartel as to both quantities and prices.

NOTES

1. *The Chemical Trade Journal and Chemical Engineer* (February 7, 1930): 140.
2. Ibid. (January 26, 1934): 64.

International Cartels in the Interwar Period: Some Aspects of the French Case

Emmanuel Chadeau

The part played by French interests and firms in international cartels has long been a neglected question among French economic historians. Some authors considered it of only marginal importance to our understanding of the national economy in the 20th century. They featured French industry as being dominated up to the 1950s by small- or medium-sized businesses that were unable to compete or cooperate with foreign producers (for instance, in textiles, steel making, machinery, and chemicals). Some other industries were supposedly dominated as early as the 1930s by oligopolies whose members shared the domestic market and neglected their international competitiveness (i.e., the automobile industry with big firms like Renault, Peugeot, and Citröen). And other industries (for instance, oil refining and electronics) were supposedly controlled by foreign multinationals that applied to their French subsidiaries or subcontractors various cartelized strategies designed and decided in Germany, Great Britain, or the United States. In France, the formation of international cartels was alluded to in leading texts and papers, but rarely studied for itself, except in the case of steel. And this attitude reflected an irrevocable fact: in the 1920s and 1930s, while proposals to organize cartels were debated in France as elsewhere in Europe among managers, economists, and politicians, they were never acted upon in France, whose attitude contrasted markedly with that of Germany and Italy.[1]

But our knowledge of the interwar period is broadening. Since the conventional ideas of French Malthusianism or of the dualist structure of industries is now out of date, historians have begun to study industrial organization. Finally, the ability of French industry to be internationally competitive in the interwar period is levelled, and the benefits of capitalism and the market economy are more frankly accepted by economic historians.

In such a perspective, the question of the role of French interests or firms in the formation of interwar international cartels should be reviewed. Starting with the case study of the nitrogen cartel, the present paper presents an overview of it in an attempt to place the French experience in the wider picture of the international history of cartels.

I. France Inside and Outside the Nitrogen Cartel

French producers were not involved in the birth of the international cartel of nitrogen, which was formed in June 1929 by Germany, England, Norway, and Chile under the name of the International Accord on Nitrogen. They entered this cartel when it was renewed and enlarged for another year in August 1930. The new cartel included the so-called DEN group, which founded the original 1929 cartel (DEN being the initial letters of Deutschland, England, and Norway), France, Belgium, Czechoslovakia, Netherlands, Italy, and Poland. In this second grouping, the cartel did not include Chile but acted towards this South American country as a collective partner in order to level prices and share markets abroad, especially in the United States, where the 1890 Sherman Act prohibited cartels organized by national or foreign producers or traders. In effect, this new cartel grouped producers of synthetic nitrogen of industrialized European countries involved in permanent bargaining with the main producer of natural, guano-processed nitrogen, Chile.

This second cartel was named the Convention Internationale de l'Industrie de l'Azote (CIA). Its rules were clear. According to such authorities as Ervin Hexner or Laurence Ballande, the CIA acted as a commercial agent each time one partner wanted to export nitrogen. It fixed the prices and preserved the previous position of each exporting nation in the world market. In that way, the CIA fulfilled its purpose: to prevent an excess of competition in a market where several years of overproduction led to a severe fall in prices and to overcapacities among partners. Under these rules, a formal free trade could be maintained, while inside it the consumers—the fertilizer industry and the farmers—kept some freedom in their purchases.[2]

But the CIA did not succeed in its struggle against the nitrogen crisis. As early as spring 1931, this authority was unable to stop the fall of prices, and some conflicts appeared among its members. According to Ervin Hexner, the French producers joined in a Confédération Française des Producteurs d'Azote (French Association of Nitrogen Producers), announced they would revoke their CIA membership, and asked their government to apply quotas protecting the French market while they would try to enlarge their share of market abroad. Quotas were settled in May 1931. Germany, Belgium, and Poland also applied quotas, and in the summer of 1931, the cartel ceased to operate. Hexner adds that a third cartel agreement came out of a London conference on July 26, 1932. But

Hexner gives very little information about it except to say that it was renewed in 1933 without Chile, and again in 1934, when Japan came in and when a new agreement was made to share European access to Chilean nitrogen and nitrogenous fertilizers.[3]

But Hexner is not supported by other authors. According to a United Nations enquiry of 1945–47, the 1930 agreement simply "terminated" in July 1931. The agreement with Japan came out only in 1936, the 1934 agreement with Chile was "separate," as in 1930, and the European cartel, including the same countries as in the CIA agreement of 1930, was recreated in the autumn of 1932.[4] Laurence Ballande tells us a quite different story. She explains that the 1930 agreement "was not renewed" in July 1931 because of "a persisting overproduction of synthetic nitrogen" and because of "a continuous fall of prices." She adds that "a year later . . . after laborious talks," a new agreement was signed. But the agreement she then describes was signed only in 1934. Eventually, the most important detail she gives us implies the French attitude toward the CIA after 1930: "France was now indirectly linked to the CIA" at last when it was renewed in 1934, but perhaps as early as 1932.[5]

However, it seems that the French producers withdrew as soon as May 1931. On the 5th of May, a governmental decree applied quotas, but no tariff, to nitrogen and nitrate imports. After May 1931, the Confédération Française des Producteurs d'Azote (CFPA) settled an independent policy backed by public powers. Afterwards, its role in the European cartel became fairly small. A number of bilateral agreements were signed with specified countries, especially Germany, Belgium, the Netherlands, and Great Britain. Cooperation with the cartel became lax, because the French wanted the cartel agreement to be narrowed to fertilizers and to allow negotiated access to Chilean guano in Europe.[6]

Consequently, with regard to the nitrogen cartel, the French may be described as followers and even as uncertain followers, while the Germans and the British may be characterized as leaders throughout the period 1929–38.

II. The French Nitrogen Market and Production Structure in the 1920s

In the 1920s, as before the First World War, French nitrogen consumption depended upon the international market. On the eve of the war, the farmers and munitions manufacturers used 418,500 metric tons/year of nitrogenized blends (equivalent to 69,058 tons of pure gas), but only 20.3% of it (85,000 tons) was processed in France. The products most in demand were nitrates (314,000 tons, or 75% of domestic consumption), imported almost entirely from Chile, with a smaller supply coming from Germany, which re-exported to France processed Chilean guano or provided synthetic blends. Synthetic nitrochalk came from Norway (7,600 tons/year). Finally, France produced only ammonium sulfate (85,000 tons/year), which was then blended locally into a large range of fertilizers. But it was unable to provide for the total domestic need, so 12,000 tons of ammonium sulfate were also imported from Great Britain. In both cases, the sulfate was processed from gas from coke plants or gas plants. In that time, due to the high dependence of France on foreign suppliers, nitrogenized or nitrogenous products were admitted freely in order to promote their use among farmers. So the domestic plants produced one-sixth the amount of their German competitors, but the country consumed 33% more nitrogenous fertilizers than Germany. In this context, the French prices were comparable to world prices. The War Ministry saw that the way the market worked actually would protect the country in the event of a war, since a possible conflict was predicted as nitrogen shortages would occur.[7]

Unfortunately, the First World War demonstrated how this expectation was wrong. The plants located in the north and northeast of France, which provided the main part of domestic production, were taken over by the Germans. An emergency plan for developing new capacities was drawn up in 1915, but for technical and other reasons it was applied slowly and with great pain. The national security and the munitions manufacturers depended strongly upon British and American exports and Chilean natural nitrates. The Georges Claude process was developed with public funds and overt military support, with partially satisfactory results. Some attempts were made to take control of production abroad, for instance when a joint-venture company, la Société Norvégienne de l'Azote, was taken over in 1915–16 by the electrotechnical firm Tréfileries et Laminoirs du Hâvre with large support coming from two French banks, in order to operate nitrochalk patents and plants in Norway. But in April 1917, the stock of nitrogenous products was as low as two days' supply, and the supply crisis was finally overcome only in the middle of 1918.[8]

In such a context, the ability of French industry to meet both the technical and production needs of the postwar demand was doubtful. As early as 1917, a vigorous postwar "policy of nitrogen" was prepared by the staff of the Minister of Trade, Etienne Clementel, because the minister wanted the country to cover its needs by domestic production instead of spending a large amount of foreign exchange to import Chilean or German blends. The official purpose of the proposed policy was then to strengthen national production and keep the country safe from German influence. A first opening was made in May 1919, when the Versailles Treaty gave France the right to exploit freely the Haber process for nitrosoda and nitrochalk. The Norwegian electrotechnical process was half abandoned, and the French sold their shares to the Société Norvégienne de l'Azote. Besides, the Société l'Air Liquide emphasized the Georges Claude process for producing synthetic ammonium in new plants cooperating with the Compagnie de Saint-Gobain, the largest firm in French chemicals. L'Air Liquide began also to enlarge its production capacity in coal mines and coke plants in the recovered northern region of France. Finally, the new landscape was completed when a 1921 bill authorized the state to establish a publicly owned and subsidized ammonia and nitrates plant in the southwest of France, in the city of Toulouse, where large munitions capabilities were now idle. It resulted in the creation of the Office National Industriel de l'Azote (ONIA), which would both employ the Haber process and revise Norwegian processes in its Toulouse plant after 1924.[9]

This general prospect of an increasing productivity would, it was hoped, keep pace with demand, since domestic consumption grew rather rapidly during the 1920s. Due to the demand of French farmers, it reached 809,200 tons/year by 1930, almost twice the level of 1913. Domestic plants now provided 49.4% of the need, more than twice their 1913 percentage. With 354,000 tons, French firms provided 93.7% of the consumed ammonium sulphate. With a turnover of more than one billion French francs, the market had greatly enlarged, and finally, in 1928–29, the ratio of imports/market fell in value from 74.1% (1913) to 39.3%. (See Table 1.)[10]

But, although their interests were specific, the main French producers (some 65 coke plants or coal mines, L'Air Liquide, and Saint Gobain) and also the largest consumers (the farmers and the military) felt their position remained weak. Year after year, overcapacity grew, while technical inefficiency limited the role of ONIA on the market. At the end of 1929, national capacity reached 551,000 metric tons, so the excess over effective production was nearly 27.5%. And this affected each kind of industry in a specific way. The production capacity of coke plants—or gas plants and ONIA's plant—grew sixfold after 1913, reaching 500,000 tons, essentially devoted to ammonium sulfate, of which 30% was now unemployed. But ONIA worked at full capacity (80,000 tons/year), while private firms had a third of their plants unemployed. Competition between private and state-controlled producers grew intense in a context of falling prices. Of course, it raised strong protests from companies. They suspected ONIA of dumping ammonium sulfate on the market and of thus precipitating a

TABLE 1 Main Nitrogen Fertilizers Used in France (1913–35) (in metric tons of blends)

	Years	French capability	Industry production	Imports	Consumption
Ammonium sulfate	1913–14	85,000	85,000	12,000	97,000
	1930–31	500,000	354,000[a]	24,000	378,000
	1931–32	590,000	359,000[b]	0	359,000
	1933–34	565,000	340,000[c]	0	340,000
	1934–35	515,000	345,000[d]	0	345,000
Nitrosoda	1913–14	0	0	314,000	314,000
	1930–31	2,000	2,000	355,000	357,000
	1931–32	6,000	5,000[e]	351,000	356,000
	1933–34	100,000	79,800[f]	170,200	250,000
	1934–35	165,000	130,000[g]	100,000	230,000
Nitrochalk	1913–14	0	0	0	0
	1930–31	40,000	39,000	27,800	66,800
	1931–32	90,000	84,400	16,200	100,600
	1933–34	135,000	114,000	0	114,000
	1934–35	175,000	130,000[h]	0	130,000
Ammonitrates	1913–14	0	0	0	0
	1930–31	7,000	4,400[i]	2,500	5,900
	1931–32	30,000	14,100[j]	0	14,100
	1933–34	150,000	72,100[k]	0	72,100
	1934–35	200,000	90,000[l]	0	90,000
Nitrates of ammonia	1913–14	0	0	0	0
	1930–31	2,000	1,000	0	1,000
	1931–32	10,000	6,500[m]	0	6,500
	1933–34	60,000	25,100[n]	0	25,100
	1934–35	80,000	30,000[p]	0	30,000

Source: Unions of nitrogen producers.
Share of ONIA: a&b: 80,000 t; c: 75,000 t; d: 69,000 t; e: 600 t; f: 33,300 t; g: 55,000 t; h: 4,000 t; i: 3,400; j: 11,800 t; k: 36,000 t; 1: 45,800 t; m: 4,500 t; n:7,200 t; p: 10,900 t.

fall in prices and discouraging new investments by its competitors, for its own investments were subsidized by the Treasury and had no return to provide to stockholders or banks. As a matter of fact, this was correct: the average price of French-made fertilizer neared 900FF/ton during the 1928–29 campaign, and once the big purchasers were supplied by domestic production, the others had to pay for imported blends at a higher rate, nearly 1300FF/ton.[11]

On another side, in spite of its dumping policy, the Toulouse plant was not able to capture the domestic market. Since 1927, a persisting public deficit had forced the Ministry of Finance to implement sharp cuts in its investment funds. The Toulouse plant's capacity grew more slowly. Its chief engineers claimed they could not compete with large German producers in processing sophisticated fertilizers such as nitrochalk and nitrosoda, and that in case of a new war against Germany, the largest number of French plants were still located in the northern districts, where they would be subject to strategic bombing, while the Toulouse ONIA plant would not.[12]

Finally, they pointed out that so long as ONIA was not a leading processor of nitrates, domestic performance in terms of quantity and quality would remain too weak to avoid a large stream of imports, for which most of the profits went to retailers. For instance, Chilean nitrate remained strongly in demand, from 314,000 tons in 1913 to 355,000 tons in 1929, and the decline of its share in the French market (from 75% to 44%) was only a relative one. The Chilean nitrates processing business—well developed by a dozen wealthy family firms since the expiration of a 10-year French monopoly over Peruvian guano exports in 1879—would remain influential, even over political decision-making.[13] The ONIA's technical failings strengthened the power of the Chileans still further. In spite of the heavy public investments made from 1921 to 1926, the supply of nitrochalk was provided by French private producers (39,000 tons) and foreign firms (41.7% of the market in 1928–29), because Toulouse could not reach this market. Eventually, the situation became so complicated that, while the ONIA used dumping methods to sell ammonium sulphate, the government reimbursed the farmers for a part of the difference between French and foreign prices.[14]

Also, when worldwide overcapacity began to endanger the whole industry in 1929, the French nitrogen industry was divided into three groups of antagonistic interests. First came the big farmers, joined in a powerful union of wheat producers (the Association Générale des Producteurs de Blé, or AGPB) that had a large influence over political life and rural voting all over the country. And the AGPB was the champion of nitrogen free trade because its leaders shared political interests with the traders and because the trend toward increasing imports was the best way to obtain low domestic prices from domestic producers and reimbursements to farmers from the state. Then came the Confédération Française des Producteurs d'Azote (CFPA) grouping the private firms, and its commercial branch, the Comptoir Français de l'Azote (the Nitrogen Syndicate of France), itself dominated by two large chemical firms, L'Air Liquide and Saint Gobain, and devoted to the very influential Comité des Houillères (the National Union of Coalmakers).[15] The union was well known as an enemy of any kind of free trade, and as an advocate of a state-supported policy of reorganizing coal mines and scaling down production, which meant the union wanted it since it was created as a by-product of ONIA. Of course, it defended protection by any means, including cartels that raise prices. And its claim against ONIA was based upon real facts: public subsidies twisted competition, and the Toulouse plant managed to gain a monopoly in the production process of ammonium sulfate, even when this national monopoly and its exclusive production of this blend paved the way for the incursion of German imported blends. To complete the picture, two other actors played parts in this involved drama. The gun powder administration in the War Ministry, chastened by the wartime shortages, wanted a quick and strong increase of national capacity at any price and by any means. And Treasury officials balked each time the ONIA—officially controlled by the Ministry of Agriculture, but devoted to the military—asked for new money.

III. How to Deal with the Cartel? (1929–32)

Because French interests were antagonistic to each other, more of them saw the incipient cartelization of the nitrogen market as a threat. The main danger came from the pivotal membership of Germany. If Chile shared the European market with Germany (the first selling natural nitro-soda, and the second, synthetic), its share of the French market would stabilize at around 25%. It meant that German producers would become more competitive with French producers of synthetic nitrates.[16] The leaders of the CFPA and the Confédération Française de l'Agriculture (CFA) were convinced they would lose their share because of the better quality of German blends, and because the capacity of plants grew more quickly in Germany. The fact that Norway entered the DEN agreement was another threat: the ONIA was still unable to launch the processing of nitrochalk, while private firms did not have sufficient funds to increase their investments. The diagnosis was clear: the birth of a cartel would stop the development of the domestic industry and strengthen international competition instead of reduce it.

To tell the truth, the German menace was foreseen before 1929. In 1927, during a discussion of a general French-German trade agreement closing the postwar period, the delegates of French synthetic nitrate producers attempted unsuccessfully to obtain a 15% tariff on German blends.[17] One year later, they demanded a 45% tariff, still without success: the French Minister of Trade, Maurice Bokanowski, tried to gain advantages in a general debate on tariffs with Berlin and so avoided conflict regarding the fertilizer question.[18]

Besides, farming interests mobilized against possible tariffs or quotas. On July 5, 1929, 350 members of the French Chamber of Deputies approved a protest manifesto that was then published in the *Journal Official de la République Française*. It claimed, "Our farmers will never accept barriers applied to nitrates or any other kind of fertilizer. ... They refuse to accept quotas also." Quotas or barriers would "reduce the competition between the different kinds of fertilizers" and stop "a profitable decrease in prices."[19]

In fact, foreign prices, lately higher than French ones, began to fall sharply at the end of 1929. Domestic producers were alarmed, since their capacity had grown 15% during the year on a free market; their advantageous gap in price competition vanished by the day. Moreover, the CFA failed in its attempt to export synthetic nitrates at a low price (50 FF/ton cheaper) to northern countries. On its side, the ONIA pursued its state-subsidized investments. So a new assault from private producers pushed the government toward a decree promoting a 15% tariff on German products. But, at the same time, the price of wheat fell from 1300FF to 1100FF/ton. The slightest rise in nitrogen prices would accelerate the painful crash of farmers' profits. Once more, the idea of a tariff was rejected. Now those who sought for equilibrium between farming and industrial interests found only one way open: join the cartel when it renewed in the summer of 1930.

But this agreement was just signed when the crisis started again. Fixing the market shares according to the shares of previous years offered to any partner a good challenge if consumption continued to rise. Of course, such a continuous rise was a common assumption among French producers and bureaucrats. But consumption of nitrates began to fall sharply; farmers' profits and investment were seriously damaged by an overproduction of wheat. Nevertheless, capacity of nitrogenous blend plants increased from 400,000 tons (1929) to 500,000 tons (August 1930), while the foreign suppliers now got the right to supply half of the French demand. The situation became dreadful. The risks supported by private industry grew tremendously, but the ONIA of course did not have to pay anything to its nonexistent stockholders or creditors. And, because it agreed to sign the 1930 international accord, the ONIA was given 40% of the ammonium sulphate market.[20] On the one hand, consumption of sulphates fell from 378,000 to 270,000 tons; on the other hand, the ONIA could sell 151,200 tons instead of 80,000 tons (+89%). The German Stickstoffsyndikat had 113,000 tons, and the coal and gas makers or the chemistry firms had to reduce their share from 274,000 tons to 113,000 (−41.4%). Henceforth, the employed capacity of the last would fall from 65.2% to 27%.[21]

New negotiations started in the beginning of 1931. The ONIA accepted a reduced share of 64,000 tons in order to prevent a new breakdown in sulphates currency and in the volume of market. In exchange, it received large compensations from the cartel.[22]

Last but not least, at this moment the union of private producers failed to break up. The ones who processed cheaper ammonium sulphate from by-products of coke plants or gas plants sustained the fall in production well because at the same time the slump in the whole economy damaged their upstream production. But private chemical firms saw their state-of-the-art nitrogen plants almost stop production. Their belief in the advantages of cartelization weakened since only 20% of their capacity was employed. They began to criticize some details of the 1930 agreement, for instance the fact that Belgian producers were permitted to count 50,000 tons of imported blends as if they were made in France. And finally, these firms protested against the persisting enforcement of both German and ONIA capacities.[23]

The Ministry of Trade and Public Works was then concerned. What kind of policy was to be brought before the 1930 treaty renewal next summer? The main opposition to tariff barriers and quotas still came from the farming interests, strongly backed by the Minister of Agriculture, François Poncet. At the end of April and in early May 1931, a sharp discussion took place in governmental and business circles. On May 2, at its annual conference, one of the most powerful regional farmers' associations repeated once more its refusal to accept any quota or barrier. That declaration followed a heavy campaign in the press, especially in *Le Temps*, the most influential daily among rightwing politicians and businessmen, and in *Paysans de France*, the magazine issued by the Union of Wheat Producers.[24]

But the government ignored the farmers' claim. On May 5, a decree made illegal any cooperation with the cartel: "In order to protect the major interests of our country, any import of fertilizer is temporarily subordinated to the delivery of licenses, these licenses being delivered by the Budget administration (Department of Customs) after the recommendation of the Minister of Agriculture."[25] It also emphasized the view of the military:

During the war, France noticed that one of the modern industries was lacking in her economy: the ammonium sulfate industry, from which fertilizers and explosives are processed. Our security and agriculture depended on foreign countries. . . . Actually the power of foreign organizations, the low cost of abundant natural reserves in some countries, worldwide overproduction, and the breakdown of the market endanger the future of a national industry that is actually passing through an awkward phase of internal reshaping.[26]

A second decree signed on May 12, 1931, created a special committee. Among its members were six delegates from various branches of the administration (Agriculture, Budget, Trade, Public Works, and War), five from farming interests, and eight from the nitrogen industry. Together, they were in charge of giving or refusing licenses to foreign exporters. They negotiated only with producers' unions in order to prevent excessive imports and to help the birth of an informal but efficient domestic cartel.[27]

While the DEN group and its affiliates discussed sharply and unsuccessfully the renewal of the 1930 agreement of two conferences held in Scheveningen (Netherlands) and Lucerne (Switzerland), the French committee examined a large number of import demands concerning 450,000 tons of various blends. Only 80,000 tons were licensed on July 7, 1931: 37,000 tons from Chile, 30,000 tons from Germany, 2,000 tons from the United States, 7,500 tons from Norway, and the rest from Great Britain. And the committee began to operate as a clearing house: fertilizers were admitted in France at the average French price, the difference between it and the foreign rates (German prices were 35F/ton higher, British prices 150F cheaper) being rebated to cheaper countries in order to stabilize domestic prices.[28]

Then came a second step. On December 27, 1931, the French CFA and the German Stickstoffsyndikat signed a treaty licensing 150,000 tons of nitrosoda in France. On January 29, 1932, a similar long-term contract brought 25,000 tons of nitrogeneous American blends into France. On February 15 and March 9, four contracts were signed with Norsk-Hydro for about 35,000 tons of Norwegian blends, and in May, 30,000 tons were ordered from American plants.[29]

Under the system of quotas, French industry could be reshaped. The ONIA's share was increased, and the Toulouse plant added the processing of nitrosoda to its classical line of ammonium sulfate. Compensation was paid to the farmers since they accepted higher prices.

Finally, at the end of the 1932–33 campaign, the landscape of the French nitrogen industry changed. Its total capacity (820,000 tons) reached more or less the actual consumption (800,500 tons). Imports (260,500 tons, or 32.5% of the market) were used in order to bring prices down to a realistic level (due to the low international prices) and to safeguard part of the plants in case of a war. The ONIA's share of the domestic market was secured at around 25%. The state-owned producer agreed not to expand its production of ammonium sulfate, which unfairly challenged private firms in previous years; its level (80,000 tons) was more or less equivalent that in 1929. Of course, an equilibrium was found with the international suppliers. Imports of ammonium sulfate from Germany or Great Britain were prohibited because this blend entered the processing of explosives. But the market of ammonia nitrates was shared, while the ONIA could produce one-third of French-made nitrosoda, a blend for which borders remained open in respect to French diplomacy toward Chile and in order to keep a satisfying contact with German producers in case of a renewal of the cartel.[30]

Finally, when the cartel slowly recovered in 1932 and 1934, French industry found no advantage in joining it as an active member. It simply joined it as an observer, for two purposes: to monitor prices, and as a gesture toward the integration of the largest number of partners in it.[31]

IV. From Nitrogen to Other Cartels

This study of the contradictory attitude of French interests toward the international cartel of nitrogen is rich in lessons for historians. First, it shows how theoretical debates, at least in the case of France, gave way finally to reality each time the question of participation in a cartel was raised by interests and firms facing a crisis situation. Of course, on a theoretical basis, the rather handsome *Revue des Deux Mondes* could try to influence the debate through a well-balanced review of ideas. Its March 1, 1929, issue published an essay by Henri de Peyerhimhoff, a leading business executive and the head of the Comité des Houillères, who advocated the generalization of cartels in every branch of industry, as a solution giving "a chance to France to promote its wealth." By contrast, a retired high-ranking official, Louis Le Launay, in the March 15, 1930, issue of the same magazine, criticized cartels for being, in his view, outdated organizations marked by a middle-aged attitude toward economy and responsible for the high cost of living.[32]

Such a debate certainly stimulated brains. But people in charge of public or private businesses were more cautious when they were involved in cartel business. For instance, Pierre-Etienne Flandin, a leading actor on the political scene strongly involved in national economic policies and a well-informed thinker too, suggested that whether or not cartels entered into a pragmatic approach to business depended on a clear strategy of branches or firms, one suited to the goals of industrial development.[33] Around 1940 the Sorbonne professor Henri Truchy gave a thorough review of cartels. He described their origin, form, and purpose in great detail but refrained from giving any opinion about their efficiency or their utility.[34]

Having emphasized the limits of the theoretical approach, let us suggest a second hypothesis. In the case of interwar France, joining or not joining an international cartel was perceived by managers as a provisional way to resolve domestic problems. For instance, French steel makers joined in 1926 the International Steel Cartel (ISC), not to win a preeminent position in the European market, but in order to solve a professional problem. How could they combat overcapacity resulting from the added effects of large wartime investment, of the rebuilding of furnaces in damaged areas, of the recovery of the Lorraine's districts from Germany, of the advantages given to them in Luxemburg firms by the Versailles Treaty?[35] Of course, the nitrogen industry offered a similar example of overcapacity due to the war and to recovery.

In a third hypothesis, the nitrogen case sends us on another track, as the International Steel Cartel experience does. In both cases, entering a cartel or cooperating with it was a preparatory experience leading to the reshaping of international trade agreement or treaties. A strong connection existed for a long time in France between business pressure and tariff policy. When international competition became more intense in the 1880s and 1890s, coal mine owners, chemical firms, and their customers had strongly demanded higher barriers and won the battle. In order to protect farmers, another party of powerful voters, the import of fertilizers remained free. Expensive coal changed the price of wheat and food when carried to urban consumers, and low prices for fertilizers were a compensation given to farmers. And then, until the eve of the First World War, this equilibrium was used as an argument by the Ministry of Foreign Affairs each time tariffs were renegotiated with Great Britain, Germany, or Chile.

And it was shown that the creation of the ISC in 1926 resulted from interfirm negotiation just before the crucial governmental accord of 1927 on French-German trade. A similar motive influenced the attitude of the Compagnie Française Thomson-Houston toward the recurrent rebirth of an international cartel of locomotives. The Compagnie had an advantage in the domestic market since the beginning of the 1920s in making electric-powered machines for tramways and railways. But the Mulhousian firm Société Alsacienne de Constructions Mécaniques (SACM) benefited from similar advantages in the German market due to its membership in a local railstock cartel before the First Word War (when Alsace belonged to the Reich). When French-German tariff negotiations started in 1924, this problem was compounded by others: will French and non-Alsatian producers enter the German market when the free entry given by the Versailles Treaty ends? Finally, a solution was found. The treaty of 1927 gave a narrow window to French machines under the Alsatian label. The following year, the locomotives department of SACM merged with the Thomson-Houston's one to form Alsthom, which inherited the part of the German cartelized market previously held by SACM. By the way, Alsthom entered the international cartel and protected its role in the European market.[36]

This leads us to the question of the complex interests shared by firms, industrial unions, and public administration. The individualistic way in considering French industrial strategies seems unadapted to historical experience. In the nitrogen case, organized interests led the game: the state bureaucracy as well as professional unions, syndicated firms, and lobbying interests played their parts with great efficiency. And each of them, in spite of their own tactical maneuvers, referred to the same "general purpose" through the idea that the nitrogen industry was a "strategic" one. And the literature shows us, for instance in the case of potassium, that French interests turned to cartelization and tried to use it with profit each time a domestic industry was closely related to national security or could improve the balance of payments. Here, provisional or durable accords were able to be made between two or more interests or syndicates. This fact gives us some sense of the high level of organization and cooperation among firms and between firms and other economic actors in that period. The idea of a French industry led in the interwar period by individualistic interests and by a shortsighted perspective seems an inaccurate description of the complex and deep involvement of the various actors in industrial restructuring.

Another example may illustrate our purpose. The lamp cartel was created in 1924 under the name Phoebus. In the lamp industry, France was a highly technologically dependent partner, and the product was not considered as "strategic" by public authorities. But the Compagnie des Lampes belonging to CGE (Compagnie Générale d'Electricité) entered the cartel with great satisfaction, since this permitted it to avoid or limit competition in the French market with the Philips Company and protected narrow relations between the CGE and German or American firms who gave it patents and with them a lead in the national market.[37]

To conclude, two remarks. First, the nitrogen case teaches us that heavy imports may be, for a country, an advantage almost as strong as heavy exports: industrial reality does not agree here with the statistical view of those concerned with the balance of payments. Second, we hope that the present paper helps to show how a detailed and complete story of international cartels remains an open file to economic and business historians. We hope that some of the points focused on in the present paper will be more completely dealt with as a result of added material.

NOTES

1. For instance, in the classic text of Fernand Braudel and Ernest Labrousse (eds.), *Histoire Economique et Sociale de la France de 1610 à nos jours* (Paris, 1979–81), tome IV, vol. 2, pp. 789–92. In these pages, the question of national or international cartels is mixed up, and the discussion of the general purpose is based on secondary sources, the conclusion of the author being that cartelization was weak in France for political reasons and because of "individualism" among managers.

2. Ervin Hexner, *International Cartels* (Chapel Hill, 1946); the nitrogen cartel is discussed on page 326ff. Laurence Ballande, *Essai d'entente monographique et statistique sur les ententes internationales* (Paris, 1936), especially pp. 92–104.

3. Hexner, op. cit., p. 326.

4. United Nations, *International Cartels* (New York, 1947), esp. Table 3.

5. Ballande, op. cit., pp. 94–96.

6. Edouard Bernard, *Le problème de l'Azote en France (Agriculture, industrie & défense nationale)* (Poitiers, 1933, 1936).

7. John F. Godfrey, *Capitalism at War: Industrial Policy and Bureaucracy in France, 1914–1918* (Hamburg–New York, 1987), pp. 157–78; see also Jean-Pierre Douffiagues and Armand Roux, *La politique française de l'Azote* (Paris, 1935).

8. Godfrey, op. cit.; see also Emmanuel Chadeau, "Produire pour les Electriciens: Les Tréfileries et Laminoirs du Hâvre de 1897 à 1930," in *Des Entreprises pour faire de l'electricité* (Paris, 1988), pp. 285–303; and Jean-Pierre Daviet, *Une multinationale à la Française, Saint-Gobain (1667–1989)* (Paris, 1989), pp. 136–46. De Lafargue, "Investissement Exterieur et concurrence franco-allemande: la Norvégienne de l'Azote, 1886–1926" (Ph.D. thesis Université Charles de Gaulle-Lille III, 1986), completely ignores the role of French industrial interests in this company during the First World War and supposes that the French banks operated the Norvégienne de l'Azote for their own interests. That is unfortunately a very narrow view of the matter.

9. Godfrey, op. cit.; Daviet, op. cit.; Bernard, op. cit., p. 163ff.; Douffiagues and Roux, op. cit., part 1.

10. Ibid., p. 14; and Bernard, op. cit., tables.

11. Bernard, ibid.

12. Douffiagues and Roux, op. cit., tables; Godfrey, op. cit.; and Daviet, op. cit.

13. For instance, Lucien Dior, Minister of Trade from January 1921 to March 1924, under Briand and then Poincaré, belonged to a family of Chilean guano processors and was a member of parliament elected at Granville, a small harbor on the Atlantic Ocean in Normandy, near the famous Mont Saint Michel, where his family ran its business; see Raymond Joly et al., *Dictionnaire des Parlementaires Français (de 1889 à 1940)* (Paris, 1964–71), vol. 1, pp. 89–92; Dior spent part of his ministerial time in trying successfully to delay the implementation of the law creating the ONIA and the building of the Toulouse plant. But in the left-wing government that came in after the general election of May 1924, politicians from the

Toulouse area were strong, and the decrees were published and the plant was launched. On the guano market when ruled by French interests, see Emmanuel Chadeau, *L'Economie du Risque, les Entrepreneurs (1850–1980)* (Paris, 1988), pp. 137–168.

14. Daviet, op. cit., p. 136ff. presents some of the difficulties met by the ONIA in a competitive environment; and Bernard, op. cit., p. 165ff. presents the technical problems met by the ONIA after 1924, as well as the politics of repayment settled in 1928 to avoid a drop in prices.

15. After Douffiagues and Roux, op. cit.; and Bernard, op. cit., p. 170ff.

16. Pierre Lucas, "Le marché de l'Azote va-t-il s'équilibrer?," *La Chimie industrielle*, vol. 6 (Dcember 1930).

17. Bernard, op. cit., p. 165.

18. Ibid.

19. *Journal Officiel de la République Française*, Débates, first session, Chambre des Députés, July 5, 1929.

20. Accord between the Minister of Agriculture and the CFA, August 16, 1930.

21. Bernard, op. cit., p. 172ff.

22. Ibid.

23. Ibid.

24. Ibid., p. 174.

25. *Journal Officiel de la République Française*, Lois et Décrets, May 7, 1931.

26. Ibid.

27. Ibid., May 14, 1931.

28. Bernard, op. cit., pp. 181–85.

29. Ibid.

30. Douffiagues and Roux, op. cit., part 2 and table, p. 14.

31. Ibid.

32. Henri de Peyerhimhoff, "Les formules modernes d'organisation économique," *Revue des Deux Mondes*, March 1, 1929, pp. 439–58; Louis le Launay, "Cartels internationaux et vie chère," *Revue des Deux Mondes*, March 15, 1930, pp. 200–210.

33. The Flandin papers at the Bibliothèque Nationale in Paris contain suggestive files devoted to the question of economic organization and international competition, files 42–45 and 62.

34. Henri Truchy, *Traité d'Economie Politique*, vol IV, tome 1 (Paris, 1941), pp. 125–59. In the author's mind (in fact the well-directed mind of one of his students, J. Saint-Germès), the final note of the study must be: "the struggle against abuses of concentration."

35. Reference to Eric Bussière, "The Evolution of Structures in the Iron and Steel Industry in France, Belgium, and Luxemburg," in Etsuo Abe and Yoshitaka Suzuki (eds.), *Changing Patterns of International Rivalry* (Tokyo, 1991).

36. These detailed information were given to us by a Canadian historian, Prof. Lanthier (University of Quebec, Trois Rivières), who studied in detail the strategic relations between multinational firms and French electrotechnical companies up to the end of the 1930s.

37. Compagnie Générale d'Electricité, *Rapport d'activité aux actionnaires pour l'année 1927*, allocution de l'administrateur délégué (executive chairman), M. Azaria, May 1928, archives of CGE, Paris.

Comment

Masaru Udagawa

In his interesting paper, Professor Chadeau has traced the French attitude toward the international nitrogen cartel, and the market for and structure of French nitrogen in the 1920s. Furthermore, after examining the relationship between the system of quotas and the international cartel, he discusses several important points concerning the French nitrogen industry and the international cartel. His paper gives us many useful materials and ideas for this conference. Chadeau's discussion is very clear, so I do not need to add any more. But in order to stimulate discussion, I would like to ask some questions with regard to his paper.

First, the synthetic ammonia industry was one of the "new" industries that led to the so-called Second Industrial Revolution. After World War I, several nations tried to develop domestic production of synthetic ammonia. But it was not easy to establish an indigenous industry because foreign products had been imported cheaply and quickly dominated the domestic market. Moreover, in order to survive severe international competition, domestic enterprises had to invest huge amounts of capital and to solve many technological difficulties in the early stages of their development. In these circumstances, the French synthetic ammonia industry began to compete with its German and British counterparts. So I would like to ask Chadeau the following points. How did the French enterprises bear the burden of initial costs in developing their industry? I think that the success or failure of this industry mainly depended upon the quality of the technology used and the success of its application to production. If so, why did two private firms, L'Air Liquide and Saint Gobain, decide to attempt the commercial application of the Claude process, which had not gone beyond the experimental stage when both entered this industry?

Second, according to Chadeau, when worldwide overcapacity began to endanger the industry in 1929, the French nitrogen industry was influenced by three antagonistic interests that competed with each other. The farmers' interests, represented by the powerful union of wheat producers (AGPB), requested free trade in nitrogen. The groups of private producers were not favorable to free trade and asked the government for a system of quotas and a tariff on foreign imports. And the ONIA, a public corporation, attempted dumping and tried to join the international cartel to safeguard its share in the domestic market. The ONIA's dumping policy was supported by the farmer groups, although the private producers stood against it. There were also various opinions among the ministries on the government's industrial policy. The War Ministry backed ONIA's activities; the Department of the Treasury opposed the ONIA, while the Ministry of Agriculture supported the farmers' demands.

Meanwhile, "the crisis of nitrogen" became more acute, and the French government created a special committee in 1931 in order to resolve the crisis. Its members were composed of the delegates from various branches of the government, and from the farming group and nitrogen interests. After the discussions in this committee, the various groups agreed to the adoption of a system of quotas on the condition that the nitrogen producers formed a domestic cartel. In this context, I would like to ask Chadeau several points. Why did the farmers' interest groups finally accept the system of quotas? I think that the business strategies of the enterprises and the relationship between the government and this industry changed considerably after the adoption of quotas and the formation of the domestic cartel. If so, how can such changes in business strategy and the relation between government and industry be explained?

Third, according to Chadeau, "in the case of interwar France, joining or not joining an international cartel was perceived by managers as a provisional way to resolve domestic problems." I agree and think that his view is quite important in the study of the international cartel. Finally, Chadeau suggests the necessity of cooperative work between theorists and historians in studying the international cartel. I agree and hope that he will explain the following point in more detail. If cooperation is possible, what form should it take?

Response

Emmanuel Chadeau

Professor Udagawa's comments require only brief answers. First, the question of the initial burden in developing a new industry: Because of the war, French firms did not have to pay for using German patents, and the Treaty of Versailles in June 1919 gave them free access to German technology (the Haber process being the main one) until 1923 or 1924. Also during the war, the control over the Norvegienne de l'Azote gave them access to electrochemical processes in a context of expanding demand for explosives. French companies involved in developing the Georges Claude process had a similar advantage, and high wartime profits gave them other opportunities; and finally, the ONIA's plant was subsidized by the government (more than half a billion French francs from 1921 to 1927).

Second, the war context explains the quick and hazardous development of the Claude process: the supply of munitions firms could not depend entirely on imports, for the position of France vis-à-vis its allies would have been too weak. We must remember also that the main French chemical firm before the war was Kuhlmann, whose biggest plants were located in the part of France occupied (like the main coalmining districts) from August 1914 up to the fall of 1918.

The final issue of my paper explains the position of various actors in the free-trade/protection discussion around 1930. And farmers accepted quotas for several reasons: in 1931 because the gap between domestic and international prices was repaid to the buyers, and later because the price of French wheat was lowered for several years by domestic overproduction. And we must also consider that the national committee that discussed and set quotas acted as an informal but efficient national cartel where customers were associated with decision making. Inside a system of quotas, firms' strategies were regulated: the ONIA could develop its own ambitions (a domination over the ammonium sulphate market), private firms resisted foreign competition, and the bureaucracy attained its goal of developing domestic production quicker than domestic consumption.

In conclusion, I cannot establish a program of international research on cartels singlehandedly, but we can try to draw a preliminary sketch here. For instance, the history of cartels before 1920 is a relevant topic in European history, and the persistence of cartelization after the Second World War is another one.

International Cartels in Belgium and the Netherlands during the Interwar Period: The Nitrogen Case

Greta Devos

Immediately after the First World War, there were clearly different economic situations in Belgium and the Netherlands. The Netherlands, having remained neutral during the war, had been able to catch up industrial arrears considerably. Belgium had to devote itself to restoring its industry, which had suffered serious damage under German occupation. Only as late as 1925 could Belgian industry achieve its prewar level for most of its products. A year later the currency was stabilized. The Netherlands had already returned to the gold standard in 1925.

I. The Economic Background

With their distinctly open economies, both countries were able to enjoy prosperity in the second half of the "roaring twenties," but they were equally vulnerable to the world crisis of 1929. Until 1931 the situation was bearable. However, exports received a fatal blow due to the devaluation of the pound sterling and later the American dollar. The two countries entered the gold bloc. Consequently, they were obliged to adapt their price level, and this disadvantaged especially those sectors producing for export. Moreover, these small countries were forced to limit their free-market-oriented policy. Both in Belgium and the Netherlands, quota measures for several commodities were announced starting from 1931. Nevertheless, they tried to advocate free world trade (Conventions of Oslo and Ouchy) and shunned a devaluation of the currency, which in their opinion would cause still more inflation and chaos in commercial relations. Finally, they could not withstand the pressure: Belgium devalued its currency by 28% in the spring of 1935. The Netherlands followed with a depreciation of 21.5% one year later.[1]

Exports were of vital importance. For Belgium the situation was especially critical after 1918. If its industry wanted to recover its prewar position, an extra effort would be required. The government, desiring to extend the scope of its responsibilities, also took charge of promoting exports. Therefore, it encouraged the planning and structuring of industrial sectors with the realization of national sales offices, domestic agreements, and cartels. But the organization within the various industrial sectors was seldom an objective by itself. Most often it was necessary to join international cartels. In other words, the international cartels were a consequence of domestic organization and collaboration.

The attitude of the Dutch authorities towards the creation of trusts and cartels in the 1920s appears to have been one of permissive indifference. Interference with the business world and its structuring was virtually nonexistent. Attempts to organize an enquiry about cartels and trusts were thwarted. The free trade movement was still too powerful. After the devaluation of the pound sterling in September 1931, however, a vigorous protectionist policy was pursued, which, according to some, went beyond that of Belgium.[2] Both countries introduced a kind of compulsory cartel system for the national sectors in the mid-thirties.[3]

The problems the two countries had to deal with during the crisis, and the ways they responded to them, were quite similar. Export markets had to be secured at all costs. Of course, this affected the countries' participation in the creation of international cartels.

II. The Convention Internationale de l'Azote (CIA)

During the twenties, many newcomers had been lured into the nitrogen industry by the expectation of high profits. In addition, a number of countries were concerned for security reasons about their dependence on foreign supplies and wanted to produce the basic material for their industries. The creation of factories for synthetic nitrogen threatened the strong position of the major producers, which were Chile for natural nitrogen, Germany, Great Britain, and Norway. In 1926 they alone would have reached an overproduction.[4]

In order to cope with this situation, an international conference was held in Biarritz at the end of April 1926. Representatives of about ten countries discussed the situation and the development of the nitrogen world market.[5] In late 1929 and early 1930, further talks of a more informal nature were organized. The first International Nitrogen Conference in Paris in April 1930 could not solve the problem of overproduction, but the participating countries, among which were Germany and Great Britain, could state their positions. Further internal negotiations led to a new international conference, in Ostend this time, at which eight countries were represented. German and British producers were in favor of a uniform restriction of production. The French-Belgian group wanted the supply to domestic markets to be reserved for the national industry. At the second International Nitrogen Conference in Paris starting on July 5,

1930, to which the American, Chilean, and Japanese producers were invited, the prospects were initially dark. French and Belgian, but also Dutch and Polish, producers vigorously opposed a restriction of production. In addition to the adamant attitude of the French, this could hardly facilitate the negotiations.[6] After an interruption of about two weeks, they reached a temporary agreement anyway.

The CIA would gather experience during one year in order to arrive at a more definite organization of production and trade. When, on the day of the agreement, the Chilean group joined as well, 98% of European and 80% of world nitrogen production was represented by this cartel. The United States and Japan did not participate.[7]

Although the agreement had been achieved with great difficulty, it went back to three previously subscribed agreements:

(1) The cartel of the DEN [Deutschland-England-Norway] group (July 1, 1929; and valid for ten years), which united the three largest European producers (Germany, Great Britain, and Norway) to pursue a common sales policy and to try and attract other European producers.

(2) The compromise between the DEN group and the Chilean producers, which was established in 1929.

(3) The foundation in 1930 of an international syndicate for calcium cyanamide. It covered 92% of world production and was created for a period of eight years. It granted full liberty to the producers in their domestic markets, but it defined the export quotas and the prices, which were to be reconsidered every six months, and which were dependent to a great extent on nitrogen prices.[8]

Also according to the CIA every country remained master of its domestic market, insofar as the national industry could satisfy the domestic needs. Exports to members of the cartel or to outsiders were regulated by means of special agreements that fixed the export quotas. Due to fiscal considerations, the Gesellschaft für Internationale Stickstoffindustrie A.G. was founded in Basle. Its shares were owned by members of the cartel. This organism had to safeguard profitable and stable prices. It also served as a compensation fund to make up for losses due to production restrictions, to fight outsiders, and to pay for the cartel's organization costs.[9] The cartel was virtually led by the Deutsche Stickstoffsyndikat. Production restrictions were not uniform but varied according to the country: 30% for Germany, Norway, Belgium, the Netherlands, Czechoslovakia, and Italy; 40% for Poland; 50% for Great Britain; and only 10% for France. Besides the stabilizing of prices and the restriction of imports France also enjoyed a mild attitude towards further development of its industry until it became self-supporting. Germany and

Great Britain, which were the largest producers, had to make a few sacrifices.

For Germany, which had previously been able to export about one-third to one-half of its production, the advantages of the cartel were: the guarantee of stable prices, the avoidance of a price war between the European producers, and the hope that the cartel would discourage a further extension of production capacity. For Great Britain, the only advantage was in the area of prices: the European market was virtually closed, and the domestic market accounted for about two-fifths of production as a result of the import of Chilean nitrates. The British producers, united in ICI, depended henceforth on the development of modern agriculture in the British Empire and the Far East.[10]

When the negotiations to renew the cartel started in April 1931, it appeared that several nitrogen producers asked for higher quotas to accord with their capacity, which had increased to 4 million tons nitrogen (N) in the meantime, whereas consumption had decreased to 1.5 million tons N. Conflicts of interest could not possibly be straightened out, and negotiations broke up in July 1931.

Almost all countries responded by raising import duties or by imposing license systems, contingents, or embargoes to protect the domestic market.[11] The DEN group, which still existed, tried to close deals with the countries individually. Finally, a new European regulation was established in August 1932, after close negotiations in London, Berlin, Scheveningen, and Paris. A new element was the entry of Switzerland. The French producers, on the other hand, withdrew under pressure of their government. Again, the DEN group was responsible for the sale of the export quotas, unless individual contracts stipulated otherwise. These quotas were calculated on the basis of the results of the previous campaign. Chile, which participated in the distribution, withdrew after a while. A special agreement with Japan was signed in 1934.[12] In the same year, the cartel was renewed. Henceforth, Chile was allowed to sell certain amounts to the European members of the cartel.

For the first time, penalties were also introduced when quotas were exceeded. The income from these penalties had to compensate for the premiums offered in exchange for limiting production. The fines were paid to the newly created trustee, International Nitrogen Association Ltd., in London.

The imposed uniform prices had to be reconsidered regularly in this period because of the continual changes in rates of exchange. After a year, in July 1935, a new agreement was reached, extending over three years this time. The stipulations remained roughly the same. Equally, the renewal of the cartel in 1938, which was to last till late June 1941, did not show any fundamental changes.[13]

Meanwhile, world production of synthetic nitrogen had increased gradually. It was deliberately kept slightly below the level of consumption. About 90% of the nitrogenous products were used for agricultural purposes. Consumption had risen steeply in Germany, the United States, the USSR, and France. In Asia especially, consumption had increased substantially. Two-thirds of the increase was accounted for by Japan and China.

III. The Nitrogen Industry in Belgium and the Netherlands

Before the First World War, the Belgian chemical industry used to be a rather limited business of several small companies, often family run. Even then the sector followed the tracks of the metallurgy and coal industries. The main products were fertilizers, especially superphosphates and sulfuric acids. However, the sector was dominated by the Solvay group, which had expanded far beyond Belgian territory, and which was one of the world's largest producers of alkalis.

Shortly before the First World War, limited production existed of nitrogen in the form of ammonia. It was a by-product of the coke factories. As such, 9,950 metric tons N were produced in 1913, which represents 27% of the nitrogen required for agriculture in those days. The remaining 73% was supplied by natural sodium nitrate imported from Chile via the port of Antwerp. Artificial fertilizers were among the few innovations the Belgian farmer had faith in.[14] Following the example of Germany, Great Britain, the United States, and other countries, Belgium started its production of synthetic nitrogen in 1925. In about five years nine factories were established.

The main initiatives were taken by four groups. The biggest group was the Union Chimique Belge, with important participation of the Solvay group. It was mainly a Belgian group, backed by the Société Générale. This concern, which was established through a merger, ran three nitrogen plants. The second group, Ougrée-L'Air Liquide/Sofigaz-Boerenbond, owned two nitrogen plants. It was the first to take the initiative to generate synthetic nitrogen by founding the Société Belge de l'Azote in 1923. The third group, Montecatini-Coppée/Coppée-Banque de Bruxelles, owned three companies, one of which was established in Dutch territory. The fourth and last group was the French Kuhlmann group, with two nitrogen factories (Table 1).

A remarkable feature of these foundations was the close collaboration between the coke factories, the chemical industry, and the banks. The

TABLE 1 Development of the Synthetic Nitrogen Industry in Belgium

1. Union Chimique Belge[a]

    Société Carbochimique S.S., 1928 (1930)*
    Société pour la Fabrication d'Engrais Azotés (SAFEA), 1929 (1930–31)

2. Ougrée-L'Air Liquide/Sofigaz-Boerenbond[b]

    Société Belge de l'Azote (SBA), 1923 (1925)
    Société des Produits Chimiques du Marly, 1929[c]

3. Montecatini-Coppée/Coppée-Banque de Bruxelles

    Société Ammoniaque Synthétique et Dérivés, 1926 (1928)
    Société Centrale du Centre pour la Fabrication de l'Ammoniaque Synthétique, 1928[d]

4. Kuhlmann Group

    Société des Fours à Coke de Selzaete, 1924 (1928)
    Société Belge des Engrais et Produits Chimiques de la Meuse, 1928 (1931)

Source: E. Dehnel, *Verflechtungen in der Stickstoff-Industrie und ihre Gründe* (Heidelberg, 1931), pp. 48–53; H. Grossmann and P. Weicksel, *Die Stickstoffindustrie in der Welt* (Berlin, 1930), pp. 92–94; *Le Recueil Financier* (1935).
*The year production started is in parentheses.
[a] The Union Chimique Belge owned another nitrogen plant near Ostend.
[b] The Ougrée group founded in 1928 the Société Belge d'Électrochimie for the production of calcium cyanamide.
[c] Ready in 1931–32. Production was delayed till July 1935 due to cartel agreements.
[d] Was never completed.

motives behind this were, on the one hand, a lack of sufficient chemical experience, and on the other hand, a lack of capital on the part of the coke industry. The participation of foreign chemical giants, such as the French L'Air Liquide, Kuhlmann, and the Italian Montecatini, was primarily due to the need for know-how. Montecatini owned the Fauser patent, L'Air Liquide owned the Claude patent, and Kuhlmann owned the patents of the American NEC system for France and Belgium.[15]

The Netherlands was, relatively speaking, the biggest consumer of nitrogen in Europe. Before the war, this country had at its disposal an extensive phosphoric acid industry that could easily satisfy domestic demand. For its nitrogen supply, the country depended on the extraction of ammonia from gas works and coke factories till the end of the twenties. Production had increased from 9,000 tons in 1913 to 47,000 tons in 1927. For 75% of its demand, the Netherlands was dependent on imports from abroad.[16]

Shortly after the First World War, the first nitrogen factory, the N.V. Stikstofbindingsindustrie Nederland (Nitrogen Compounding Industry of Netherlands), was founded with subsidies from the state. It focused on the production of ammonium sulphate as a by-product, urea, and natrium cyanamide.[17] The initiatives to build synthetic nitrogen plants were taken roughly simultaneously at the end of the twenties. The Koninklijke Nederlandse Hoogovens en Staalfabrieken (Royal Dutch Blast-Furnaces and Steel Factories) and the Royal Dutch Petroleum Co. established the N.V. Mij. tot Exploitatie van Kookovengas (MEKOG, Company for the Exploitation of Furnace Gas). This factory functioned according to the Mont-Cénis process and had a production capacity of 16,000 tons N.

With the assistance of Montecatini-Coppée, the Dutch State Coalmines built a factory that functioned according to the Fauser process and that could produce up to 20,000 tons N. Although the production capacity of these two plants was more than sufficient to supply the domestic market, a third initiative was undertaken by the same Belgian-Italian group. It started its own factory, the Cie. Néerlandaise de l'Azote (CNA), close to the Belgian-Dutch border at Sluiskil. Its supply of raw materials was provided by a French company, the Association Coopérative Zélandaise de Carbonisation, which delivered coke-oven gas for a capacity of 30,000 to 40,000 tons N. The CNA did not belong to the Dutch group of the cartel; it enjoyed special regulations. In the subsequent cartel agreements, it was granted a separate export quota that was around 2%. The plant, which had the greatest production capacity for ammonium sulfate, produced almost exclusively for export. The three nitrogen plants on Dutch territory started their activities respectively in March, June, and December 1930.[18]

Domestic consumption absorbed roughly the same quantity in both countries during the thirties: about 60,000 tons N. Production capacity was around 190,000 tons N in Belgium (1935 and 1938) and 135,000 tons N in the Netherlands (1935). As young producers, both countries started with the production of ammonium sulfate, which was technically much easier to fabricate. In this way, they could in the beginning avoid additional investments necessary for diversification in the production process.[19] This also explains why they had to reduce their output and why they were dependent on imports of nitrates in the early thirties.

IV. The Cartel and the Belgian and Dutch Nitrogen Industries

The Belgian fertilizer industry was already organized to some extent before the First World War. Since 1895 there was in Brussels the Comptoir Belge des Engrais Chimiques, which represented approximately 60% of the producers and which concentrated on sales.[20] After the war the

Comptoir Belge des Engrais Azotés was founded. This organization was responsible for the sale of nitrogen and nitrogen compounds. Not all producers were members from the start. The Kuhlmann group and the Ougrée-L'Air Liquide group joined the organization in 1930, and by the end of the thirties a small part of the domestic sales were still made outside the Comptoir.[21] In 1932 the Fédération Belge des Producteurs de l'Azote came into being, which is regarded by some as a domestic cartel and which looked after all interests of the producers, with the exception of sales.[22] Since the mid-twenties, an agreement supposedly existed between the Comptoir Français de l'Azote and the Belgian Comptoir. This agreement covered both countries' sales on foreign markets and the German nitrogen supplies related to its reparations payments. After the conference in Biarritz in 1926, the literature mentions an agreement of the Deutsche Stickstoffsyndikat with the French and the Belgian sales offices, on the one hand, and with a Dutch sales organization, on the other hand. Both concerned German imports.[23] In fact, those countries were then still much dependent on the German nitrogen industry. In early 1930 the Belgian producers had made agreements with the members of the DEN group with the purpose of escaping German dumping prices.[24]

Meanwhile, the chemical industry was in rather bad shape. Fusion and concentration movements came to an end. After the overcapitalization in the previous years, the yields dropped from 30.46% in 1927 to 2.11% in 1932 and to 1.99% in 1933. There was a clear overcapacity for the production of ammonium sulfate. It evolved from 131,000 tons in 1929 to 256,000 tons in 1930 and to 237,000 tons in 1931, and it would soon have exceeded the capacity of Great Britain. Consumption, on the other hand, amounted to 178,000, 212,000, and 131,000 tons respectively.[25] The "grève des engrais" made the situation even more critical. The older nitrogen companies were able to cope with the problems more easily, but the situation was worse for those factories that had been planned in the boom days of the late twenties and were still under development.[26] The disintegration of the CIA in July 1931 added to the chaos. Very soon the Belgian manufacturers closed a new deal with the DEN group. It extended over one year. The agreement was almost immediately copied by the German and the Belgian governments on August 17, 1931. Belgium had imposed a license duty on the import of nitrogen and that was contrary to the German-Belgian Commercial Treaty of 1925, which stipulated that this product could be imported freely. After all, this treaty dated from a period when the supply of nitrogen was of vital importance to Belgium.

As far as the scarce data can be trusted, the Belgian production capacity of synthetic nitrogen was not extended any further after the first years of the thirties. It fluctuated around 190,000 tons N. Although, according to Stocking and Watkins, "the cartel did not publicly acknowledge curtailment of capacity as an objective," it tried to stop expansion of capacity in Belgium. One factory that had been planned but was never completed enjoyed considerable amounts of compensation during the thirties. In 1938 it was paid 75 million Belgian francs in quarterly payments of 3.7 million francs over a period of five years for its liquidation, with the understanding that, if a third party bought the plant, buildings, or equipment, the property would not be used to produce synthetic ammonia for eight years.[27] Measures were taken to reduce the output. The Belgian group was entitled to produce 73,500 tons N during the campaign of 1930–31, but it would receive compensations if it produced less. And it did produce less. In the German-Belgian agreement signed in August 1931, reduction seems to be enforced. As a compensation, the DEN group was to indemnify the Belgian producers with a fixed amount and with an amount proportional to German nitrogen imports (the import of ammonium sulfate was forbidden) into the Belgian market. Apparently all Belgian nitrogen plants were more or less affected by restrictions. It was the Fédération, the inland cartel, that decided on the repartition of production among the producers.

As a consequence of cartel membership, the different factories concentrated on diversifying their production. After all, it had already become clear in 1930 that the overproduction involved mainly ammonium sulphate. Increasingly, the manufacturers tried to become independent of imports. As a result, only sodanitrates from Chile, a little urea, and 11,000 tons of calcium cyanamide (from Yugoslavia and Norway) had to be imported by the end of the thirties.[28]

As mentioned above, the Netherlands started its production of synthetic nitrogen later, but it caught up with the Belgian production level very fast. The output of the very young Dutch nitrogen industry was in 1930–31 fixed at 28,400 tons N or 45,900 tons N, including CNA. The restriction of the output was less severe, although from the beginning CNA had immediately been hit by a reduction of its output by two-thirds. Later agreements continued to restrict it in return to a yearly amount of 4.5 million RM.[29]

The State Coalmines and MEKOG quickly specialized in the production of other nitrogenous products. No doubt, the sharp decline in prices encouraged the conversion to nitrates. In this way, domestic consumption, which had increased annually throughout the decade, shifted: the share of ammonium sulfate dropped from 70.4% in 1931–32 to 19.3% in 1937–38.[30] The rapid increase of the use of calcium ammonium nitrate was remarkable: from 0.7% in 1929–30 to 50.5% in 1937–38. This was unlike the situation in Belgium, where the use of ammonium sulfate had been propagated unilaterally. In terms of produced quantities, ammonium sulfate remained in the Netherlands the most important product. It was more or less the only nitrogenous export product and amounted to 98.8% and 97% of total nitrogen exports in 1937 and 1938, respectively.

In 1930, the year in which the new factories started their production, 64% was still supplied by the German chemical industry. When Dutch production met the domestic demand for ammonium sulfate, the import of nitrogenous products by the DEN group (exclusively Germany and Norway) continued. Because of the low Dutch prices, the Netherlands became a major exporter of German nitrogen to the United States, after the latter had decreed the antidumping law.[31] Even after the introduction of quota restrictions by the Dutch government in January 1934, German imports persisted. According to the "Zusatz-Verträge" (additional agreements), the German nitrogen producers could export to the Netherlands first one-half, and later one-third, of Dutch domestic consumption. They had to share this quota with CNA.

Theoretically the domestic markets were more or less protected by the cartel agreements, although the protectionist measures taken by the government seem to have been more effective. This is clearly shown by the import figures of ammonium sulfate in the Belgium-Luxembourg Economic Union (BLEU) and the Netherlands (Table 2). In the latter, lower quotas were imposed by the government than those allowed by the cartel. This happened when, in late 1933, rumors were spread about protectionist measures to be taken. As a result, the Dutch market was flooded with foreign, mainly German, nitrogen. To get rid of the enormous stock—the cartel had specified that only 50,000 tons of foreign goods could be stored—a gentleman's agreement was made with the cartel partners to strongly limit the imports during one year. Only 50% instead of 100% of the quota of the previous year was allowed to enter the country. The measure remained valid. It had been a good excuse for the Dutch to lower imports. At the same time they hoped to hold a stonger position at the renewal of the cartel in the summer of 1935.[32]

Chilean imports had decreased remarkably: for the BLEU they went down during the thirties by 87% and for the Netherlands by 58%. In 1932 Chile set up exchange controls that were used to force the purchase of Chilean nitrate. From 1934 on the cartel specified that Chile could make separate agreements with all the European cartel members. Especially, the Dutch producers tried to limit the Chilean imports. At the clearing negotiations they insisted on basing imports upon the figures of the previous campaign, whereas the Chileans tried to base their imports upon the

TABLE 2 Import and Export of Ammonium Sulfate (BLEU and the
Netherlands) (in metric tons)

	BLEU		The Netherlands	
	Import	Export	Import	Export
1923	13,958	22,327	21,354	27,058
1924	22,046	8,409	44,963	21,784
1925	24,006	9,862	69,097	28,180
1926	38,389	5,786	78,721	25,418
1927	46,053	6,468	108,200	35,436
1928	50,581	16,588	139,105	31,318
1929	38,890	57,824	126,472	32,896
1930	36,630	80,398	30,720	91,792
1931	70,656	175,770	172,614	254,685
1932	10,347	161,582	139,905	377,022
1933	266	130,618	144,449	298,628
1934	131	120,378	66,941	249,264
1935	115	101,776	53,748	267,321
1936	768	143,525	3,051	182,532
1937	65	190,588	331	247,648
1938	56	146,978	402	223,392
1939	–	130,791	25,699	136,959

Source: BLEU, "Tableau mensuel du commerce avec les pays étrangers," 1923–
31; "Bulletin mensuel du commerce avec les pays étrangers," 1932–39;
CBS, "Jaarstatistiek van den in-, uit- en doorvoer," 1923–39.

figures of the twenties.[33] In the course of time the Dutch even tried to
substitute homemade calcium nitrate for natural nitrates. The Belgian
attitude towards Chilean imports was more obliging. According to Belgian sources, the Chilean share in the Belgian market was always higher
than had been settled between the two parties before. Nevertheless, the
Belgian producers turned a blind eye to this situation, hoping to create
goodwill at the cartel talks in mid-1938.

The Belgian and Dutch export quotas fluctuated around 10% and 8%,
respectively, of the total cartel export quantities in the mid-thirties. The
division among the cartel members was fixed before mid-June each year
by the DEN group in consultation with the partners. Only Sluiskil had no
right to compete for an export quota.

If we examine the destination of Dutch and Belgian ammonium sulphate, it strikes us that in the early thirties the exports were more directed
to the home market of the other cartel members. Further regular outlets
for both countries were Spain and Portugal. Exports to the United States

were important to the Dutch producers, who also re-exported German
nitrogen. Dutch exports to Central America became clearly visible from
1932 on. The growing consumption of synthetic fertilizers in Asia was
another characteristic. First, there were the Dutch East Indies, where
the Dutch producers held the leading position. Their import quantity
rose from 4,000 tons in 1926 to 38,000 tons in 1931, and to 50,000 tons
in 1939, which meant 36% of the total Dutch exports of ammonium sulfate. For Belgium, countries such as Egypt, British India, and China
were regular buyers. Exports to Japan became considerable from 1934
on for the Netherlands and two years later for the BLEU.

From 1936 on, export sales opportunities for countries like the Netherlands and Belgium appeared to diminish. Due to the events in Spain and
China, parts of the export market were lost. Moreover, the free nitrogen
market started to collapse. Smaller cartel members suffered from this
situation. In these circumstances Sluiskil attempted to conquer a share of
the domestic market commensurate with its capacity. It came to a national deal: only when the CIA agreement expired would the home market be
newly divided. The competition on the domestic market might have led
eventually to a serious price war, since CNA (Sluiskil) could produce at
lower cost. Its advantageous geographical location and its technical
equipment contributed to this.[34]

The cartel agreement of July 1st, 1938, provided a number of "safety
valves" to secure the exports of the smaller groups. It was stipulated that
the Dutch group (with a share of 5,000 to 20,000 tons N) was granted the
opportunity to export calcium nitrate instead of ammonium sulfate.
Possibly part of German exports to the Netherlands would be taken
over by the Dutch State Coalmines and MEKOG. This, however, would
weaken the Dutch clearing position. Another solution to the problem
would be that the DEN group would take over the dead stock and would
pay a "fair price" (half of the proceeds).[35] But it did not come to any of
that. When the cartel disintegrated because of the start of the war in August 1939, it appeared that the demand in the major export markets was
met mainly by the Dutch, Belgian, and Norwegian nitrogen industries.
For that purpose, the producers of those countries founded a limited cartel. They tried to increase production and to make the most of their capacity, but an insufficient supply of raw materials rendered this impossible.[36]

V. Domestic Responses to the Cartel

Although the domestic markets were left undisturbed by the CIA, they
were nevertheless subject to its influence. At first sight, the agreements
between the Comptoir Belge des Produits Azotés and the DEN group in

the early thirties had little effect on domestic prices of ammonium sulfate. Belgian producers could keep up their prices in agreement with the Germans.

The realization of the CIA in August 1930 occasioned a slight drop and, from early 1931 on, a slight rise in prices. When the first probationary year expired and the negotiations to establish a new international agreement failed, the prices suddenly fell to 52% in July 1931. The breakdown of the international negotiations in Paris compelled the Belgian government into a protectionist reaction against the abnormally high imports at extremely low prices. It imposed a license system "in order to guarantee the country's vital commodities." By a royal decree of August 20, 1931, the import of about five nitrogenous fertilizers was subjected to control.[37] In order to cope with the protest from domestic consumers, the government had long negotiations with the producers of nitrogen about price reductions. In the end, a minimum reduction of 30% was granted on the condition that the prices in 1931–32 would never be lower than two-thirds of the prices in 1930–31. After the agreement with the government, the Chilean producers were also willing to grant a reduction of 20%.[38]

The drop in domestic prices by nearly a half, following the breakup of the CIA, had stirred up bad feelings among the farmers. The critics claimed that the producers had enriched themselves all these past years at the expense of the farmers, who had already had plenty of difficulties to deal with because of the crisis. They charged that it was their group who paid the compensation for the partial or total shutdown of the factories. Animosity was stirred up even more when it was announced that the "Boerenbond," the most powerful corporation of farmers in the country, had important participations in at least three nitrogen companies. Being an important shareholder, the union was accused of having enriched itself by charging the farmer-members high prices.[39] Moreover, the Minister of Agriculture at that time was known to be a political mandatary of the union. Consequently, interpellations in parliament were frequent and vehement.

All these facts incited the press, and especially the farmers' press, to keep the movements of the cartel under close observation for years. After the devaluation of the Belgian currency in the spring of 1935 and after the consultation with the government, the producers waited for five months before adjusting their prices, but then, in 1936, prices went up. The growing criticism of the cartelization movement in general gave the nitrogen industry a hard time in 1937–38. In concrete terms, it boiled down to calling agriculture the victim of a monopoly. Indignation rose so high that the Fédération Belge des Producteurs de l'Azote thought fit to publish some kind of white paper, replete with data. It was hoped that this would appease public opinion and at the same time protect its members.[40] The violent nature of the attacks was related to the plight of agriculture, which could not profit to the same extent as industry from the revival of the economy after the devaluation. Sensitivity among farmers had grown so explosive that the government had to take further action.

The question of nitrogen was investigated by a newly founded Commission for the Reorientation of Agriculture (CORA). The results of that study were not published. This report would have been incomplete anyway, since the producers of nitrogen refused access to their books. The authorities did not stop at that: they appointed a special commissioner in consultation with representatives of farmers' unions and the nitrogen industry. This commissioner was to start a thorough investigation of the factories themselves.[41]

Dutch synthetic ammonium sulfate was cheap from the start of national production in order to counter the low prices that German dumping had created. This German penetration of the nonprotected domestic market was also fought through internal agreements between producers and farmers' associations; the latter boycotted German products as much as possible and, in exchange, producers guaranteed the farmers lower prices than in neighboring countries.[42] The Netherlands was among the few West European countries that did not take any protectionist measures immediately after the failure of the cartel negotiatons in July 1931. The reason for this was primarily the inability of the national industry to cover the entire domestic market rather than a so-called free-trade-oriented attitude. But already one year later Dutch producers did appeal to the government to interfere. Only as late as January 1, 1934, did the government impose quota systems on nitrogenous fertilizers, at a moment when the CIA was functioning again.[43] One of the official reasons for this was the fear of exaggerated imports by outsiders such as Japan, the United States, and especially Hungary, the latter being a major producer of calcium ammonium nitrate.

Moreover, the government expected the quota systems to support the Dutch producers and their negotiating power at the renewal of the cartel. It directly linked a price control system and a close supervision of the companies' accounts to its support.[44] Since Dutch prices, especially for ammonium sulfate, were extremely low—the producers would have been willing to sell below official prices—neither the rationing system nor the cartel evoked any resistance by farmers' organizations.[45] Neither did these have any objections to the slight price increases in the second half of the thirties. In comparison to the Belgian and the Danish prices, ammonium sulphate was especially cheap. Other fertilizers temporarily had somewhat higher prices.

However, protest did arise after 1935, and it originated in the distribution sector. When new sales conditions were announced that year—a subject in which the German Stickstoffsyndikat was involved as well—the matter was brought before parliament. The reason for this was the fact that, instead of three distributors, the Centraal Stikstof Verkoopbureau (CSV, Central Nitrogen Sales Office) at Heerlen gained the monopoly for the distribution. In this way, both domestic and import trade were centralized by the largest Dutch producer.[46] Especially the system of confidential orders and the rebate scales by CSV seemed to be arbitrary and discriminatory and hence caused dissatisfaction, primarily among buyers with less financial means. In order to restrict the power of the sales office, the government started to advocate the appointment of a contact commissioner with supervising authority.[47]

Thus the domestic responses to the cartel strenghtened in both countries the governments' grip on the nitrogen industry.

NOTES

1. G. Van Roon, *Kleine landen in crisistijd. Van Oslostaten tot Benelux, 1930–1940* (Amsterdam-Brussels, 1985), pp. 64–65; H. Van der Wee and K. Tavernier, *De Nationale Bank van België en het monetaire gebeuren tussen de twee wereldoorlogen* (Brussels, 1975), p. 288.

2. P.E. de Hen, *Actieve en re-actieve industriepolitiek in Nederland. De overheid en de ontwikkelinq van de Nederlandse industrie in de jaren dertig en tussen 1945 en 1950* (Amsterdam, 1980), pp. 32, 301.

3. G. Vantemsche, "De Belgische overheid en de kartels tijdens het Interbellum," *Belgisch Tijdschrift voor Filologie en Geschiedenis* No. 3 (1983): 851–94; H.H. Vleesenbeek, "Overheid, parlement en economische mededinging. Analyse van de parlementaire diskussie n.a.v. de wet tot het algemeen verbindend en onverbindend verklaren van de ondernemingovereenskomsten, 1934/35," in J. van Herwaarden (ed.), *Lof der Historie. Opstellen over geschiedenis en maatschappij* (Rotterdam, 1973), p. 381.

4. *Bulletin d'Information et de Documentation de la Banque Nationale de Belgique* (10.9.1931): 180.

5. E. Dehnel, *Verflechtungen in der Stickstoff-Industrie und ihre Gründe* (Heidelberg, 1931), p. 85.

6. P. Kypriotis, *Les cartels internationaux* (Paris, 1936), pp. 152–53; Dehnel, op. cit., pp. 86–89.

7. AMFAB (Archives of the Ministry of Foreign Affairs, Brussels), 2607bis, Enquête sur la situation actuelle des Ententes Internationales à participation belge AMFAB, Presse 412, II, Production et commerce. La Convention

Internationale de l'Azote; *Les Cartels Internationaux* (Recueils et Monographies, no. 32) (Paris, 1954), pp. 194–95; E. Hexner, *International Cartels* (Chapel Hill, N.C., 1946), p. 327.

8. AMFAB, 2607bis, Syndicat International de la Cyanamide de chaux.

9. H. Grossmann and P. Weicksel, *Die Stickstoffindustrie in der Welt* (Berlin, 1930), pp. 92–94.

10. AMFAB, Presse 412, II, La Convention Internationale de l'Azote, pp. 7–8.

11. AMFAB, Presse 412, II, Agence économique et financière, 2.7.1931; Hexner, op. cit., p. 326(6).

12. Ibid., p. 327.

13. Ibid., pp. 327–28.

14. R.L., Hogg, *Structural Rigidities and Policy Inertia in Inter-War Belgium* (Verhandelingen van de Koninklijke Academie voor Wetenschappen, Letteren en Schone Kunsten van België, Klasse der Letteren, 48, 1986, no. 118), p. 100.

15. Dehnel, op. cit., pp. 48–53; Grossmann and Weicksel, op. cit., pp. 92–94.

16. Ibid., p. 156.

17. H. Koopman, *Vijftig jaar scheikundige nijverheid in Nederland* (Delft, 1967), p. 39.

18. D.H. Wester, *Synthetische petroleum, het wereld-stikstofprobleem, kunstzijde* (Leiden, 1931), pp. 32–34; P. Puype, G. Beauchez, and M. Jongsma, *Van kiem tot korrel. Nederlandse Stikstof Mij. N.V., 1929–1979* (n.p., 1979), pp. 76–77; *Het Stikstof-bindingsbedrijf van de Staatsmijnen in Limburg* (n.p., n.d.), p. 6.

19. R. Lachmann-Mosse, *Die Stickstoffindustrie und ihre internationale Kartellierung* (Zurich, 1940), p. 87.

20. G. De Leener, *Les Syndicats Industriels en Belgique* (Brussels, 1903), p. 131.

21. Grossmann and Weicksel, op. cit., p. 96; Archives Boerenbond, 22.5.3., Het Stikstofvraagstuk, p. 4.

22. *Bulletin d'Information et de Documentation de la Banque Nationale de Belgique* (24.10.1931): 275.

23. Dehnel, op. cit., p. 85.

24. AMFAB, Presse 412, I, Berliner Börsen Courier, 21.1.1930.

25. *Bulletin d'Information et de Documentation de la Banque Nationale de Belgique* (25.8.1932): 121.

26. Ibid., p. 125.

27. G.W. Stocking and M.W. Watkins, *Cartels in Action: Case Studies in International Business Diplomacy* (New York, 1947), p. 161.

28. Archives Boerenbond, 22.5.3., Het Stikstofvraagstuk, p. 4.

29. Ibid., p. 160.

30. P.S. Pels, *Een economisch en statistisch onderzoek naar de chemische industrie in Nederland* (Haarlem, 1943), p. 68.

31. ARA-II, Dir. H & N 1905–1943, 7336, no. 1141.

32. Ibid., 7344, nos. 40, 288, and 325.

33. *Documenten betreffende de Buitenlandse Politiek van Nederland. 1919–1945. III 1.3.1933–26.6.1934* (RGP, Grote serie 212) (The Hague, 1990), p. 332.

34. Ibid., 7335, no. 682 and 7336, no. 1039.

35. Ibid., 7351, no. 4981a.

36. *Le Recueil Financier* (1940) II: 120.

37. *Moniteur Belge* (20.8.1931): 4762.

38. *Annales Parlementaires*, Chambre des Représentants, 8.12.1931, p. 224.

39. L. Van Molle, *Ieder voor Allen. De Belgische Boerenbond 1890–1990* (Louvain, 1990), p. 243.

40. Belgische Federatie der voortbrengers van stikstof, *De Stikstofnijverheid en de prijzen der stikstofmesten* (Brussels, 1937).

41. Archives Boerenbond, 22.5.3., Het Stikstofvraagstuk, p. 5.

42. Puype, Beauchez, and Jongsma, op. cit., p. 109.

43. A. Van Schaick, *Crisis en protectie onder Colijn. Over economische doelmatigheid en maatschappelijke aanvaardbaarheid van de Nederlandse handelspolitiek in de jaren dertig* (Amsterdam, 1986), pp. 378–79.

44. ARA-II, Dir. H & N 1905–1943, 7339, no. 2169.

45. Ibid., 7334, no. 541.

46. Ibid., 7337, no. 1326; 7339, no. 2067 and 7340, no. 2426.

47. Ibid., 7543, no. 3395a.

Comment

Hideaki Miyajima

Professor Devos's paper examines the relation between the nitrogen industry of Belgium and the Netherlands and the international nitrogen cartel, CIA. First of all, the paper clarifies the differences in economic structures of the two countries, and then it investigates the following four points: (1) the growth of the nitrogen industry in the interwar period, (2) the development of the international cartel, (3) the domestic situation in the two countries under the framework of CIA, and (4) the response of government and farmers to the nitrogen cartel.

Since information about Belgium and the Netherlands in the interwar period is very limited for the Japanese researcher, this paper certainly gives interesting insights into this period. It also sheds light on similar Japanese cases, because Belgium and the Netherlands have the same characteristics as Japan in that they are peripheral countries in the international cartel and their interests are very different from those of the core countries, in this case, the DEN group.

First, I would like to look at the international cartel from the standpoint of the core countries. This may not be the main issue of this paper, but an important aspect nonetheless. There are three points here. The first is the main strategy that the DEN group has adopted towards Belgium and the Netherlands. The second is the measures that the DEN group has taken to actualize the strategy. The third is whether the strategy of the DEN group succeeded or not in the 1930s.

I think the second point needs to be explained in detail. The DEN group paid compensation to Belgium and the Netherlands in return for the restriction of production and exports. This is quite interesting because this was not the case with Japan. As far as I know, Japanese firms have never accepted compensation in order to keep a cooperative relationship with the international cartel. Also, Belgium and the Netherlands were developing nations in the nitrogen industry, so they should maintain the operation because of their large investments. From this point of view, I would like to know the principle behind the large compensation the DEN group has paid and the degree of its cost and advantage.

Next, let us look at the international cartel from the standpoint of Belgium and the Netherlands. I can understand why nitrogen firms in Belgium joined the international cartel—they wanted to secure their domestic market and to stabilize domestic prices. But I cannot understand the Netherlands' case. Under the CIA agreement the domestic market in the Netherlands was still not completely secured by the Dutch firms, although the Netherlands market was relatively larger than the Belgium one. Why were the Dutch firms unable to secure the domestic market under the CIA agreement? What advantage did they receive when they joined the CIA?

This paper has concentrated much on the trade policy and cartel policy of both governments. It is clear that these policies were very effective in restricting imports, since Table 2 shows that nitrogen imports dropped sharply a year after the government's intervention. Unfortunately, however, there was no clear description of the relation between the government's policy and the formation of the international cartel, including the Belgian-Dutch negotiations with the DEN group. I feel that the following points should be considered: What influence did the import license system in Belgium in 1931 have on the negotiations with the DEN group? What influence did the quota system in 1934 in the Netherlands have on the renewal of the CIA agreement?

In Japan during the interwar period, the government's policy helped to change the strategy of international oligopolistic firms towards Japan. In other words, when we examine the international cartel from the standpoint of the peripheral countries, we should not analyze it as a two-person game between core and peripheral parties, but as a three-person game, adding the government as another main player.

As in the case of the Netherlands and Belgium, Japan was a latecomer in the nitrogen industry. In the period of the Great Depression, Japan's cooperation with the DEN group was a problem of a budding industry. However, as Ōshio's paper has shown, the relationship between our country's nitrogen industry and the DEN group was quite different from the case of the two countries under consideration in that (1) no agreement was formed during 1930–31, when the price fell at the bottom; and (2) the agreement formed in 1934 had no restrictions on domestic productive capacity and output. I would like to point out some reasons why these differences emerged.

First of all, there were three external factors: (1) In Japan the domestic market was relatively large, because Japan had about seven to eight times the population of the Netherlands and Belgium, and the agricultural population was 50% out of the working population. (2) The interests of the agricultural population influenced the policies of the Diet. (3) Japan had abolished the gold standard at the end of 1931, one of the first nations to do so. Factor 1 was emphasized by the high price elasticity of the nitrogen fertilizer demand. In spite of the increase of newly entering firms in Japan, this factor had worked to avoid excess capacity in the domestic market. And because of this factor, exports did not become a serious problem, as they did for companies in the Netherlands and Belgium. Factor 2 blocked international agreements that would restrict productive capacity and raise domestic prices. Factor 3 reduced the pressure of competitors after 1932 and made it impossible for the DEN group to expand its exports to Japan. As a result, the DEN group lost its chief negotiating weapon and completely changed its strategy to one of maintaining its markets in East Asia rather than expanding its sales in the Japanese market.

Second, there were two internal factors: (1) the established companies and the latecomers that had entered the field at the time of the world economic crisis (of 1929) were all aggressive in management; and (2) the market was thoroughly organized by the general trading companies and manufacturers. Factor 2 enabled the industry to protect its domestic market from imported goods during the Depression. After the agreement with the DEN group, this factor was the reason that imported goods could be treated as a marginal supplier of the domestic market. And factor 1 shows the fact that all the companies adopted the following strategy: instead of delaying the investment project or stabilizing prices by controlling production, the firms tried to reduce costs through realizing economies of scale by enlarging production capacity when the price was lowered. This was realized by the entrepreneurial spirit of managers and the great funds of zaibatsu. The aggressive management policy practiced by Japanese firms eventually avoided any agreement with the DEN group that had a restriction of production capability. Even in 1934 when the agreement was finally made, production capability and output were not included.

Response

Greta Devos

It is obvious that Belgian and still more Dutch producers of synthetic nitrogen entered the world market rather late. They built or expanded

their plants at a moment when the overcapacity in the world was generally known and even at a stage when the most important producers had
already made agreements in the hope of controlling the situation. The
race against time was especially evident with the Dutch industry, which
built its plants very rapidly in the hope of obtaining an advantageous
share and negotiating position at the international nitrogen talks in the
summer of 1930. The arrival of the two new producers on the world market dealt a serious blow to the DEN group and more specifically to the
German producers. They not only lost two important markets, but worse,
it looked like the two new producing countries could develop into danger-
ous competitors in foreign markets. The loss of the Belgian and Dutch
market was at first not too bad, because the more advanced German industry could supply them with more sophisticated nitrogenous products.
Much worse was the threatening competition, especially when the two
countries claimed higher export quotas. The DEN group was willing to
pay compensation to limit production capacity and output, especially export. This policy seemed to be successful, as the capacity was apparently
not expanded during the late thirties.

The reasons both countries were anxious to join the cartel were to secure their share of the market and to protect the domestic market. As the
Deutsche Stickstoffsyndikat was responsible for sales, they could also
profit from its market experience. And one could wonder if their extremely
low prices, especially after 1931, due to the deflationary policy of the
government, were not compensated for by more remunerable prices on
foreign markets.

It is striking that both countries, which at first sight had to contend
with similar difficulties, were obviously treated in a different way by the
cartel. But one has to consider that the Belgian nitrogen industry had
already started its production in 1925 and could gradually expand it during the boom years of the late twenties. The sector was well organized and
was backed by important financial-industrial groups, which had diversified their interests. It preferred to accept compensation in exchange for a
reduction of output. Although it obtained a larger export quota, the effective export figures of ammonium sulfate, the main export product, were
lower than the Dutch ones. As far as the scarce data allow any conclusion,
the Belgian strategy seems to have been less energetic. The strategy of the
very young Dutch nitrogen sector, which in plain crisis initially lacked any
governmental help—except for the subsidies of the State Coalmines—had
to be more aggressive. The protectionist measures of the government
came three years later than in other producing countries. But once issued,
they were extremely useful to strengthen the position of the Dutch nitrogen sector within the cartel.

Finally, it does not suffice to study the national situation of a sector and its position in an international cartel. Data do indicate that further attention should be paid—especially concerning the Belgian nitrogen industry and the CNA—to the international links of the giant chemical multinationals, with their wide range of products and their mutual deals.

National Goals, Industry Structure, and Corporate Strategies: Chemical Cartels between the Wars

John Kenly Smith, Jr.

The theme of this conference is "the rationalization of production and formation of organized markets that were brought about by international competition and cooperation of rival companies in the world." My paper is on the chemical industry, which both on the national and international levels tried to rationalize production and organize markets. There is an immense documentary record collected by the Antitrust Division of the Department of Justice in the late 1930s and early 1940s which shows the enormous amount of time and energy that the leaders of the world chemical industry put into negotiating about prices, markets, and patents.[1] At the time these documents were cited as proof that business had sought to avoid competition and maintain high levels of profit. According to neoclassical economic theory, any subversion of the balancing of supply and demand through markets led to economic inefficiencies in the short run and economic ruin in the long run.[2] Since historians are not bound to neoclassical economic theory, we can analyze a situation from other perspectives, the historical, the diplomatic, and the structural.

From the historical point of view, it can be argued that the interwar cartels were the product of unique historical circumstances. World War I had disrupted the international networks of commerce, leaving many countries desperate for chemical products such as Chilean nitrates or German dyes and pharmaceuticals. The Germans had shown the strategic importance of having a dynamic chemical industry by synthesizing ammonia to replace Chilean nitrates for use in munitions and fertilizer, and by using its dyestuffs plants to produce new high explosives, such as TNT and poison gases. These wartime developments led to the recognition that a strong domestic chemical industry was important for national defense. With the removal of German organic chemicals from international commerce during the war, businessmen and governments invested in new facilities to produce what previously had been imported. After the war, worldwide capacity in dyestuffs particularly had risen far above demand, which was weak because of the economic devastation caused by the war. Soon other countries would be building enormous ammonia synthesis plants to insure national self-sufficiency in this strategic material. Because of the enormous economies of scale in ammonia plants and because of optimistic forecasts of peacetime use in fertilizer, world production of ammonia skyrocketed in the late 1920s. In 1929 the Great Depression began, which reduced levels of industrial activity dramatically and depressed farm prices and income to very low levels. The chemical industry was once again saddled with overcapacity in dyestuffs, ammonia, and other chemicals. The cartel arrangements of this era can be seen as attempts to divide remaining markets along national lines, since exiting these strategic fields was economically and politically undesirable.[3]

This historical argument leads to the conclusion that cartel arrangements were responses to extraordinary circumstances, such as war and depression, but during "normal" periods, regulation by markets would replace regulation by agreement. Historically, however, there are some problems with this argument. In particular one sees a continuity of cartel arrangements from the late 19th century up to World War II. The desire to reach agreements may have intensified during depressions, but the discussions never seem to have stopped except during hostilities. Overall, the historical explanation is inadequate to explain the cartels in the chemical industry.

A second way to understand cartels is in terms of international diplomacy; that is, by using the same methods of analysis that political and military historians use. From this point of view each nation and its chemical companies attempted to maximize their economic potential through negotiation. The outcome of these negotiations between companies was determined by assessments of each other's strengths and weaknesses. If an agreement could not be reached, then the commercial equivalent of war was waged by promoting higher tariffs at home or invading the other country's exclusive territories or home turf. This type of analysis sheds considerable light on the chemical industry between the wars.

I. The Structure of the International Chemical Industry

The international chemical industry between the wars was in a transition period that represented the culmination of older trends and the early development of new ones. The older "chemical industry" had consisted of a disparate set of industries that did some chemical operations as part of their manufacturing processes. These chemical operations included purely physical processes, such as filtration, crystallization, and distillation. Thus the chemical industry included sugar refining, paint manufacture, heavy chemicals, electrochemicals, explosives, industrial gases, dyestuffs, pharmaceuticals, insecticides, soap, and myriad cellulose products. In the 20th century, however, this broad collection of industries began a process of technological convergence that would be completed in the decade after the end of World War II.[4] The chemical industry had traditionally supplied chemicals to other industries for use in their operations. Reagents such as sulfuric acid or alkalis were used in numerous industrial processes. In this period the demand for chemicals and the types of chemicals produced was determined primarily by the consumers, not the chemical producers. Two pronounced trends changed this relationship in the 20th century. First, chemical companies began to do research on their customers' processes, especially in fields such as leather, rubber, and textiles. Out of this work came new chemical products that were sold to the processors. In this way the downstream processors became dependent on chemical companies for improving their processes. The other strategy was to replace naturally derived raw materials used in processing industries with chemically manufactured ones. The first dramatic example of this was the synthesis of alizarin and indigo that replaced the natural red and blue dyes in the late 19th century. With the beginnings of polymer processing, first with cellulose derivatives such as celluloid and rayon, chemical manufacturers saw the potential to synthesize materials, not just chemical reagents. The first man-made polymer, Bakelite, made from phenol and formaldehyde, suggested that all kinds of chemicals could be combined to make new materials.[5] Bakelite was first sold in the 1910s, and by 1939 plastics was a bigger seller than synthetic dyes, sales of which were $70 million.[6] Plastics sales in the United States had grown rapidly during the Depression, but more important for the future were the new discoveries made during that decade.

The development of polymer science in the 1920s and early 1930s gave chemists the tools that they needed to investigate the polymerization of organic compounds. Not surprisingly, many new polymers were discovered. This list included polyethylene, several types of synthetic rubber, acrylic plastics, polystyrene, Teflon, and nylon. In most cases, however, these research breakthroughs did not become immediate commercial successes because large-scale polymerization technology had not been developed, raw materials were expensive if available at all, and markets for the new materials appeared to be small.[7]

In the prewar period raw materials for polymeric plastics were derived from coal tar, which also had been the basis for synthetic dyes. Although supplies of coal tar products were adequate in the interwar period, there was increasing interest in making chemicals out of petroleum and natural gas. One of the pioneers in this area was Union Carbide, which initiated a radical diverisification attempt in the 1920s based on making ethylene from natural gas. The first big success was ethylene glycol used as antifreeze in automobile radiators. Other companies such as Dow, Shell, and Standard Oil were also working on petrochemicals in this period.[8]

During World War II polymers and petrochemicals both made tremendous advances and in the postwar world would come to dominate the chemical industry. The war brought about the large-scale manufacture of synthetic rubber from butadiene and styrene in Germany and the United States. Other plastics, such as polystyrene and polyvinylchloride, served as substitutes for metal and leather, respectively. Some polymers performed critical functions in military equipment: polyethylene in radar, acrylic sheets in aircraft, and Teflon in proximity fuses. After the war, demand for plastics and polymers continued to expand, especially in synthetic fibers, where nylon, acrylonitrile, and polyester fibers grew rapidly. In addition to fibers, polymers found use as structural plastics, films, and paints. Increasingly these polymers would be made from petroleum and natural gas instead of from coal tar derivatives.[9] The shift to a chemical industry dominated by polymers and petrochemicals probably would have occurred without the stimulus of World War II, although the transition would have happened more slowly. The impact of cartels on the industry can only be understood within the above framework. During the 1920s and 1930s, chemical companies tried to protect their mature businesses and to develop new products upon which future growth would depend.

II. The Chemical Industry and National Economies

Throughout this period, the United States possessed the singular advantage of being the largest national economy in the world. In general, in this era chemical consumption was derivative of overall industrial activity. In most cases the demand for chemical products resulted from the growth of other industries that provided goods directly to consumers. For example, in the United States between the wars, the growth of the automobile, radio, consumer appliance, and food-processing industries created large demand for chemicals of all kinds.[10] Even though the American economy slumped badly between 1929 and 1939, the chemical industry remained remarkably healthy. Wall Street labeled it "depression proof."[11] At the bottom of the decline in the spring of 1933, sales of the chemical industry had fallen 39% below the frenzied 1929 peak, but total output quickly rebounded and passed the 1929 record in 1934. During the Depression the total assets of the industry increased by over 25%.[12] That the American chemical industry outperformed the economy as a whole during the interwar years implies that it was becoming more than just a supplier of chemicals to other industries.

Not only did the United States have the largest economy, but its economy was also growing more rapidly than that of its two chief competitors, Great Britain and Germany. America's manufacturing production increased 86% from the prewar level of 1913 to 1937. Over the same period, Great Britain's and Germany's increased by 28% and 38%, respectively.[13]

For the chemical industry the size of a national economy was important because of the large economies of scale that new technologies were achieving. The most dramatic example of this phenomenon was synthetic ammonia plants. The gigantic I.G. Farben plant at Oppau could supply the entire German market with 50% of its capacity. In Great Britain, the situation was even worse. British farmers were already well supplied with ammonium sulfate recovered from coking of coal for steel making. Much of the Imperial Chemical Industries' (ICI) projected output of 180,000 tons per year of ammonia from its Billingham plant would have to find markets overseas. In the United States two plants, those of Allied and Du Pont at 210,000 tons/year and 70,000 tons/year, respectively, supplied the domestic market with three-quarters of its capacity.[14] Synthetic ammonia was the most dramatic example of economies of scale; for most technologies the American market was large enough to absorb the output of several large plants. In fact, exports represented less than 10% of American chemical sales in the interwar period. With tariff protection and an increasingly strong bargaining position, American companies, with few exceptions, were able to preserve the domestic market for themselves. Imports accounted for only about 10% of chemical sales in this period.[15] Direct foreign investment in America was not widespread, the major exceptions being I.G. Farben in dyestuffs and the British textile firm Courtalds in rayon. In contrast to the American situation, the Europeans needed foreign markets to operate plants of competitive size. Regardless of comparative technological strengths of the competing countries, a major advantage of the Americans was that the home market was large and relatively free from foreign penetration. This situation was the basic asymmetry in the diplomatic relations between the Americans and the Europeans. For the Europeans, cartel arrangements were necessary for the survival of nationally based industries. Americans hoped to acquire advanced technologies and insure protection of the domestic market.[16]

Another factor in the strategic analysis of the international chemical industry was the characteristics of the major companies in each country. The three biggest companies in the world were I.G. Farben in Germany, ICI in Great Britain, and Du Pont in the United States. Whereas the first two companies dominated their respective domestic markets, Du Pont had somewhere between one-quarter and one-third of the American market. In the interwar years its major competitors were the Allied Chemical Company, American Cyanamid, and Union Carbide.[17] In the following section I will summarize the strengths and weaknesses of the three major players in the international chemical industry.

III. The Big Three Chemical Companies

The German chemical combine formed in 1925 by the merger of Bayer, BASF, Hoechst, and numerous smaller companies had three major strengths: technological leadership in dyestuffs and synthetic ammonia, and an extremely capable research organization, which worked closely with Germany's outstanding academic chemists. Each of these strengths, however, concealed weaknesses. In the pre-Nazi era Farben's fortunes were tied very closely to its two largest product groups—ammonia and dyes—which accounted for about two-thirds of its sales and profits. Over half of these sales were exports.[18] Both dyestuffs and ammonia gave the I.G. headaches. For the former, World War I had led to the establishment of an American dye industry that was protected by tariffs. By 1930, however, Farben had traded its technical expertise—it still dominated the higher priced dyestuffs markets—to regain control of its prewar American company. In the 1930s Farben controlled about one-quarter of the American dye business. Even with its technological advantages, Farben did not make large profits on dyes because the business was not changing or growing rapidly.[19] In addition, as the competence of Farben's competitors increased, they began to eat away at Farben's market share, which worldwide declined from 46% to 25% between 1925 and 1936. I.G.'s ammonia business, which provided 65% of the company's profits in 1926, was hit first by rapidly expanding world capacity in the late 1920s and second by reduced demand caused by worldwide depression.[20] The I.G. desperately needed some new products to restore the firm's growth and profits.

The economic and political instability of Germany in the late 1920s and early 1930s limited the effectiveness of Farben's research. Its researchers made many important breakthroughs, particularly in polymers, but the transformation of research knowledge into new products lagged because of the sluggish German economy.[21] Compounding this problem was the I.G.'s disdain for consumer markets such as rayon, which was probably the most important new product of the interwar era, in favor of producing chemical commodities in large-scale plants.[22] Pursuing this strategy, Farben's head, Carl Bosch, tried to repeat his earlier success with ammonia by using similar technology to transform coal into gasoline. When new oil discoveries and decreased demand for petroleum occurred after 1929, the synthetic gasoline project looked like a very expensive mistake. After the Nazis came into power and emphasized economic self-sufficiency, the I.G. fortuitously was able to save its investment in synthetic gasoline and develop some of its other research discoveries, such as synthetic rubber.[23] Overall, the performance of I.G. Farben in the interwar years was not outstanding. Sales doubled from the depth of the Depression in 1932 to 1939, a 10% per year rate of growth, but from the peak of the late 1920s sales had only increased 30% in a decade.[24]

In Great Britain, the Imperial Chemical Industries, Ltd., was created as a response to the formation of I.G. Farben one year earlier. In the late 1920s, ICI's largest businesses were heavy chemicals, especially alkalis (33%), nonferrous metals (16%), explosives (16%), and dyestuffs (12%). Its only major new product in the interwar era was synthetic ammonia, which by 1937 accounted for 20% of the company's sales.[25] Like I.G. Farben before the Nazi regime, ICI was an old-fashioned chemical company that produced basic goods that were consumed by other industries. It followed from this that its growth was dependent on the overall growth of its domestic economy and its success in cornering world markets. Also like I.G. Farben, ICI developed an outstanding research capability that made several important discoveries such as polyethylene and acrylic plastics. By the late 1930s, however, neither of these developments had been turned into successful businesses. All told, between 1927 and 1937 ICI's sales doubled, representing a growth rate of 7% per year.[26]

Neither I.G. Farben nor ICI could match the performance of Du Pont in the interwar years. The latter company increased its sales by a factor of four between 1925 and 1939 because of the growth of certain sectors of the American economy generally and its willingness to produce more complex goods that were closer to the consumer than traditional chemical products.[27] It is hard to exaggerate the importance of the automobile to the American economy in this era. Approximately 50 million cars were manufactured in America between 1920 and 1940, and as late as 1929 U.S. automobile companies produced 85% of the world's output.[28] This large industry provided many opportunities for chemical manufacturers. In the mid- and late 1920s Du Pont's largest and most profitable division was the one that made paint. The company's first major innovation—Duco lacquers—dramatically decreased the time needed to finish an automobile body and made color finishes more durable. Du Pont was also the sole manufacturer of tetraethyllead (TEL), an effective engine knock suppressor in gasoline.[29]

The interwar years in America witnessed a flourishing consumer culture encouraged by the burgeoning business of advertising and the new medium of radio. Du Pont capitalized on this phenomenon in several ways but most successfully with its most important new products of the interwar era, rayon fibers and cellophane film. Both were produced through a complex series of chemical reactions that first made cellulose soluble and then, after extrusion as either a fiber or film, regenerated a solid cellulosic product. Worldwide production of rayon increased one hundred times between 1919 and 1939, reaching 2.2 billion pounds in the latter year, which generated about one billion dollars in sales. In the United States, Du Pont ranked second in rayon production to the American Viscose Company, a subsidiary of the British firm Courtalds. For rayon, the 1920s was a decade of high growth and high profits; in the subsequent decade growth continued but at much lower levels of profitability.

In the Depression decade, Du Pont maintained its profits with cellophane, which found increasing use as the packaging that sold its contents. By 1939, United States cellophane production reached 100 million pounds, and sales totaled $40 million. Du Pont had three-quarters of the market of this very profitable product. Because of their technological similarity, rayon and cellophane were manufactured by the Rayon Department, which in the late 1930s generated about one-quarter of Du Pont's sales and earnings.[30] By this time Du Pont was a very diversified corporation, so much so that its international competitors' mainstay products, dyestuffs and ammonia, represented less than 20% of the company's sales and profits.[31] This would be an important point in Du Pont's international negotiations.

IV. Cartels in the Chemical Industry

To understand the impact of the cartels on the industry, it is necessary to understand what each party hoped to achieve, how successful it was in achieving its goals, and what the impact of the negotiations and agreements were. First and foremost, the international diplomacy of the chemical industry was about division of world markets. The usual formula was North America for Du Pont, the British Empire for ICI (Canada, which happened to be both in the Empire and North America, was handled through a joint venture agreement), and Europe for I.G. Farben. The rest of the world was subject to negotiation, but with few exceptions these markets were not so large as to have a major impact on the parent companies' fortunes. That the major companies spent considerable time and effort arguing over small markets probably had more to do with maintaining prestige than making money. The competitors would, however, join forces in South American and Asian countries to discourage local producers through price cutting and other means.[32] From the perspective of markets, the chemical industry was rather well ordered and disputes were usually settled diplomatically rather than by invading other's territories.

To determine the impact of this structure on the industry requires an analysis of what would have transpired if the diplomatic structure did not exist. The questions then become would the volume of exports have been greater, would companies have invested directly in foreign production facilities, and would the industry have been more innovative? From the perspective of neoclassical economics the answer to all these questions would have been yes, but there are other perspectives from which to assess the industry. One such perspective is the goals that each major company sought to achieve.

I.G. Farben faced the problem of regaining its foreign markets after a decade of war and depression had weakened the German economy and raised obstacles against exports. To counter these disadvantages, the I.G. used its strengths in dyestuffs and high pressure technology and research to regain its prewar markets. The I.G. had two principal weapons: the threat to invade others' territories and the ability to hinder innovations in other countries through patenting. The I.G. attempted to capitalize on its research capability by taking out large numbers of patents. In the United States in 1936 the I.G. held 4,000 patents and was receiving new ones at the rate of about 300 per year.[33] Not only did the I.G. have a lot of patents, but it tried to make the claims in them as broad as possible. In general the I.G. did not have a coherent strategy in the late 1920s and early 1930s. During this time period, the investment in synthetic gasoline continued, while its chances for commercial success dimmed. After 1933 the Nazi government not only saved the synthetic gasoline project, but gave the I.G. a strategy: to help make Germany self-sufficient in critical materials.[34]

From Du Pont's point of view, the international agreements were never critical to the future of the firm. As mentioned earlier, the diversified nature of the company's business reduced its vulnerability in any one particular area. In the 1920s, the company's leaders did work very hard to get help for the dyestuffs and ammonia efforts, both of which were struggling from technological problems. As late as 1929, Du Pont tried to form a joint venture with I.G. Farben in dyestuffs in America but could not complete the deal because Du Pont insisted on majority control. In the 1930s, Du Pont wanted to stabilize prices in areas that were threatened by overcapacity, particularly ammonia, but overall engaged in international diplomacy to assert its position as America's leading chemical company and out of the necessity to exchange patent rights in the rapidly developing field of polymer technology.[35]

The keystone of Du Pont's foreign relations became its 1929 patents and processes agreement with ICI. The wording of the agreement stipulated that Du Pont and ICI would combine forces technologically by sharing know-how and R & D results. By basing the agreement primarily on patents, Du Pont maintained that stipulating sales territories was legal under the patent monopoly. At one level, the agreement was clearly an attempt to circumvent the U.S. antitrust laws. The technological exchanges, however, were real and important to both companies. Because technology is primarily a cumulative learning process, the exposure of each company to the other's experience broadened the perspective of both.[36]

The goal of ICI under the leadership of Sir Harry McGowan was to maintain a viable British chemical industry. According to William J. Reader, ICI was a combination of private corporation and public service institution. McGowan saw ICI as an old-fashioned chemical company that made high volume chemicals in large continuously operating plants. He was not very interested in becoming a more consumer-oriented company like Du Pont or developing new businesses such as plastics. McGowan, backed by the British government, sought to protect the domestic chemical industry through negotiation to maintain large enough markets to absorb the output of plants that were almost all located on British soil.[37]

Overall the three companies were each fairly successful in achieving their aims in the interwar era. The European firms survived the post-World War I chaos and the Great Depression. No firm had to abandon a major investment, although World War II saved I.G. Farben's and ICI's synthetic gasoline plants. Of the three companies, Du Pont did the best during this time period, and had World War II not occurred its strategic position would have continued to improve as its major competitors would have had to deal with the synthetic gasoline problem.

What about the industry as a whole? How well did it perform under this system? Given the political and economic instability of this period, the cooperative relations between the major companies established some stability in the international chemical industry. It was relatively easy to save businesses suffering from overcapacity by agreeing not to dump excess products in each other's countries. But even this was not a great accomplishment because in this highly nationalistic era, this problem could have been solved through tariffs rather than negotiation. Also, as historians of the cartel era have shown, international cartel agreements were not really enforceable by law, so companies abided by them when it was to their advantage and violated them when it was not.[38] What was more important was that the chemical companies sought to solve their problems through cooperation rather than competition. Within any particular country, though, the situation was different, primarily because patents are legally enforceable and in this era were used by companies as strategic instruments.[39] Where the extensive relations between the chemical companies could have had their greatest impact was on the dynamic element of the industry, the coming of the polymer and petrochemical revolution.

V. Cartels and Innovation

Perhaps the best way to understand the workings of the international system is through examples of how it actually worked. One major innovation of the interwar period was acrylic plastics; it later became a critical war material as lightweight, shatterproof windows for aircraft. Acrylic polymers had their beginning in the work of Dr. Otto Rohm, who founded the German Rohm and Haas company to sell a leather-processing chemical. Rohm had done his doctoral research early in the 20th century on reactions of acrylic acid. In 1920, looking to diversify his product line, Rohm returned to acrylic chemistry. Seven years later Rohm and his assistant Dr. Walter Bauer introduced a polymethylacrylate polymer as a substitute for nitrocellulose as the flexible interlayer in safety glass for automobiles. This product enjoyed modest sales and was profitable until the late 1930s, when polyvinylbutyral resins replaced acrylates in safety glass.[40] Continuing his acrylic research, Bauer in 1931 produced a polymer from methylmethacrylate, which was clear like glass yet weighed only half as much and was shatterproof. Chemists at Du Pont and ICI made the same discovery at approximately the same time. The I.G. had also been active in this area, especially in acrylate research.[41] The final actor in this drama was the American Rohm and Haas company, which had been formed by Otto Haas in 1909 to market Rohm's original product in America. During World War I, the American and German companies were separated legally, but after the war Haas created a nonvoting stock trust for his former partner. Based on their personal friendship, relations between Rohm and Haas remained close throughout the interwar period. During this era, Haas looked to Rohm and Bauer in Germany for new products, of which acrylic polymers looked like a promising one.[42]

In the mid-1930s acrylic polymers, like most of the new polymers being manufactured at that time, had difficulty finding large volume uses. The first large market would be for windows in the increasing number of airplanes that were being produced as political tensions increased in Europe in the late 1930s.[43] The key to producing clear sheeting was discovered by Bauer in 1932 while he was attempting to cast a polymethylmethacrylate

(PMMA) interlayer between sheets of glass to make safety glass. When the hardened PMMA layer did not adhere to the glass, Bauer had a thin clear sheet of plastic. After solving other problems with shrinking and warping during the polymerization process, Bauer had a successful method for making clear sheets.[44]

As the technology developed, the inevitable negotiations began to determine who would sell what products and where they could be sold. The I.G. had staked out the field of acrylates by doing some research and then applying for rather broad patents. In 1934, Rohm and the I.G. reached an agreement whereby Rohm gave the field of acrylic and methacrylic polymers over to the I.G. except for the production of PMMA sheets.[45] Sheldon Hochheiser, in his history of the American Rohm and Haas, states that Rohm was strapped for cash and licensed his rights hoping to gain future royalties.[46] Given the state of the acrylics business, however, there would not have been any appreciable royalties in the near future. It seems likely that the I.G. might have used its size to bully the smaller firm into the agreement.

Although PMMA appeared to be a Rohm development, it was not uncontested by other companies. Neither Rohm in Germany nor Haas in America had applied for a patent on the new polymer. In Great Britain, ICI employee Rowland Hill had independently discovered PMMA and had applied for an American patent that would be granted in 1934.[47] ICI also developed a superior process for making the methylmethacrylate monomer. In 1936 Rohm gave ICI access to its sheet-making process—both Du Pont and ICI had previously made sheet by casting blocks and sawing them into thin sheets—in exchange for its monomer process. Of course, this agreement restricted each company's market to its exclusive territory domain.[48]

Now the relationships became rather complicated. Because of the Du Pont-ICI agreement, both the Hill patent and the monomer process had to be offered to Du Pont, but ICI also had access to the sheet-making process, which could not be shown to Du Pont. Similarly, Rohm could not license Haas to use the ICI monomer process. Confusion over who owned what apparently led ICI to inadvertently disclose the secret sheet-making process to Du Pont, which soon began to use it. In 1939, Haas got an American patent on the process that gave him a strong bargaining chip to use against Du Pont, which held the Hill patent on PMMA.[49] Rather than fight it out in the courts or the marketplace, Haas and Du Pont reached an agreement based on mutual assessments of the strength of each side. One reason for this outcome was that PMMA was a new product that appeared to have considerable potential even though sales were currently small. Both companies wanted to see PMMA become successful, and both could achieve rapid sales growth when the product took off. Also, if the Hill patent was ruled invalid in the courts, it would open the way for other competitors to enter the PMMA field. Lawyers at Du Pont and Rohm and Haas agreed that the Hill patent was weak because of earlier anticipations of the invention, especially Rohm's work, which dated back to the turn of the century. The key bargaining chip turned out to be the sheet-process patent, which allowed Rohm and Haas to limit Du Pont's market share to one-third in the sheet business.[50] For some reason Du Pont did not bring the ICI monomer process into the negotiations, so Rohm and Haas had to use a more costly process. Rohm and Haas, however, was able to overcome this disadvantage with other economies of scale achieved by being the largest producer of PMMA.

This example shows that a small company could be successful in challenging larger ones when it was protected by strong patents that gave legitimacy to its claims. The problem with international negotiations was that there was no legal framework within which the companies operated. As long as the goal of the negotiations was to keep the business arranged along national lines, patents were of limited value in resolving international disputes. The primary battles would be fought between domestic producers, who looked to overseas relationships to improve their respective positions.

The most infamous cartel arrangement was that between Standard Oil and I.G. Farben, which became headline material when America suddenly found itself without a substitute for rubber when the war with Japan cut off supplies of that critical material. This episode is important because it shows the effect of cartel arrangements on innovation and it highlights problems that were caused by the changing structure of the chemical industry. Although usually it was chemical manufacturers who worried about oil companies invading their turf, the Standard-I.G. marriage came about for the opposite reason. Worried by predictions that demand for oil would soon outstrip supplies, Standard opened negotiations with the I.G. in the late 1920s to gain access to the latter's hydrogenation technology.[51] Whereas the Germans were planning to convert coal to oil, Standard hoped to hydrogenate heavy crudes to gasoline. In the agreement with the I.G., Standard laid claim to the oil industry outside Germany, and the I.G. was given the entire world in non-petrochemical developments. In the gray area in between, arrangements were made to share developments. To gain the critical hydrogenation technology know-how, Standard also gave the I.G. $30 million of Standard stock.[52]

The agreement was signed on November 9, 1929, just a few weeks after the stock market crash that signaled the beginning of a worldwide depression. At approximately the same time, a big new oil strike was made in Oklahoma, and one year later massive new fields would be discovered in east Texas. The combined result of the Depression and new sources of oil sent the price of gasoline tumbling. Standard no longer needed to look for new sources of gasoline.[53] This did not end Standard's relationship with the I.G., however.

In September 1930, Standard and the I.G. set up the jointly owned Joint American Study Company (Jasco) to make experiments and to act as a licensing agency for the exploitation of new chemical processes that were based on petrochemicals. The stockholding in the firm was 50–50, but the originator of a new process was to receive five-eighths of the royalties.[54] By the late 1930s, Standard began to focus on one I.G. development that looked increasingly important, synthetic rubber. In the late 1920s and early 1930s, I.G. chemists developed synthetic rubbers based on emulsion polymerization of butadiene with either styrene or acrylonitrile as a copolymer. Following the trend of oil and other commodities, however, rubber prices fell dramatically during the Depression, and interest in replacing natural rubber waned in the early 1930s.[55]

In the mid-1930s synthetic rubber research was revived because of a new Du Pont product, neoprene, and the German government's policy of autarky. Neoprene was discovered serendipitously during research on polymerization of acetylene in 1930, and within a few years Du Pont was marketing it as a premium price rubber for uses for which natural rubber was unsuited, such as in oily or greasy environments. This new product created the field of specialty rubber.[56] Standard established its position in 1937 with its discovery of butyl rubber made from isobutylene. As interest in the field increased generally, Standard sought to get the I.G. to release its synthetic rubber patents and know-how to Jasco. Probably because of government restrictions on such critical information, the I.G. kept putting off Standard's requests. Believing in I.G.'s good faith, Standard in 1938 turned over its butyl rubber patents and know-how to the I.G. but got nothing in return. A year later, after war broke out in Europe, the I.G. turned over its American synthetic rubber rights to Standard, which began to get inquiries from the rubber companies about licensing agreements.[57]

Most of the interest at this point was in the butadiene-acrylonitrile copolymer that had properties similar to Du Pont's neoprene. The I.G. had actually been exporting small quantities to the United States before the war.[58] This was probably a minor strategic thrust against Du Pont, which was engaged in negotiations with the I.G. on a broad front. In the mid-1930s, the I.G. believed that neoprene was the best candidate for a general-purpose rubber. Soon the I.G. reversed its conclusion after learning of difficulties involved in producing neoprene and after having improved its own rubber.[59] The I.G had withheld its Buna N patents from Jasco, in part to keep them as a bargaining chip with Du Pont, but after 1939 Standard was free to license them. The terms of the agreement that was offered restricted the products to specialty markets, because Standard wished to retain the large general market for itself, and required that the licensee surrender all improvement patents to Standard.

During 1939 and 1940, Standard pondered ways in which the rubber companies could be brought into the synthetic rubber field without surrendering any control over the business. Proposals included a joint venture to be controlled by Standard.[60] When the United States entered the war, the government intervened and forced Standard, through antitrust action, to relinquish its demands.[61] In 1942 the U.S. government launched a massive cooperative program between the chemical, oil, and rubber companies to establish an American general-purpose synthetic rubber industry that produced over 1.5 billion pounds two years later.[62]

Much attention has been focused on Standard's relationship with the I.G. and the initial bureaucratic problems that the synthetic rubber program had. What has not been emphasized is that until the government stepped in to run the project there had not been sufficient need for a general-purpose synthetic rubber or a single company that had all the skills necessary to accomplish the task. That the synthetic rubber patents ended up in an oil company that had limited experience in chemical manufacture, generally, or polymerization, specifically, was unfortunate. On the other hand, even if Du Pont had owned these patents instead of Standard, it is doubtful that the industry could have gotten off the ground without government support. The investment necessary and the scale of the operations made it really unattractive to any single American company. In Germany, I.G. Farben, which had already taken a similar risk with synthetic gasoline, took on the rubber project with government support. Overall, technological and economic constraints inhibited the development of the industry much more than the cartel arrangements.

VI. Chemical Technology and Industry Structure

In general, the structure of the industry gave it considerable stability and defined its territory. The structure of an industry is not just a politically contrived entity but is shaped by its economic and technological organization. Of course, political agreements can temporarily stabilize a given configuration, but they cannot completely harness the dynamic force of technological and economic change. In fact, if one wants to find an example of a rationalized industry in which competition had been channeled into narrow areas, the American chemical industry between the wars is a fine example. Contemporary commentators noted the lack of price competition among companies and the small number of producers of many chemicals.[63] It can be argued that the underlying structure of the industry shaped its economic characteristics.

The chemical industry in this era consisted of a diverse set of industries that were only loosely connected to one another. Du Pont and the second largest "chemical" company, Union Carbide, had almost no direct overlap in their product lines.[64] Competition between them was mostly the result of each company following the trajectory of its own technological capabilities. For example, Du Pont entered the manufacture of methanol to capitalize on the know-how that it had developed to make ammonia.[65] A lucrative market for this basic chemical turned out to be antifreeze. Union Carbide developed a competitive product, ethylene glycol, as an antifreeze out of its research initiative to make chemicals from natural gas.[66] Comparisons between other companies would also show a lack of congruence between product lines. This did not represent a conspiracy to avoid competition, but reflected the nature of chemical production. The chemical industry used so many chemicals as raw materials or intermediates in multistep processes that no single company could hope to own an economically efficient scale plant for every chemical it needed.

The large economies of scale in chemical production led to the conclusion that it was more efficient for only a few companies to build large plants that would serve not only internal needs but other companies as well. When Du Pont needed acetic acid for making cellulose acetate fibers or acetylene for making neoprene, it bought these chemicals from Union Carbide rather than made them. The best customer of any given chemical company, generally, was other chemical companies.[67] These intimate relationships tended to dampen competition because there were numerous ways for a competitor to retaliate.

The American chemical industry between the wars was structured in a way that reflected the economic and technological realities of the era. The executives of the major companies recognized this order and sought to sustain it through legal sanctions based on patent monopolies. Although these executives had to put the welfare of their own companies first, they also had a larger mission to promote the expansion of the industry in general. Armed with its research capabilities, the chemical industry produced thousands of new products that replaced naturally derived chemicals or materials in other industries.[68] In this era the goal of the chemicalization of all industry provided a common target that all chemical companies, large and small, shared. Rather than compete with each other, they worked together to open up large markets that would provide healthy growth rates for everyone. And to a remarkable degree they were successful.

At the time that the chemical industry was most ordered—the 1930s—forces were gathering that would destroy the existing system. As discussed above, the development of petrochemical and polymer technology opened the floodgates for competition. The ascendance of the new chemical industry was accelerated by World War II. In its new mode the industry continued to grow rapidly, but price competition began to erode profits in many areas. The new competitive chemical industry was a product of technological change, not a creation of public policy or international cooperation.

VII. Conclusion

The cartel arrangements of the interwar years in the chemical industry reflected the technological and economic realities of the times and the various countries. On the international level there was no overarching consensus on aims or goals. Each company entered into cartel arrangements opportunistically when it appeared to its advantage to do so. Companies could violate cartel arrangements whenever it was deemed to their advantage to do so. In an era of economic nationalism, threats by foreign concerns to companies that were protected by tariffs or other government actions were not that serious. In this era, rationalized production could best be found at the national level. In Germany and Great Britain, I.G. Farben and ICI dominated their respective national industries. In the United States, the diverse nature of chemical technologies and the patent system created a managed industry that competed only in mutually agreed upon ways. The companies also shared a common goal of chemicalizing other industries and providing growth opportunities for everyone. The success of this system is reflected in the healthy growth rates of the American companies, large and small, in economic boom and bust in the interwar years.

NOTES

1. The best introduction to the literature is George W. Stocking and Myron W. Watkins, *Cartels in Action: Case Studies in International Business Diplomacy* (New York, 1946).

2. This is the general position of Stocking and Watkins. For example, in discussing the nitrogen cartel, they assert that nitrogen prices "declined much further than the general price level between 1919 and 1939. Despite substantial recovery in the late thirties, nitrogen was relatively cheap. *Nevertheless nitrogen prices were no*

doubt higher than they would have been without the cartel" (emphasis added), ibid., pp. 164–65.

3. This general point of view is presented by William J. Reader, *Imperial Chemical Industries: A History*, vol. II (London, 1975).

4. On the structure of the chemical industry see John Kenly Smith, Jr., "World War II and the Transformation of the American Chemical Industry," in Everett Mendelsohn, Merritt Roe Smith, and Peter Weingart (eds.), *Science, Technology, and the Military* (Boston, 1988), pp. 307–22.

5. John Kenly Smith, Jr., "The Evolution of the Chemical Industry: A Technological Perspective," paper delivered at the conference "Chemical Sciences in the Modern World," in Philadelphia, May 1990.

6. The sales figures are from Williams Haynes, *American Chemical Industry: Decade of New Products*, vol. 5 (New York, 1954), pp. 508, 510. Total plastics sales are from Howard C.E. Johnson, "In the Stillness a Giant Was Stirring," *Chemical Week* (November 16, 1968): p. 128.

7. Smith, op. cit. (1988).

8. Peter H. Spitz, *Petrochemicals: The Rise of an Industry* (New York, 1988), chapters 2, 5, 6.

9. Ibid., chapter 6; and Smith, op. cit. (1988).

10. On the chemical industry in this era see Haynes, op. cit., vols. 4 and 5.

11. Ibid., vol. 5, chapter 3.

12. Johnson, op. cit., p. 120.

13. Paul Kennedy, *The Rise and Fall of the Great Powers* (New York, 1989), p. 299.

14. Reader, op. cit., vol. 2, p. 108; and "Nitrogen IV: We Hoped to Make Money," *Fortune*, August 1932: 58–70.

15. On imports and exports, see Anna Hazel Swift, "Changes in the Chemical Industry during the Past Twenty-Five Years," *Industrial and Engineering Chemistry* 20 (June 1928): 657; and "What Is Chemical Industry?" *Chemical and Metallurgical Engineering* (September 1939): 568.

16. Stocking and Watkins, op, cit., chapter 9.

17. The Du Pont figures are an estimate based on the ratio of its investment to that of its competitors. In 1939 Du Pont represented 35% of the total investment of the forty largest chemical companies (Stocking and Watkins, op. cit., p. 381). In 1937 *Fortune* estimated that the big three, Du Pont, Union Carbide, and Allied, had two-thirds of the assets of the industry ("The Chemical Industry I," *Fortune*, December 1937: 37). For Du Pont's market share in various industries, see "Approximate Percent of United States Market Enjoyed by Du Pont Products," Du Pont-General Motors Antitrust Suit Printed Documents, p. 3789, Hagley Museum and Library, Wilmington, Delaware.

18. On the I.G.'s ammonia and dyestuffs businesses, see Peter Hayes, *Industry and Ideology: I.G. Farben in the Nazi Era* (New York, 1987), chapter 2; and Alfred D. Chandler, Jr., *Scale and Scope: The Dynamics of Industrial Enterprise* (Cambridge, Mass., 1990), pp. 580–82.

19. On Farben's dye business, see Stocking and Watkins, op. cit., pp. 505–11. On the declining importance of dyestuffs, see L.F. Haber, *The Chemical Industry, 1900–1930* (Oxford, 1971), p. 273.

20. Hayes, op. cit., pp. 33–35.

21. On research at I.G. Farben in this era, see Christopher Freeman, *The Economics of Industrial Innovation*, 2nd ed. (Cambridge, Mass., 1986), pp. 52–64.

22. On I.G. Farben and rayon, see Hayes, op. cit., pp. 145–48.

23. Ibid., pp. 36–42.

24. Chandler, op. cit., p. 580.

25. Reader, op. cit., vol. 2, p. 499.

26. On the overall strategy of ICI, see Reader, op. cit., vol. 2, chapter 1. On ICI research, see ibid., pp. 81–94, 338–64. For sales statistics see ibid., p. 497.

27. For Du Pont sales statistics, see David A. Hounshell and John Kenly Smith, Jr., *Science and Corporate Strategy, Du Pont R & D, 1902–1980* (New York, 1988), pp. 602–3.

28. The 1929 production percentage is from Jean-Pierre Bardou et al., *The Automobile Revolution: The Impact of an Industry* (Chapel Hill, N.C., 1982), p. 120. The total production estimate is from John B. Rae, *The American Automobile* (Chicago, 1965), p. 238.

29. On Du Pont's paints business, see Hounshell and Smith, op. cit., chapter 6. On TEL, see ibid., chapter 7.

30. Ibid., chapter 8. Worldwide production figures are from Williams Haynes *Cellulose: The Chemical That Grows* (Garden City, N.Y., 1953), pp. 348–50.

31. For Du Pont ammonia sales in this period, see "Annual Research Expenditures . . . ," Accession 1814, Box 34, Hagley Museum and Library. For dyestuffs sales, see Stocking and Watkins, op. cit., p. 508.

32. For a general discussion of cartels, see Stocking and Watkins, op. cit. The large, surviving body of correspondence concerning cartel arrangements is in "Patents," Hearings Before the Committee on Patents, 77th Congress, 2nd Session, on S2303 and S491; "Investigation of the National Defense Program," Hearings Before a Special Committee Investigating the National Defense Program, U.S. Senate, 77th Congress, 1st Session, pursuant to S. Res. 71; and the United States v. E.I. du Pont de Nemours, Imperial Chemical Industries, et al., Civil Action 24–13, Southern District of New York, 1944.

33. "Patents," p. 2264.

34. On the I.G. in the 1930s, see Hayes, op. cit., chapter 4.

35. Graham Taylor and Patricia Sudnik, *Du Pont and the International Chemical Industry* (Boston, 1984), chapter 5.

36. Hounshell and Smith, op. cit., chapter 10.

37. Reader, op. cit., vol. 2, chapter 1.

38. Stocking and Watkins, op. cit., document the relative failure of the cartels to achieve market and price stability during the 1920s and 1930s.

39. On the use of patents to order markets, see "Patents."

40. Sheldon Hochheiser, *Rohm and Haas: History of a Chemical Company* (Philadelphia, 1986), p. 55–56.

41. Ibid., pp. 56–57. For the ICI discovery, see Reader, op. cit., vol . 2, p. 346. On Du Pont, see Hounshell and Smith, op. cit., p. 476. See also "Patents," pp. 663–749.

42. Hochheiser, op. cit., chapters 2–4.

43. Ibid., pp. 60–65.

44. Ibid., p. 57; and "Patents," pp. 691–701.

45. "Patents," p. 670.

46. Hochheiser, op. cit., p. 57.

47. "Patents," pp . 684–85.

48. Hochheiser, op. cit., p. 58; and "Patents," p. 701.

49. "Patents," pp. 685–90, 699–702.

50. Ibid.

51. Stocking and Watkins, op. cit., pp. 491–505.

52. Ibid.

53. Henrietta Larson, Evelyn H. Knowlton, and Charles S. Popple, *History of Standard Oil Company (N.J.): New Horizons, 1927–1950* (New York, 1971), pp. 153–59.

54. Stocking and Watkins, op. cit., pp. 91–95.

55. On the early synthetic rubber research, see Vernon Herbert and Attilio Bisio, *Synthetic Rubber: A Project That Had To Succeed* (Westport, Conn., 1985), pp. 27–33.

56. On neoprene, see John Kenly Smith, Jr., "The Ten-Year Invention: Neoprene and Du Pont Research, 1930–1939," *Technology and Culture* 26 (January 1985): 48.

57. Stocking and Watkins, op. cit., pp. 97–108.

58. [Standard Oil Company], "Memorandum Re Manufacture of Buna and Prebunan in USA," October 31, 1939, "Patents," pp. 2930–31.

59. Stocking and Watkins, op. cit., pp. 108–12.

60. [Standard Oil Company], "Memorandum—Synthetic Rubber," January 2, 1940, "Patents," pp. 2962–65.

61. Herbert and Bisio, op. cit., pp. 59–61.

62. Ibid., chapter 11.

63. See for example "Chemical Industry I," *Fortune* (December 1937): 157; and Stocking and Watkins, op. cit., pp. 386–92.

64. Stocking and Watkins, op. cit., pp. 386–87.

65. Hounshell and Smith, op. cit., pp. 186–88.

66. Spitz, op. cit., pp. 69–80; and "Carbide & Carbon Chemicals," *Fortune* (September 1941): 62.

67. Stocking and Watkins, op. cit., pp. 386–87; on sales to consuming industries, see "What Is Chemical Industry?"

68. On the chemicalization of industry, see Haynes, op. cit., vol. 4, p. 430.

Comment

Katsuyuki Ozawa

In his paper, Professor Smith emphasizes the relation between techno-logical change and international cooperation in the chemical industy. The international chemical industry between the wars was in a transition period that represented the culmination of older trends and the early de-velopment of new ones. The older chemical industry had supplied chemi-cals to other industries for use in their operations. The older chemicals had consisted of heavy chemicals, explosives, and dyestuffs. The new chemical industry supplied chemicals directly to the consumer. The new chemical products consisted of neoprene, nylon, and plastics. Technologically, it needed the polymerization of organic compounds. The raw material soon changed from coal tar to petroleum.

From the viewpoint of economic conditions, American manufacturing production increased 86% from 1913 to 1937. Over the same period Great Britain's and Germany's increased by 28% and 38%, respectively. This was largely due to the fact that the United States was a flourishing con-sumer culture, and the market for new chemicals had grown very rapidly.

As other nations became self-sufficient in dyestuffs after World War I, German chemical companies were consolidated as I.G. Farben in 1925 and made international cartel arrangements with other countries to con-trol the European market. But Germany hardly developed the new consumer-oriented chemical industry because it lacked the immense mar-ket for these new chemicals that the United States had.

In Great Britain, like Germany, chemical companies were consolidated into ICI in 1926 and took part in the international dyestuffs cartel in 1931 to keep the British Empire market. But Great Britain also did not develop the new chemical industry.

In the United States, high economic growth had continued, and a serious overcapacity of production had not occurred. Many companies con-tinued to produce the older chemicals independently, and new chemi-cals like polymers were developed rapidly. Du Pont had been developing the new chemicals enthusiastically, and the company's business was diversified. From Du Pont's of view, the international agreements were never critical to the future of the firm. The keystone of Du Pont's foreign relation became its 1929 patents and processes agreement with ICI. Because technology is primarily a cumulative learning process, the exposure of each company to another's experience broadened the perspective of both.

Although Smith's paper is very persuasive, I have two questions. First, whenever I consider the international chemical cartel, I think of the 1897 Jamesburg Agreement between Du Pont and the predecessors of I.G. Farben and ICI. International chemical agreements during the interwar period usually divided the world market into North America for Du Pont, the British Empire for ICI, and Europe for I.G. Farben. It was the same formula as the agreement of 1897. Leaving aside for the moment technological change, were the international chemical agreements of this era influenced by the old relations between these companies that had been built in 1897?

Second, Du Pont developed the new chemicals enthusiastically, but I.G. Farben and ICI did not. This difference was due mostly to economic conditions in each country. Is there, however, another important reason? Were the top management and the management structure of these three companies important factors? Irénée and Lammot were familiar with chemical technology and rational management. Carl Bosch was a good chemist, but was not familiar with rational management. McGowan was not familiar with technology and rational management. Du Pont had a top management that could plan strategy and a decentralized divisional organization in which divisions were profit centers. I.G. Farben and ICI had not made such rational management structures.

Response

John Kenly Smith, Jr.

Professor Ozawa asked if the international agreements between chemical companies in the interwar era were influenced by older cartel arrangements dating back to the late 19th century. Yes, relationships and agreements between chemical companies had been established in this earlier era. Many of the interwar agreements were explicitly seen as extensions of prewar relationships. For example, Du Pont had participated in the original 1897 Nobel Dynamite Trust and sought to re-establish it in 1920. Not only had companies developed business relationships but personal ones as well. The Du Ponts became very close friends with Harry McGowan, the head of the Nobel company in Great Britain. A major difference between the prewar and postwar cartels was that the former tried to prevent overcapacity in the industry, whereas the latter had to deal with overcapacity that resulted from wartime expansion and national security concerns in the postwar era.

Ozawa also noted that I attributed the difference in the development of the chemical industry in the United States and Europe mostly to economic factors. He then went on to ask if there are, however, other factors, especially the attitudes of top managers, that account for these differences. There were important differences in attitudes of the management of Du Pont, ICI, and I.G. Farben. In the 1920s the Du Pont company evolved a strategy of developing sophisticated products for use in expanding consumer markets. For a number of reasons, including management attitudes, both ICI and I.G. Farben pursued the older strategies of producing bulk chemicals. But one must ask the question, would the Du Pont strategy have worked in Great Britain and Germany? I believe that the answer is no, because of the weakness of consumer spending in both countries. The most striking difference between America and Europe in the 1920s was the mass production of automobiles in the United States. Automobiles, of course, created opportunities for many new chemical products, such as plastics, paints, synthetic rubber, safety glass, and gasoline additives, all of which Du Pont manufactured.

II. The Electrical Industry

Competition and Cooperation in the Japanese Electrical Machinery Industry

Shin Hasegawa

I. Introduction

It is well known that international agreements in the electrical machinery industry have been repeatedly concluded since the end of the 19th century. The aim of this paper is to analyze the effects of international agreements on Japanese electrical machinery manufacturers from 1903 to 1936, especially heavy electrical equipment manufacturers and electric lamp manufacturers.

The substance of the international agreements among electrical machinery manufacturers was, first, the exchange of patents and inventions, and second, the market division among major producers. The cartel organization and management based on the international agreements has already been studied to some extent. It is usually considered that the agreements, by which major producers were supposed to enjoy technical advantages and strong market shares, were helpful in controlling competition in the market. However, in these studies, they have rarely mentioned the effects on Japanese electrical machinery producers. In addition, the influence of international agreements depended on the electrical machinery producers' behavior and the market structure in each country.

During the interwar period, the active investment of the electric power industry expanded the electrical machinery market in Japan (Figure 1). Domestic electrical machinery manufacturers rapidly developed, actively competing against each other. So, have the international agreements had no influence on Japanese electrical machinery producers and their market? In this paper, considering the rapid growth of the Japanese electrical machinery industry and the competitive market structure, I will examine the effects of international agreements on Japanese producers and their market structure, not only short-term effects on the market but also long-term effects like technology transfer.

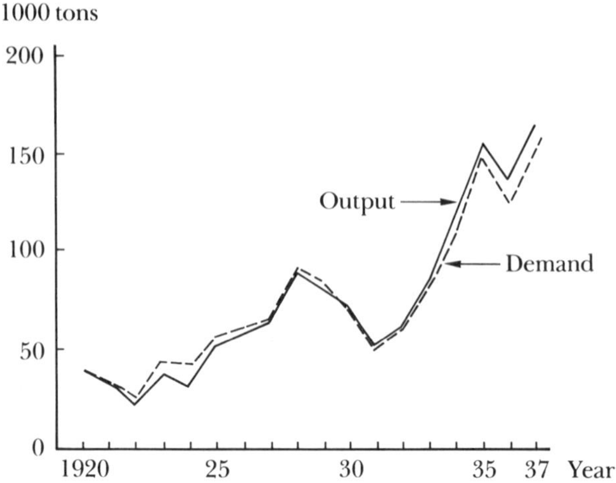

Fig. 1 Output and Demand by Quantity

Source: Hasegawa Shin, "Jūdenki Cartel (Satsukikai)" (Heavy Electrical Machinery Cartel), in Hashimoto Jurō and Takeda Haruhito (eds.), *Ryōtaisenkanki Nihon no Cartel* (Japan's Cartels in the Interwar Period) (Tokyo, 1985), pp. 277–78.

II. The Heavy Electrical Equipment Manufacturers and the International Agreements

1. The International Agreement in 1903 and Its Effects on Japan before World War I

GE-AEG Agreement of 1903.   The International Agreement between General Electric Co. (GE) and Allgemeine Elektrizitäts-Gesellschaft (AEG) was concluded on October 19, 1903. The gist of the agreement was as follows:[1]

(1) The exchange of patents and inventions, except when a party has a specific contract with others, e.g., for steam turbines and generators.

(2) Territory: AEG: Germany, Austria-Hungary, European and Asiatic Russia, Finland, Holland, Belgium, Sweden, Norway, Denmark, Switzerland, Turkey, and the Balkan states;

GE: The United States of America and its dependencies, and Canada.

(3) The territory of the General la Compagnie pour l'Exploitation des Procedes, Thomson-Houston, the Medi-Thomson Company, and the British Thomson Houston Company shall be considered by both parties as autonomous and neutral.

In this agreement there was no item that directly referred to Japan. Only an item on exports to the rest of the world was related to Japan. It

TABLE 1 Demand for Electrical Machines, 1909–14 (¥ 1000)

	Electrical Machinery	%	Generators, etc.	%
Imported goods	25,427	100.0	17,779	100.0
United Kingdom	4,144	16.3	3,217	18.1
U.S.A.	10,873	42.8	7,640	43.0
Germany	6,167	24.3	3,246	18.3
Switzerland	289	1.1	211	1.2
Others	3,954	15.6	3,465	19.5
Domestic goods	17,103	—	2,375	—

Source: Ministry of Communications, *Denki Jigyō Yōran*, 1917.
Note: Electrical machinery includes generators, motors, transformers, etc.

said that the exports of the two corporations to the rest of the world should be proportionate, according to the conditions in each country:

> Export business for the rest of the world shall be done by both parties hereto on a general basis that each party shall be entitled to a certain part proportional to the amount billed out by it on its books for electrical machinery, apparatus and supplies, not including cable & wire, as compared with a similar business done by the other party in the same time in the territory to which said export business relates.

The agreement had the tendency to accelerate the competition in the rest of the world because the export drive to the rest of the world was enhanced by the restriction of export to the excluded territory. But the objectives of the agreement between GE and AEG were mainly exchange of technology and confirmation of the excluded territory. Regarding the territory, it was important for both parties to maintain the areas of North America and Europe. Controlling the exports to the rest of the world was not an urgent issue. Probably both GE and AEG had an understanding that exports to Japan were free. Therefore, though the proportion of the Japanese market according to the agreement in 1903 should be respected by both GE and AEG, the contract as to Japan was not made at once.

The Tie-up of Shibaura Seisakusho with GE and Its Effects. GE tied up with the electric lamp producer Tokyo Denki (Tokyo Electric Co.) in 1905 and further tied up with the heavy electrical machine manufacturer Shibaura Seisakusho (Shibaura Manufacturing Co.) in 1909. As regards the electrical machine imports during the period from 1909 to 1914, Germany provided 24%, next to America, whose ratio was 42% (Table 1). German producers were powerful competitors against American producers, not only in the world market but also in Japan. It was necessary for GE to secure a base for production in Japan, because GE's prices were not so competitive as those of German producers. But GE's strategy was aimed at something else. Shibaura began to use GE's patents thanks to the contract, and the patents were registered in Japan from 1909 to 1910. At the same time, disagreement on the patent right for the turbine and the electric lamp arose between GE and AEG. A letter from GE to AEG dated January 6, 1910, included the statement:

> Of course these manufacturing and selling concerns in Japan will have the exclusive right for a limited period under the Japanese patents which are issued on inventions acquired for that territory by the General Electric Company, either through its employees or otherwise, and will expect that the patents will be respected.

GE warned AEG that Shibaura and Mitsui Bussan (Mitsui and Co.) had the exclusive right of GE's patents in Japan and it should be respected by AEG. AEG replied to GE in a letter that as of February 22, 1910, Ōkura-Gumi (Ōkura & Co.) was AEG's agent and would continue its services. At the time, the trouble was that Ōkura-Gumi imported AEG turbines that were based on the patent of the Courtis turbine. As noted previously, GE and AEG had an agreement as to the turbine, turbine generator, and its accessories. GE insisted that AEG could not export to Japan, which was part of GE's territory, whereas AEG argued that the exports to Japan should be free.

The reason the trouble arose as late as 1910 was related to the tie-up of Shibaura and GE in 1909. With the tie-up, GE began to assign its patents to Shibaura and insisted on the exclusive right of Shibaura in Japan. Thus GE expanded its own territory in substance under the pretext of respecting Shibaura's territory. A memorandum of Ōkura-Gumi dated July 18, 1910, reads as follows:

> This patent question cannot be settled in Japan by Ōkura and Mitsui (who in a way control Shibaura) and Tokyo Lamp Co. which is not Mitsui but is more of G.E's. The settlement must be made between the principals A.E.G. and G.E.
>
> The question for A.E.G. is not really Japan alone. It has a grave relation on all neutral markets, such as South America, South Africa, & Australia & c (*sic*).

Ōkura-Gumi, which was not a party to the agreement, prepared a memorandum that it hoped would be of use to the negotiations between

AEG and GE scheduled to be held in London in September. Ōkura's wish was that AEG should construct an electrical machinery factory in Japan, because losing the AEG business would be a great blow to Ōkura-Gumi. Besides, problems like this, which AEG had not expected at all, might occur in all of the neutral areas. The problem of the AEG turbines was settled by compensation to Shibaura around October 1910. But similar problems might recur in Japan unless AEG and Shibaura (or GE) reached an agreement with regard to the exports of AEG.

The Shibaura-AEG Agreement of 1913.　　Shibaura concluded a seven-year agreement with AEG on February 23, 1913. The substance of the agreement was basically as follows:[2]

(1) Both Shibaura and GE assign the sales right to AEG in Japan and Korea. AEG assigns the right for manufacturing and sales to Shibaura.

(2) In Japan, AEG pays the patent fee or 4% commission for the turbine that AEG sells, and 2.5% for other products.

(3) The ratio of GE and Shibaura to AEG is decided by the sales volume for the past four years; if the ratio is exceeded, each party pays 15% for the turbine, and 10% for the others.

The agreement between Shibaura and AEG, which might be called an extension of the GE-AEG agreement of 1903, solved the problem for the time being. It enabled AEG to continue exporting to Japan and Ōkura-Gumi to remain the sales agent for AEG after this. But AEG's assignment of the right for manufacturing in Japan to Shibaura was a great concession, because under the agreement AEG was not permitted to build factories in Japan.

Though the trouble between GE and AEG ended to the advantage of GE, which used patents as a weapon, it is doubtful that the agreement would be effective in controlling competition. Siemens-Schuckertwerke (SSW), stronger than AEG, was another competitor of GE. Around 1910, adopting an aggressive sales policy by lowering prices, SSW was trying to advance into the Japanese market.[3]

2. International Agreements and Domestic Competition in the 1920s
Changes in the World Market and the Proliferation of International Agreements.
After World War I the world electrical machinery market changed considerably (Table 2). American manufacturers increased production and enlarged their export share in the world market. German manufacturers recovered their lost export share but were not able to reach their prewar level by the middle of the 1920s. In 1919, GE established the International General Electric Co. (IGE), and GE transferred its foreign

TABLE 2 Demand, Output, and Export in the World Market (million
         Reichsmark)

	1913		
	Demand	Output	Exports
1. U.S.A.	1,292	1,400	112
2. Germany	983	1,300	330
3. U.K.	498	600	156
4. France	151	150	30
5. Austria	139	120	10
6. Japan	103	90	1
	1925		
	Demand	Output	Exports
1. U.S.A.	6,457	6,800	353
2. Germany	1,765	2,100	356
3. U.K.	1,150	1,400	352
4. Japan	409	360	11
5. France	380	420	78
6. Canada	235	170	12

Source: League of Nations, *Electrical Industry* (Geneva, 1927), pp. 21, 26.
Note: Demand = Output + Import − Export

activities to IGE. As a result, in June 1919, one of the two parties to the
Japanese producers' contracts with GE changed from GE to IGE. A
new contract between Shibaura and IGE gave the exclusive territory to
Shibaura.

With the recovery of the German electrical machinery industry, in
January 1922 another international agreement between GE and AEG was
concluded. Compared with the agreement of 1903, the exclusive territories
of AEG in the new agreement were reduced in size. This shows that the
growth of GE was remarkable. In 1924 an international agreement between Westinghouse (WH) and SSW was concluded. The agreement included the exchange of technology and confirmed each other's territory.
SSW was allowed a territory about the same size as that of AEG.[4]

Both the GE-AEG agreement and the WH-SSW agreement were concluded by the first half of the 1920s. The network of international agreements was expanded in the 1920s. But the two groups, GE and AEG
versus WH and SSW, were competing with each other in export markets,
as there was no agreement between the two.

During World War I, it was difficult for European producers to export
to Japan. American manufacturers increased their share in the trade with

TABLE 3 Imports by Value (¥ 1000, %)

Year	U.S.A.	U.K.	Germany	Switzerland	Sweden	Total
1914	1,211	695	1,151	55	111	3,326
	36	21	35	2	3	100
1920	7,995	583	25	236	231	9,244
	86	6	0	3	2	100
1925	8,099	2,354	2,228	1,946	192	15,105
	54	16	15	13	1	100
1930	1,916	1,903	1,241	635	156	6,150
	31	31	20	10	3	100

Source: Ministry of Finance, *Dainihon Gaikoku Bōeki Nenpyō.*

Japan immediately after World War I. The share of the Americans in import value was 86% in 1920 (Table 3). At the time American producers enjoyed a clear advantage in Japan as well as in the rest of the world. But around 1922 European goods began to flow into Japan, first those of Swiss manufacturers, and then German products. From 1921 on, high power stations and power lines above 150,000 volts were constructed one after another, which created a demand for heavy electrical machines that Japanese producers could not satisfy. In addition, the country was undergoing a reconstruction boom after the Great Kantō Earthquake in 1923. As a result, the dependence on imports increased from 1923 to 1924 (Figure 2).

But the competitive power of Japanese producers was becoming stronger, with the exception of heavy electrical machinery. American products had higher prices than German products. Moreover, the competitiveness of German manufacturers was further strengthened since their import prices were reduced sharply thanks to the fall in the exchange rate from 1921 to 1922. From 1923 on, however, the advantage of German manufacturers was disappearing because the import prices of their products went up with the rise in the exchange rate. After World War I, the competitiveness of Japanese producers such as Hitachi Seisakusho (Hitachi Manufacturing Co.), Mitsubishi Denki, and Okumura Denki Shōkai, as well as Shibaura Seisakusho, improved. In the middle of the 1920s, in the lower capacity machines Japanese producers gained a distinct advantage.[5] The annual report of the Ministry of Finance said about foreign trade in 1925:

Since the domestic makers reduced their prices after the summer, the prices became lower than the import prices of German manufacturers.

    S. Hasegawa

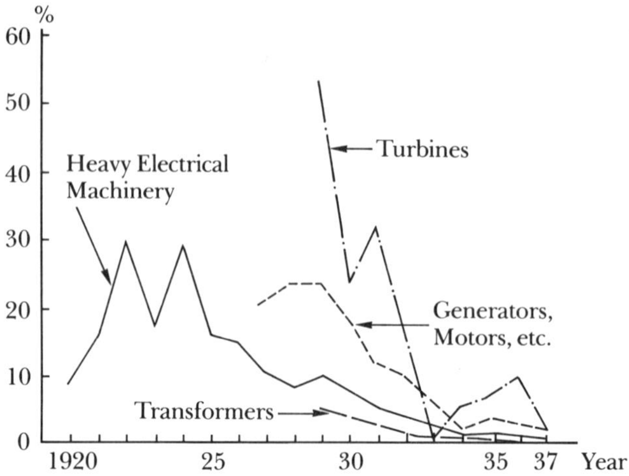

Fig. 2 Dependence on Imports
Source: Same as Figure 1.

With the rise of the nationalistic call for domestic-made goods, Japanese producers' goods enjoyed an advantage. The German Siemens company tried to recover the market by a 10% price reduction but failed.[6]

The sales policy of foreign producers had to be re-examined. WH had already joined with Mitsubishi Denki in November 1923, and SSW had joined with Furukawa Denki Kōgyō in August 1923 to establish a new company in Japan.

The Competition for the Technical Tie-up. The factories of Mitsubishi Zōsen (Mitsubishi Shipbuilding Co.), which is the predecessor of Mitsubishi Denki, had manufactured electrical machinery for ships and mines since the Meiji era. During World War I, the production of electrical machines expanded, and the electrical machine division broke off from Mitsubishi Zōsen in 1919. Subsequently, Mitsubishi Denki (Mitsubishi Electric Co.) started in 1921. In the beginning, Mitsubishi Denki faced many problems, like the breakdown of transmission equipment for the Ministry of Railways and the failure of ten thousand electric fans. It also lacked accumulated experience in factory management. To resolve these difficulties, it was clearly necessary for Mitsubishi Denki to tie up with a foreign manufacturer. It began to look for a foreign company suitable for the tie-up and selected as candidates WH, Metropolitan Vickers (MV), and SSW. In June 1921, the executive director, Tachihara Jin, made a trip to inspect manufacturing plants in the United States and Europe. At first Mitsubishi Denki negotiated with MV in order to acquire technology for its electric railway equipment. However, Mitsubishi failed in the negotiations because Suzuki Shōten (Suzuki Trading Co.) became the sales agent for MV in Japan.[7]

In the negotiations with SSW, the condition offered by SSW was unfavorable for Mitsubishi Denki. In the case of WH, the severe condition that Mitsubishi Denki should assign one-third of its shares to WH by free distribution was proposed in 1921. Being informed that Mitsubishi was in contact with SSW, WH proposed a new condition: one-fifteenth of shares by free distribution should be assigned and one-thirtieth at face value. In November 1923 these terms were accepted.

The tie-up of Furukawa zaibatsu with Siemens had been discussed between the parties since 1919. The board of directors of Siemens decided to construct an electrical machine factory in Japan and selected Furukawa & Co. as the most likely candidate for a tie-up. The negotiations started between Siemens and Furukawa & Co., but Furukawa suffered a setback with the failure of Furukawa Shōji (Furukawa Trading Co.) caused by the crisis after World War I in March 1920.[8]

The negotiations with Siemens—this time, however, the party was Furukawa Denki Kōgyō (Furukawa Electric Manufacturing Co.), in place of Furukawa & Co.—were reopened in January 1921. The memorandum drafted by the two parties on June 1, 1921, reads as follows:[9]

(1) The new company's business includes the manufacturing and sales of heavy electric machines, such as generators, motors, and transformers, telephone and telegram instruments, etc., and the sale of Siemens's goods.

(2) The new company is assigned the patents, inventions, and know-how by Siemens on manufacturing machines, and is able to utilize them in Japan.

(3) Siemens subscribes one-fifth of the new company's shares, which is paid by Furukawa Denki Kōgyō. The patent fee which the new company will pay to Siemens is assigned to Furukawa Denki Kōgyō as shares' payment of the new company.

(4) Siemens should avoid competing with Furukawa and the new company in Japan.

And a further memorandum dated March 23, 1922:

(1) Siemens subscribes one-twentieth of the new company's shares at face value.

(2) The new company is able to export to foreign markets except Europe, and it should avoid competing with Siemens.

Eventually Siemens subscribed 30% of the new company's shares, but the actual payment of Siemens was only 10%. The new company, Fuji Denki Seizō (Fuji Electric Manufacturing Co.), was established in August 1923. At first the main business of Fuji Denki was the importing of Siemens's goods. After the factory was completed in April 1925, the production of a switchboard that used Siemens's parts started. Fuji Denki succeeded in making heavy electrical machines, generators, motors, transformers, etc., in the latter half of the 1920s.

When we examine the case of the tie-ups of Mitsubishi Denki and Fuji Denki, it is clear that Japanese manufacturers took a positive attitude toward the tie-ups with foreign corporations. According to the unpublished diary of the president of Hitachi Seisakusho, Odaira Namihei, Hitachi Seisakusho was also in contact with foreign companies, i.e., MV and AEG, in 1925. In the first half of the 1920s, Japanese producers faced the necessity of improving technology with technical assistance from foreign producers. But in spite of serious competition for tying up on the part of Japanese manufacturers, the terms of the contracts changed and became more liberal. It shows that the competition among foreign companies for the tie-up was stronger than among the Japanese companies. Three major companies, though not Hitachi Seisakusho, joined with foreign companies. What were the effects of these joint ventures?

First, the absorption of the patents, inventions, and know-how that Japanese companies were assigned by the foreign companies promoted the Japanese manufacturers' technical progress and led to their success in producing high-capacity machines, such as turbines and generators. Of course the agreements had some restrictions with respect to technical assistance. For example, Mitsubishi Denki had not been able to make a high-capacity transformer above 110,000 volts until 1933 because of the restrictive terms of the agreement with WH. In the case of Shibaura, according to the memoir of Ōtaguro Jūgorō, the director of the company up to 1920, the agreement with GE restricted the manufacture of steam turbines.[10] Joining with Ishikawajima Zōsenjo (Ishikawajima Shipbuilding Co.), Shibaura began to produce turbines in 1929 with technical advice from GE. But the restrictions were not fixed ones; they were subject to modification according to the progress of the Japanese manufacturers' technology and the increase of domestic demand.

Second, the uncontrolled exports to Japan from GE, WH, and SSW came to an end because the three Japanese makers, Shibaura Seisakusho,

Mitsubishi Denki, and Fuji Denki, were given exclusive rights in the domestic market.

Excessive Competition and Plant Investment in the Latter Half of the 1920s. The decline of the domestic price by 54% from 1924 to 1932 shows how vehement the competition in Japan became in the latter half of the 1920s (Figure 3). One of the factors behind this phenomenon was the importation of foreign manufacturers' goods. The dependence on imports of high-capacity turbines, generators, etc., which Japanese manufacturers had difficulties producing, was still high (Figure 2). Looking at each country's import value, the ratio of the United States fell, while the ratio of Britain, Germany, and Switzerland rose in the latter half of the 1920s (Table 3).

But, as a whole, import dependence in the latter half of the 1920s was obviously lower than it was in the first half. The raising of customs duties in 1926 was helpful in strengthening the competitiveness of Japanese producers and in lessening import dependence. The customs duties were more effective in blocking the flow of American goods than European goods, which were less expensive. However, the European companies did not lower the export price to the degree of dumping, such as we had witnessed in the steel industry.

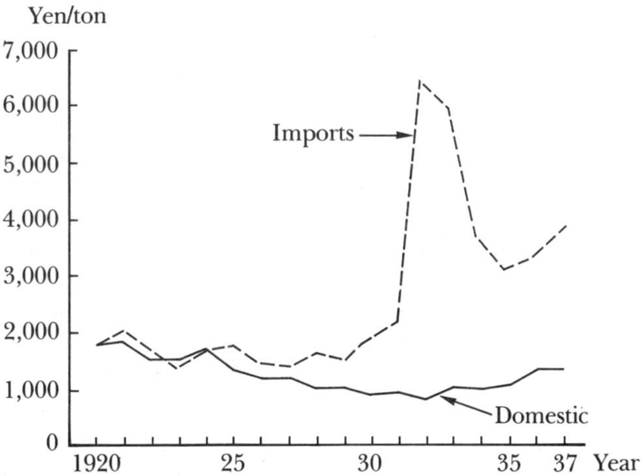

FIG. 3 Unit Price of Heavy Electrical Machinery
Source: Same as Figure 1.

The main factor accelerating competition was the rapid growth of domestic producers.[11] As demand expanded and high-capacity electrical machines increased, the major domestic manufacturers enlarged their factories and equipment. Shibaura constructed the Tsurumi Works, replacing Shibaura Works, which was destroyed by the Great Kantō Earthquake in September 1923. The total production capacity of Shibaura Seisakusho increased by 80% in the latter half of the 1920s, compared with the period of World War I. Hitachi Seisakusho expanded the Hitachi Works and decided to construct Hitachi Kaigan Kōjō (Hitachi Seaside Works) in 1927. Mitsubishi Denki began to construct a factory in Nagoya in 1925, and Fuji Denki also started to build a new factory in 1923. These investments remarkably increased the production capacity of the Japanese industry. On the other hand, the investment of the electric power industry, which was an electrical machine user, declined from 1927, and therefore competition became quite intense.

In the latter half of the 1920s, while they were still importing foreign manufactures, Japanese producers grew rapidly; this is why the competition became vehement to the degree of excess. On November 11, 1929, at a meeting between Furukawa and Siemens, Dr. Carl Köttgen, the chairman of the board of directors of SSW, said that the market prices of electrical machines in Japan were about 30% below the world market prices.[12]

The factors that influenced competition in the latter half of the 1920s were:

(1) International agreements and their network expanded, with the GE-AEG agreement in 1922, the WH-SSW agreement in 1923, the WH-Mitsubishi Denki agreement in 1923, and the SSW-Furukawa agreement in 1922. In these agreements the Japanese manufacturers, Shibaura, Mitsubishi Denki, and Fuji Denki, were each granted territories so that the major foreign manufacturers, GE, AEG, SSW, and WH, could not freely export to Japan. But the absence of an agreement between GE and SSW was a factor accelerating the competition in Japan.

(2) The rise of customs duties, as mentioned previously, strengthened the competitiveness of the Japanese producers and suppressed imports.

(3) The effects of the domestic cartel, as discussed later in detail, were not so remarkable in the latter half of the 1920s. The cartel agreement between Shibaura and Hitachi Seisakusho formed in 1925 did not last long.

(4) Though European imports continued, total imports from foreign manufacturers were gradually decreasing.

(5) The plant investment on the part of the Japanese manufacturers, which increased the production capacity, accelerated the competition in the domestic market.

Among these factors the ones relaxing competition were (1), (2), and (3), while the ones stepping up competition were (4) and (5), factor (5) primarily. With regard to (5), the Japanese producers' behavior and its effects should be especially noted:

Japanese manufacturers join with foreign manufacturers and attain technological progress with the foreign companies' technical assistance. With the technology transfer, Japanese manufacturers expand their plant investment eagerly. The production capacity of the Japanese industry, which is increased by this investment, exceeds the domestic demand. As a result, competition is intensified, and the market prices decline steeply. The decline of prices leads to the exclusion of foreign manufactures and an expansion of domestic demand. Furthermore, the competition accelerates the technology transfer. In these circumstances, the technical tie-up ends up intensifying competition; in other words, there is feedback between the technical tie-up and competition in the domestic market. It is not always correct, then, to argue that the expansion of international agreements is a factor relaxing competition. As stated above, international agreements sometimes play a part in intensifying competition rather than relaxing it.

3. Cooperation and Competition in the 1930s

The International Notification and Compensation Agreement (INCA) was concluded in December 1930. The original participants were the following nine companies: AEG, SSW, the British Thomson Houston Co., the English Electric Co., the General Electric Co., Metropolitan Vickers Electrical Export Co., Brown Boveri & Cie., Westinghouse Electric International Co., and International General Electric Co. INCA claimed as its territory all areas of the world excluding the following: Europe; the territories of the USSR; the United States and its territories and dependencies; the Dominion of Canada and Newfoundland; the French colonies, protectorates, and mandated territories; the Spanish colonies; the Empire of Japan, including its mandated and leased territories and the South Manchurian Railway zone.[13] The agreement did not apply to the excluded territory of the participants and the exclusive territory where the participants allowed the other producers to use patents and inventions. As a result INCA covered the following areas: the Near and Middle East, China, Oceania, South America, Africa, etc., which were not main markets for the electrical machinery industry.

INCA selected a manufacturer who would become a bidder and controlled the difference in bidding prices between a bidder and other manufacturers. In this way, INCA could distribute orders among the participants of the agreement. INCA's management was similar to that of the domestic cartels. As the number of orders grew, INCA faced the need to subdivide the organization and rearrange the way it controlled the market for individual electrical machines. In 1936 the International Electrical Association (IEA), which consisted of fifteen sections and thirty manufacturers, was established, so that the control of cartels became more strict. The international agreements, INCA and its successors, were effective in controlling exports in the mid-1930s. Adding to existing agreements, including those covering technical assistance, the network of the international agreements covered the entire globe.

INCA excluded as its territory the Empire of Japan, including its mandated and leased territories, and the South Manchurian Railway zone. The Japanese producers did not have any direct relation to the agreement. Bound by the restrictive terms for exports in their contracts for technical assistance, they were mostly enclosed in the domestic market, Japan and its colonies.

The Japanese producers could have easily become outsiders disturbing the control of INCA in the 1930s. The exports of Japanese producers, mainly to Manchuria, increased in the mid-1930s. Actually, Hitachi Seisakusho exported motors, transformers, electric fans, etc., to India, Malaya, and Java, in addition to Manchuria.[14] In 1936, Hitachi bid for the generator and other machines in Mysore, India, though it ended in failure. Hitachi, whose territory was not restricted by the technical tie-up except in connection with the turbine, had the possibility of export expansion. But the competitiveness of the Japanese manufacturers was not enough to enable exports in the 1930s. Besides, since Japanese producers took on many orders beyond their capacity in the mid-1930s, there was little possibility of expansion of exports, except in the Manchuria area. In the 1930s contracts relating to the issue of territories between Japanese and foreign manufacturers were not necessary because Japanese manufacturers were virtually shut in the domestic market.

Cooperation among Japanese manufacturers started in the mid-1920s. Denki Kyōkai (the Electric Association), with which the electric power companies and the electrical machinery producers were affiliated, appealed for cooperation in order to expand the use of domestic goods. In December 1925, four manufacturers, Shibaura, Hitachi, Mitsubishi Denki, and Fuji Denki, met in the first of a series of meetings. In March 1926, Hitachi and Shibaura reached a consensus about Tokyo Electric

Power Company's order for transmission equipment for its 150,000 volt power line. But the cooperation lasted only for two months, because Hitachi was doubtful about the cooperativeness of Shibaura. Moreover, a consensus between only the two parties could not suppress the competition, because at this time WH succeeded in supplying high-capacity transformers to Tokyo Electric Power Company.[15]

The conditions for a producers' cartel improved in the 1930s. The import price had been rising since 1930, and imports decreased. At the same time, orders to Japanese producers were reduced under the influence of the economic crisis of 1929. Cooperation among Japanese producers became a pressing need. On May 15, 1931, a cartel agreement was concluded among Shibaura, Hitachi, Mitsubishi Denki, and Fuji Denki. In March 1932, Yasukawa Denki Seisakusho (Yasukawa Electric Manufacturing Co.) joined in the agreement, and further in December 1933, Meidensha (Meidensha Electric Manufacturing Co.) was affiliated with it, too.

The cartel, called Satsukikai, settled the sales ratio of each company and tried to achieve them by making the participants take turns at accepting large orders for electrical machines. The fall of the exchange rate and the rise of customs duties by 35% caused import prices to rise rapidly in 1932, which meant that the dependence on imports of electrical machines, including high-capacity machines, was reduced.

In addition to these objective conditions, it seems the advice of the top management of the foreign companies tied up with Japanese companies was helpful in concluding the agreement and operating the cartel. In November 1929, at a meeting between Furukawa and Siemens, Dr. Carl Köttgen emphasized the effects of the domestic cartels in Germany and the United Kingdom, and moreover he stated that a cartel should be introduced also in Japan and referred to the concrete operation of cartels.

The cartel Satsukikai was not always effective in regulating competition in the domestic market. In the expanding electrical machine market, new products emerged, and the market structure was changing. In these markets the major Japanese manufacturers took a positive attitude toward the new market and tried to expand their sales share. The market for equipment for steam generation was a typical case. With the increase of steam generation in the 1930s, the demand for steam turbines, generators, and their accessories enlarged rapidly. Until then only two Japanese producers, Mitsubishi Denki, affiliated with Mitsubishi Zōsen, and Shibaura Seisakusho, affiliated with Ishikawajima Zōsenjo, supplied steam turbines and their companion generators. The entry of Hitachi Seisakusho in 1933 stepped up the competition. Affiliated with AEG in 1931, Hitachi began to manufacture turbines in Hitachi Kaigan Kōjō. Hitachi manufactured the first turbine model, with the help of AEG's patents, drawings, materials, and know-how. But the second turbine model was manufactured from Hitachi's own drawings.[16] The smooth absorption of turbine technology is evidence of the development of the Japanese electrical machine industry.

On the other hand, the technical assistance received for the AEG turbine represented a new type of technical tie-up in the electrical machine industry. While the technical tie-up had been accompanied by capital participation so far, the tie-up of Hitachi with AEG was confined to technical assistance that furnished patents, drawings, and know-how. The AEG policy regarding the Japanese market and Japanese producers was switched from an export drive to technical assistance through Ōkura Shōji (Ōkura Trading Co.), as a result of the growth of the Japanese industry. AEG also provided Yasukawa Denki with the patent for a motor in 1932. It seems that AEG was able to export its patents separately because the contents of the 1913 agreement between Shibaura and AEG were modified.

The development of the Japanese electrical machine industry made possible separate technical assistance, and the separate technical assistance promoted the technical progress of Japanese manufacturers. The Japanese manufacturers which could not enter into a comprehensive tie-up had a chance to absorb advanced technology through separate technical tie-ups, the consequence of which was that technological progress played a part in intensifying competition in the expanding domestic market.

III. The Electric Lamp Manufacturers and the International Cartel

Tokyo Denki (Tokyo Electric Co.), the largest electric lamp manufacturer in Japan, joined with GE and obtained the exclusive right to manufacture incandescent lamps in the domestic market. Tokyo Denki, as a subsidiary of GE, came to play an important role in the competition against German incandescent lamps.

As well as heavy current machines, GE and Tokyo Denki tried to drive away the German incandescent lamps. GE warned Ōkura-Gumi, AEG's import agency, that the import of the metallized carbon filament lamps would be an infringement of GE's patent right as of May 7, 1910.[17] AEG protested to GE, saying that the exports of the AEG lamp to Japan were to be free according to the agreement of October 19, 1903. But GE insisted once more that AEG should stop the exports, respecting the exclusive right of Tokyo Denki. The trouble was over around October 1910 along with that of AEG turbines, because Ōkura-Gumi reluctantly stopped importing the AEG lamps. With regard to the Japanese electric lamp market, Tokyo Denki concluded an agreement with AEG in 1914; it was helpful in stabilizing the domestic market.[18] Moreover, Tokyo Denki joined with the major producers in Japan to stabilize the domestic market. Tokyo Denki was responsible for 67% of the domestic production of electric lamps in 1915. In Japan, a monopolistic market was being formed and maintained by the force of GE's patent, especially its patent for the tungsten bulb.

With the outbreak of the First World War, Tokyo Denki, which had been researching foreign markets, like China, Manchuria, Indochina, Dutch East Indies, and the South Sea Islands, established the Dairen sales office in 1916 and the Shanghai sales office in 1918 and made inroads into the South Sea Islands market from 1919. With the entry of Tokyo Denki's lamp into the foreign market, the terms of the agreement between GE and Tokyo Denki were changed. The territories of Tokyo Denki, limited to Japan and Korea in the first agreement, were altered in a new agreement on April 29, 1918:[19]

(1) Tokyo Denki has an exclusive right of manufacturing and selling incandescent lamps and sockets, etc., in Japan.

(2) In China, Tokyo Denki has a nonexclusive and nonassigned right of manufacturing and selling incandescent lamps.

(3) Tokyo Denki has no right of manufacturing and selling them in areas except Japan including Korea, Taiwan, the southern half of Sakhalin, and China.

The export expansion of Tokyo Denki to China brought about modification of the terms of the contract between Tokyo Denki and GE. Moreover, the contract between Tokyo Denki and IGE on June 3, 1919, allowed the former to get the nonexclusive right to sell incandescent lamps in the Dutch East Indies, Sumatra, the South Sea Islands, and the Straits Settlement. After World War I, Tokyo Denki found its way into China and parts of Southeast Asia. In 1924, Tokyo Denki participated in the international electric lamp cartel, Phoebus, because GE had allowed exports by Tokyo Denki to foreign markets at the times of alterations of the contracts in 1918 and 1919.

Using electric lamp patents as a weapon, Tokyo Denki urged the major domestic producers to accept capital participation and technical tie-ups. But Tokyo Denki did not succeed in excluding small electric lamp producers. In 1922 the small electric lamp manufacturers started the "Kokusan Denkyū Undō," a nationalistic movement to promote domestic lamps instead of those produced by Tokyo Denki tied up with GE, and organized electric lamp manufacturers' associations.[20]

TABLE 4 Indices of the Japanese Electric Lamp Industry (¥ 1000, %)

Year	Total Output	Tokyo Denki Sales	Share of Tokyo Denki	Exports	Export Dependence
1915	4,264	2,855	67.0	—	0.0
1920	11,665	8,124	69.6	2,146	18.4
1925	17,089	8,945	52.3	2,956	17.3
1930	15,192	8,248	54.3	5,316	35.0
1933	21,971	8,557	38.9	10,167	46.3
1935	21,210	9,534	45.0	7,637	36.0

Sources: Ministry of International Trade and Industry, *Kōgyō Tōkei 50 Nenshi, Shiryōhen* 2, 1969 (reprint); Tokyo Shibaura Denki, *Tokyo Shibaura Denki Kabushiki Kaisha 85 Nenshi*, 1963, p. 936; Tōyō Keizai Shinpōsha, *Nihon Bōeki Seiran*, 1975 (reprint).

Considering the fact that some producers were affiliated with Tokyo Denki, the market share of Tokyo Denki in the domestic market decreased obviously from the 1920s to the 1930s (Table 4), since great numbers of small electric lamp manufacturers joined the market one after another. In another change of circumstances, the original technology of the electric lamp had become obsolete. We can see this in the fact that an extension of the gas-filled lamp patent was not granted in 1932. This also affected the decline of the market share of Tokyo Denki.

From the latter half of the 1920s on, especially from 1932, small lamp producers rapidly increased their exports all over the world, which caused such troubles as a suit against the infringement of patents, the rise of customs duties, and import restrictions. The small Japanese lamp manufacturers grew to be influential outsiders for the international incandescent lamp cartel (Phoebus). But Phoebus was not able to stop the advance of the small Japanese manufacturers. Finally, import restrictions, like the civil agreement about electric lamps between Japan and the United Kingdom in 1934, were adopted to check the advance of the Japanese electric lamp industry.

The Japanese government urged small manufacturers to form an association to control exports in view of the difficulties caused by the spread of import restrictions. Under its administrative guidance, the Japanese Electric Lamp & Allied Manufacturers Association, Nihon Denkyū Kōgyō Kumiai Rengōkai, was established in October 1933. Tokyo Denki became a member of it in November 1934, and then an agreement between the Allied Association and Tokyo Denki was made for the purpose of controlling the domestic market. But the agreement did not work immediately because it was necessary to organize a joint selling company and the outsiders were still there.

According to a letter from the embassy in Berlin to the Japanese Ministry of Foreign Affairs dated November 14, 1935, the international incandescent lamp cartel invited the Japanese Allied Association to join it.[21] The Ministry of Foreign Affairs conveyed the gist of this letter to the Ministry of Commerce and Industry on December 9, 1935. Phoebus offered the invitation again in February 1936, this time through the embassy in London. But the response of the Japanese government was delayed. The letters dated June 6 and September 4, 1936, from the embassy in London to the Ministry of Foreign Affairs said that the representative of Phoebus had explained some advantages of the cartel and requested a reply. On September 25, 1936, the consul of the Japanese embassy notified the representative of Phoebus that the Allied Association could not become a member of Phoebus immediately. The reasons were as follows:

(1) The Japanese government and electric lamp manufacturers had been making efforts to establish an organization for the control of exports and the domestic market. However, the trouble was that the organization for sales control was not set up on account of opposition between the manufacturers' association and the export association.

(2) The smaller Japanese producers were anxious that after joining Phoebus they might be oppressed as newcomers.

(3) It was doubtful that the international cartel would be effective, since Russian and American manufacturers were not members.

At that time the representative of Phoebus was understanding; he was sympathetic toward Japan's indecisiveness about immediate participation in Phoebus. He suggested that Phoebus would concede several territorries, such as the South Sea Islands, Latin America, parts of the British Empire, etc., to the Japanese manufacturers, or permit them to manufacture certain kinds of lamps to export. And furthermore he explained that Phoebus was currently in contact with Russia and that Phoebus had been closely associated with American manufacturers from the start. Phoebus did not choose a policy that would exclude Japanese producers by means of patents; it adopted another strategy: to compromise with them and extend the areas of Phoebus.

In spite of the fairly generous concession made by Phoebus, Japanese manufacturers did not agree to the proposal. This is because the Allied Association consisted of many small producers who could control neither exports nor the domestic market. It was difficult for the Japanese electric lamp industry to cooperate with the international cartel because of the lack of domestic cartel control. Only import restrictions were able to limit the Japanese electric lamp industry, which grew into a formidable outsider in East Asia.

IV. Conclusion

This paper has discussed the effects of international agreements on Japanese electrical machinery manufacturers and their markets. The effects of the international agreements have two sides: the division of market and the technical tie-up.

First, the market division of the international agreements had scarcely anything to do with the Japanese manufacturers. The agreements—for example, the GE-AEG agreement in 1903—did not refer to Japan directly. Japanese producers or their domestic cartel had not been affiliated with the international agreements except for the participation of Tokyo Denki in Phoebus. This was because the Japanese producers were limited in the domestic market, as far as the heavy electrical machinery industry was concerned. As for the electric lamp industry, though the smaller electric lamp manufacturers made their way into the foreign market, an agreement between the Japanese producers and Phoebus was not realized because the domestic cartel, the Japanese Electric Lamp & Allied Manufacturers Association, lacked the capacity to control the domestic market. In both cases, the Japanese producers did not have direct relations with the international cartels.

Second, the international agreements were effective in the field of technology transfer from foreign manufacturers to Japanese manufacturers. In the heavy electrical machinery industry, technology transfer through technical tie-ups and plant investment enlarged production capacity, which led to excessive competition. The competition expanded the domestic market through price reduction and the import decrease. Moreover, the expanding demand was a stimulus to the introduction of foreign technology. There was a feedback between technology transfer and competition, typically seen in the 1920s. On the other hand, in the case of the electric lamp industry, the technical tie-up with foreign manufacturers contributed to the monopolistic market structure. But with the spread of electric lamp technology, the smaller producers grew remarkably. It became difficult to control not only the exports but also the domestic market. Therefore, the international cartel could not stop the advance of the small Japanese manufacturers. Regarding the two cases, the heavy electrical machinery industry and the electric lamp industry, international agreements were more effective in intensifying competition rather than suppressing it in the domestic market.

Finally, whether the international agreements intensify competition or suppress it depends on the entrepreneurial activities of Japanese producers. The stimulators of competition were not only the Japanese producers affiliated with foreign companies, but also other unaffiliated Japanese producers who expanded their plant investment and activities.[22] Technology transfer became more active due to the positive attitude of the Japanese producers, such as Hitachi Seisakusho, the small electric lamp manufacturers, and others. The Japanese electrical machinery industry, which was still enclosed in the domestic market, had grown up to be a virtual outsider with great potential to launch into the world market in the near future.

NOTES

1. The agreement is included in "Ōkura Shōji Shiryō" (Historical Materials of Ōkura Trading Co.), in the Tokyo Keizai University collection. Later quotations from the agreement are taken from this source.

2. Mitsui Bussan, "Dai 2 Kai Shitenchō Shimonkaigi Gijiroku" (The 2nd Advisory Meeting of Branch Managers), 1913.

3. Takenaka Tōru, "Dai-ichiji Taisenzen ni okeru Siemens-sha no Tainichi Gyōseki" (Geshäftsergebnisse des Japangeschäfts von Siemens vor dem Ersten Weltkrieg), *Proceedings of the Faculty of Letters of Tōkai University*, no. 49 (1988): 107.

4. Federal Trade Commission, *Supply of Electrical Equipment and Competitive Conditions* (Washington, D.C., 1928), pp. 139–44.

5. See Hasegawa Shin, "1920 Nendai no Denkikikai Shijō" (The Japanese Electrical Equipment Market in the 1920s), *Shakai Keizai Shigaku*, vol. 45, no. 4.

6. Ministry of Finance, *Shōwa 2 nen Gaikoku Bōeki Gairan* (Annual Report on Foreign Trade), 1920, p. 300.

7. Mitsubishi Denki, *Kengyō Kaiko* (History and Memoirs of Mitsubishi Denki) (Tokyo, 1951), pp. 64–67.

8. Fuji Denki, *Fuji Denki Shashi* (History of Fuji Denki) (1957), pp. 4–7.

9. In the memorandum, Siemens was a general term for Siemens-Schuckertwerke, Siemens & Halske & Co., and Siemens Schuckert Denki Kabushiki Kaisha.

10. Ōtaguro Jūgorō, *Omoide o Kataru* (Memoirs of Ōtaguro), 1936, pp. 261–63.

11. See Hasegawa Shin, "The Electrical Equipment Industry in the 1920s," *Rekishigaku Kenkyū* (Journal of Historical Studies), no. 486 (1980); and idem., "The Development of Yasukawa Electric Co. and Its Entrepreneurial Activities," *Japanese Yearbook on Business History 1987* (Tokyo, 1987).

12. "Furukawa-kanbu to Siemens-sha Köttgen Hakase to Ikenkōkan Yōryōsho" (A Summary of the Views Exchanged between Furukawa and Siemens), dated November 11, 1929.

13. Federal Trade Commission, *Report of the Federal Trade Commission on International Electrical Equipment Cartels* (Washington, D.C., 1948), pp. 3–5.

14. Hitachi Seisakusho, *Hitachi Seisakushoshi* (History of Hitachi Seisakusho, Ltd.), 1949, pp. 217–20.

15. See Hasegawa Shin, "Jūdenki Cartel (Satsukikai)" (Heavy Electrical Machinery Cartel), in Hashimoto Jurō and Takeda Haruhito (eds.), *Ryōtaisenkanki Nihon no Cartel* (Japan's Cartels in the Interwar Period) (Tokyo, 1985).

16. *Hitachi Seisakusho Shashi Shiryō* (Historical Materials of Hitachi Seisakusho).

17. "Ōkura Shōji Shiryō," op. cit.

18. Tokyo Denki, *Tokyo Denki 50 Nenshi* (50-year History of Tokyo Denki), 1940, p. 139.

19. *Toshiba Shashi Hensan Shiryō* (Historical Materials of Tokyo Shibaura Denki).

20. Nihon Denkyū Kōgyōkai (Japan Electric Lamp Manufacturers Association), *Nihon Denkyū Kōgyōshi* (History of the Japanese Electric Lamp Industry), 1963.

21. "Kokusai Cartel Kankei-zakken" (Miscellaneous Matters Regarding the International Cartel) in the Archives of the Ministry of Foreign Affairs.

22. See Hasegawa, op. cit. (1987).

Comment

Namiko Harumi

When international relations in the electrical machinery industry during the interwar period are discussed, two major countries, the United States and Germany, are generally focused on, and Japan is considered as a marginal player in the easternmost part of Asia. However, Professor Hasegawa has presented an interesting analysis of the international relationships of Japan. He says that from the 1920s through the 1930s, the Japanese electrical machinery industry had grown to be a virtual outsider with great potential to launch into the world market in the near future. How was it possible for Japan to realize such growth when major firms in the developed countries led by GE of the United States had oligopolistic control in the world market through international agreements and cartels? Yet major Japanese firms also made some international agreements in those days. What role did these agreements play in those circumstances? These are the most important issues in Hasegawa's paper. They can be divided into three points.

(1) The international agreements were effective for technology transfers from foreign to Japanese manufacturers.

(2) The technology transfers made through technical tie-ups and plant investments brought about the rapid growth and the feedback between technology transfer and competition in the Japanese electrical machinery industry.

(3) International agreements helped to step up competition in the domestic market.

There are two questions about the first point. First, what kind of agreement was most effective for technology transfers? When a company grants a license to another company, it usually gets royalties and offers its technology with the intention of monopolizing the technology and market. The agreements made between Shibaura Manufacturing Co. and GE before World War I were of this kind. It seems that agreements made after the 1920s were, on the contrary, preferably for technology transfers. I would like to pursue this aspect in more detail. Second, how did the

Japanese persuade foreign firms to enter into agreements that would improve their counterparts' technological ability and intensify competition? Hasegawa pointed out that the competition among the foreign manufacturers was as intense as that among Japanese manufacturers, in terms of seeking technical tie-ups. Such circumstances seem unique to Japan. Am I right if I think that such attitudes of foreign firms had a great influence on the negotiating process and the contents of the agreements?

Next I would like to ask about the second point. Under what conditions and to what extent did the introduced technology influence the feedback between technology transfer and competition? Hasegawa pointed out that in the heavy electrical machinery industry in the 1920s, Hitachi Manufacturing Co., which made it its motto to resort to only domestic technology, boasted that its own technology was comparable to that of Shibaura Manufacturing Co., which had a technical affiliation with GE. He also pointed out that in the electric lamp manufacturing industry, a technological monopoly of Tokyo Electric Co., which had a technical affiliation with GE, was broken by domestic small and medium-sized manufacturers. Such cases seem to be unique to Japan. What was the relationship between those cases and "the effects of international agreements on technical transfers"?

Finally, I would like to refer to the relationship between the international cartels and Japan, relating to the third point. Naturally, it was of no use for the Japanese heavy electrical machinery industry to join an international cartel since it did not have the ability to export. Additionally, it was natural for the Japanese Electric Lamp & Allied Manufacturers Association to decline to join the international incandescent lamp cartel (Phoebus) as it would be at a disadvantage as a newcomer.

On the other hand, why could the international cartels not include Japan as one of the objects of their restrictions? As far as the world market of heavy electrical machinery industry was concerned, Asia and Japan were not part of the exclusive territory in the United States–Germany Agreement for market division made after World War I. Moreover, in the INCA, which was intended for the nonexclusive territory, Japan was also excluded from the territory, although Asia was included. It is interesting that the prospective Japanese market had been a free market for other countries since before World War I.

Response

Shin Hasegawa

Professor Harumi made three main points in her comments. I shall make clear my position on these points. First, let us briefly examine the case of the tie-up of Shibaura with GE in 1909. Shibaura assigned 24% of its shares to GE, but the management right was not shared; it belonged to Japanese executives of Shibaura and Mitsui Gōmei (the holding company of Mitsui zaibatsu). Shibaura could use GE's patents and inventions. Actually they dispatched engineers to GE to acquire know-how and designs. Shibaura paid the royalty, 1% of sales value, and this rate was not very high. It means GE's objective was the extension of GE's influence in the Japanese market rather than the gain of patent fees. The foreign manufacturers, such as GE, WH, SSW, and AEG, were under the necessity of tying up with Japanese producers in order to compete with each other. This is why the Japanese producers could make the agreements for the technology transfer to their own advantage.

Second, it is difficult to estimate exactly the degree of the contribution of technology transfer to the technical progress of Japanese manufacturers. But in the case of Mitsubishi Denki and Fuji Denki, the late starters, they could not have acquired their production system in the latter half of the 1920s without foreign technical assistance. The facts show the importance of technology transfer. In addition, Japanese producers like Hitachi Seisakusho that did not tie up with foreign firms played an important role in promoting the technology transfer. The competition among Japanese producers accelerated the technology transfer from foreign manufacturers; in other words, feedback between technology transfer and competition began in the 1920s.

Third, the reason the international cartel did not include the Japanese market directly should be explained by the foreign manufacturers' strategy. In industrializing nations like Japan, foreign firms, such as GE, WH, SSW, and AEG, preferred direct investment so as to maintain their influence. When this led to the formation of plural joint ventures, the foreign firms tended to promote the formation of the domestic cartels and left the control of the domestic market to those joint firms. It was difficult and not necessary for the foreign manufacturers to control the Japanese market directly.

The Power Equipment Cartels: The International Agreement and the Italian Case in the 1930s

Renato Giannetti

I. Introduction

The theme of cartelization is obviously only a part of the analysis of market behavior. The characters of the products involved and the phases of their development are also very important. A cartel in raw materials or in the monoproduct sectors is different from a cartel in multiproduct industries; analogously, collusive behavior in new products is different from collusive behavior in mature products.

According to this we shall briefly describe the "technological and market trajectory" of the heavy electrical equipment industry from the 1880s to the 1930s, which favored the rise and consolidation of an early international oligopoly. Then we shall describe the origins of the international heavy electrical equipment cartel in 1930, which was primarily a defensive cartel formed to face a strong decrease of international demand and to prevent disruptive competition on prices. Finally, we shall describe the origins of a national cartel, the ANIEM (Accordo Nazionale Imprese Elettro-Meccaniche) agreement in Italy, which was at the crossroads of the international big concerns and the smaller Italian firms.

II. The Rise and Growth of an International Market for Heavy Electrical Equipment from the 1880s to 1914

1. The First Phase (1880–1900)

In this phase there was prevalently a struggle between enterprises at the national level. It was the phase of the early standardization of systems (e.g., the battle of the systems between a.c. and d.c.) in the United States and Germany, which were technological leaders and also large markets. In these countries a national oligopolistic structure of the sector emerged, characterized by a few big enterprises that extended their influence abroad in the second phase. They were General Electric and Westinghouse in the United States, AEG and Siemens in Germany, and Brown Boveri in Switzerland.[1]

TABLE 1 Foreign and National Electrical Machinery in Italy (a.c., d.c.), 1898–1908 (%)

	1898				
	d.c.	Monophase	Biphase	Triphase	Total
Italian	35	8	42	4	23
Foreign	65	92	58	96	77
Total	57	15	2	26	
	1908				
Italian	29	56	63	30	30
Foreign	71	44	37	70	70
Total	17	2		81	

Source: Ministry of Agriculture, Industry and Commerce, *Notizie statistiche sugli impianti elettrici esistenti in Italia alla fine del 1908 e cenni sulle industrie elettriche in Italia a tutto il 1911* (Rome, 1911).

In Italy, the presence of foreign enterprises prevailed already before the turn of the century. Two surveys carried out by the Ministry of Agriculture, Industry, and Commerce, in 1898 and in 1908, showed a quota of foreign-made generators of around 70% (see Table 1). The domestic manufacturers, Tecnomasio-Cabella, Officine di Savigliano, Officine Morelli, Franco e Bonamico, Guzzi, etc., equipped the small plants, which were widely diffused in Italy. The presence, among the leading four enterprises in the sector, of AEG Thomson-Houston and Brown Boveri (with its affiliate Tecnomasio) from 1904 and of Westinghouse from 1908 is further proof of this situation (see Table 2). The national industry was more successful in mechanical areas, like the production of hydraulic turbines by Officine Riva (1885), Officine Riunite Italiane (1892), and Officine Calzoni e Parenti (1885).

2. The Second Phase (1900–1914)
In this phase, the big enterprises began to extend their influence to foreign countries. The advancements in the field of long-distance transmission and the standardization of parts militated against the expansion of big enterprises, which entered the markets of many European and South American countries at local enterprises' expense. In Italy, Brown Boveri established its subsidiary in 1903, AEG Thomson-Houston in 1904, and Westinghouse in 1908. Through this strategy of direct investment, the multinational companies got a more effective control over foreign markets, especially in respect to licensing of technology by foreign enterprises.[2] The

TABLE 2 The Four Leading Enterprises (1904–36)

Year	Enterprises	Capital (thousands of current lire)
1904	AEG Thomson-Houston	4,500
	Nazionale delle Officine di Savigliano	2,500
	Tecnomasio italiano Brown Boveri	1,580
1908	AEG Thomson-Houston	9,000
	Tecnomasio Italiano Brown Boveri	6,000
	Società elettrotecnica Galileo Ferraris (Westinghouse)	6,000
	Officine meccaniche Stigler	5,000
1912	Società elettrotecnica Galileo Ferraris (Westinghouse)	9,000
	Nazionale delle Officine de Savigliano	6,000
	Tecnomasio Italiano Brown Boveri	6,000
	Officine meccaniche Stigler	5,000
1916	Nazionale delle Officine di Savigliano	6,000
	Tecnomasio Italiano Brown Boveri	6,000
	Officine meccaniche Stigler	5,000
	Officine Elettroferroviarie Tallero	3,000
1920	Officine Galileo	30,000
	Nazionale delle Officine di Savigliano	20,000
	Ercole Marelli & C.	15,000
	Società italiano dei forni elettrici	14,000
1924	Tecnomasio Italiano Brown Boveri	45,930
	Compagnia Generale di Elettricità (General Electric)	40,000
	Ercole Marelli & C.	30,000
	Compagnia Nazionale delle officine di Savigliano	30,000
1928	Tecnomasio Italiano Brown Boveri	60,000
	Cemsa	40,000
	Compagnia Generale di elettricità (General Electric)	40,000
	Ercole Marelli & C.	30,000
1932	Ercole Marelli & C.	60,000
	Tecnomasio Italiano Brown Boveri	60,000
	Compagnia Generale di elettricità (General Electric)	40,000
	Ing. V. Tedeschi & C.	40,000
1936	Compagnia Generale di elettricità (General Electric)	64,000
	Tecnomasio Italiano Brown Boveri	60,000
	Officine Galileo	53,000
	Ercole Marelli & C.	51,000

Source: Renato Giannetti, *Tecnologia, imprese mercati: l'industria elettromeccanica italiana (1883–1940)* (Florence, 1991).

division of labor between the parent company and its foreign subsidiaries aimed, on the one hand, to retain sophisticated technology in the home country, and, on the other, to achieve a better utilization of the parent company's production facilities. At the beginning, foreign subsidiaries only assembled imported parts and components; afterwards, the electric parts of transformers and switchgears were imported by the parent company, while mechanical parts were manufactured locally by Italian enterprises such as Unione Elettrotecnica.

Several initiatives to promote integration in electrical equipment were undertaken also at the technical level. An international committee began in 1904 to promote a more rapid standardization of units of measurement, rules of operations of plants, transmission and distribution, etc.[3] Two "technological styles" of standardization emerged: the first one defined only some general rules of performance, letting the different enterprises define the technical rules to build and run electrical machinery; the other, on the contrary, specified very detailed rules. Only German enterprises adopted the latter approach, while other enterprises limited themselves to setting guidelines of performance, as the early international organizations even did. An oligopolistic struggle began to emerge among the major enterprises that tried to extend their standards to foreign countries in order to control the market. In Italy, a struggle between American, Swiss, and German standards emerged, especially in the field of electric traction, where Swiss-German triphase a.c. standard prevailed over American d.c. standard.

III. The Penetration and the Defense of Foreign Markets

1. The First Phase (1900–1918): Financing Utilities and Direct Investment
At the very beginning of the sector, in the 1880s, many countries developed local capabilities. The rapidly changing technology and the low level of standardization in the construction of parts and components favored the existence of many small firms. With the relative stabilization of the electric system around the end of the century, competition at the national level reduced the number of enterprises and, finally, the penetration into foreign markets began.

Some countries tried to react to this foreign penetration. Generally, they had as much expertise in the field of electricity as Italy had, and sometimes they even had a favorable environment. Italy and Sweden, for example, relied prevalently on hydroelectrically generated power that required control and a promoting role by the state. This role could be exercised in many ways. We shall limit ourselves to underline two points in order to explain why Italy, unlike Sweden, missed this opportunity.[4]

The first point was a legal organization of the exploitation of rivers that could promote a coordinated exploitation of water resources. Between 1884 and 1904, a large body of legislation on the concession and procedure of derivation of water was established, but Italian legislation was not able to establish efficient forms of coordinating between electrical and agricultural uses.[5]

The second one was the capital formation and the role of the state in promoting power companies through different institutional and financial arrangements: enforcing standards, direct financing of plants, etc. The Italian state had largely financed the building of dams to regulate river flows already at the turn of the 19th century but was not able to improve the coordination of the exploitation of these dams. As to the enforcing of standards, a prerequisite to establish a national electromechanical industry, the state attempted it only in the field of electric traction of the nationalized railway system, but this too failed because it established "a wrong standard"—the a.c. triphase, which insulated the Italian railway network from the successful technology, and the d.c., up to the end of the 1920s.[6]

2. The Rise of National "Electrical Systems" (1918–30) and the Consolidation of International Trusts

In this phase, the technology of the electrotechnical industry began to be relatively established. New problems arose in the field of the transmission and distribution of a growing volume of electricity at long distances and were a strong impulse for an increase of the cumulativity and appropriability of technical change. For example, large laboratories to test the electric machinery were built in order to solve some problems arising from the stability of machinery in large systems, especially switchgears. Only few large firms were able to build them, such as Siemens and General Electric. At the same time, technical change multiplied the range of products, and the capability to exploit commercially these technical advances became more and more important. The "building of networks" was the critical point of this phase. It greatly enlarged the demand for electric energy, but at the same time required more complex skills to manage simultaneously the problems of the consumers and of the network. Consumers wanted a much greater reliable supply, which was very difficult to obtain with the new, unexpected problems of stability arising from the higher voltage of transmission and the growing variability of load.

The big multinational enterprises reinforced their technological leadership, increasing their foreign penetration, but a big reshuffling of the leadership also occurred, due to the effects of the First World War. In electrical machinery, for example, the German share decreased from 38.5% in 1913 to 15.7% in 1925, while the U.S. share grew from 16.5% to 23.7% and Great Britain's from 27.6% to 35.3%.

Cooperation among international enterprises also increased. For example, a survey of the British Electrical and Allied Manufacturers Association (BEAMA) in 1927[7] pointed out that both Siemens-Schuckert and AEG were linked up with American firms for the interchange of manufacturing, research, and patent information—Siemens and Schuckert with Westinghouse, AEG with General Electric—while the same report suggested a possible association between AEG and Brown Boveri.

The reduction of German firms' share of total production immediately after World War I permitted some national electromechanical firms to exploit this temporary situation to build up a national system and electromechanical enterprises to furnish the equipment. Figures of the League of Nations show an increase in the foreign exports of France from 2% to 4.4.% but, more significantly, of Sweden, which grew from 3% to 7.1%. Italy, on the other hand, stagnated from 1.2% in 1913 to 1.3% in 1925 (see Table 3).

One of the main causes of this failure of the Italian electromechanical industry was the persisting fragmentation and diversity of demand. The Italian network grew around eleven private regional groups (Società

TABLE 3 Share of Various Countries in Exports of Electrical Machinery

| | 1913 | | | 1925 |
	Reichsmark 1000	%	Reichsmark 1000	%
Germany	64,400	38.5	51,803	15.7
France	3,334	2	14,627	4.4
Belgium		0	2,202	0.6
U.K.	46,296	27.6	116,966	35.3
Italy	2,012	1.2	4,466	1.3
Netherlands			4,827	1.5
Switzerland	16,485	9.8	22,742	6.9
Austria[a]	1,264	0.8	7,909	2.4
Sweden	5,051	3	23,654	7.1
U.S.A.	27,598	16.5	78,506	23.7
Japan	987	0.6	3,667	1.1
Total	167,427	100	331,369	100

Source: League of Nations, International Economic Conference, Geneva, May 1927, *Documentation on Electrical Industry*, Feb. 7, 1927.
[a]Austrian figures are at 1913 boundaries.

Idroelletrica Piemontese, or SIP, previously Alta Italia, Piemontese di elettricità e Piemonte Centrale di elettricità, Edison, Adamello, Adriatica, Unione Esercizi Elettrici, Tridentina, Trentino, Elettricità e Gas di Roma, Ligure-Toscana e Valdarno, and Meridionale di elettricità) that were able to attain financial independence from international concerns. However, in order to maintain this independence they never integrated vertically with electromechanical producers. For example, Edison, the most important electric utility from the turn of the century, bought its machinery from TIBB (the Italian affiliate of Brown Boveri) and AEG[8] and later from Compagnia Generale di Elettricità (CGE, the Italian affiliate of International General Electric), too, in order to diversify its suppliers. This strategy helped Edison to realize independence as an electrical utility, but damaged the chances of establishing of a national network, which, at that time, was everywhere, and especially in small countries, a prerequisite to building up a national electromechanical sector. The various regional systems operated in different ways; e.g., in the 1920s, 50 Mhz was not the standard frequency of operation of the "Italian systems." This prevented them from obtaining the advantages derived from static economies of scale, as in the case of turbine-generators, where large economies, particularly in machining blades and casting, were realized in large-scale plants during the 1920s. They were not able even to enjoy the advantages deriving from integration. For example, the small Italian firms producing transformers generally bought laminations from steel suppliers, but this was never as satisfactory as being able to produce them in-house as and when they were required.

The lack of adequate investment in R&D is a more important factor of backwardness. The point is that the Italian enterprises not only did not invest in basic advancement of equipment as the international concerns did—probably Italian enterprises would not have been able to develop laboratories to test large prototypes of transformers and switchgears, for they lacked the accumulated skills and adequate financial capabilities—but they also failed to undertake research and development in the field of low-cost designs and efficient manufacturing techniques. Finally, a central issue was the strategic behavior of governments interacting with the behavior of the firms. The building up of a national network is again a good example. As we said above, this was the strategic choice to enlarge and unify the market for electrical machinery. This option was strongly debated in Italy in the early 1920s, but what resulted from this was a lot of uncoordinated measures—subsidies, tariff protection, etc.—that showed primarily the working of outstanding lobbying skills.[9]

IV. The International Power Equipment Cartel of 1931:
A Defensive Cartel

The power equipment cartel was one of the last cartels to be established in the rush of cartelization of the late twenties.[10] It came after a period of turmoil in international markets. Almost everywhere in the more advanced countries the network was already built up during the 1920s, and there was an overcapacity in the sector. The competition among international producers grew as they sought to enlarge their share at the expense of other producers. General Electric, for example, tried to massively enter the European market in 1929, but the European producers opposed this initiative successfully. In order to avoid disruptive competition, American and some European enterprises met to negotiate an international electric equipment cartel agreement, limited, for the most part, to those regions and markets of the world that were not already covered by contracts for patent and licensing and exchange of manufacturing know-how.

As we said above, agreements on international competition were introduced from the early 1920s in licensing agreements that carried the obligation not to sell in markets where there was another manufacturer using the same patents or license. Consequently, international competition was minimal. With the exhaustion of the great rush of "systems" construction and the severe restriction on business with the crisis of 1929, international enterprises wished to extend their agreement to the countries not yet covered by a license agreement, as the International Notification and Compensation Agreement (INCA) clearly stated.[11] The territories covered were all countries excluding Europe; the territories of the USSR; the United States of America and its possessions and dependencies; Canada and Newfoundland; Turkey; the Empire of Japan, including its colonies and mandated and leased territories and the South Manchurian Railway zone; French colonies, protectorates, and mandated territories; Spanish colonies; and any of the countries included in this agreement if the apparatus were to be ordered from German members on the reparations account.

On December 13, 1931, in the Paris office of General Electric, eight companies joined INCA, which was an omnibus agreement, i.e., included both notification and compensation rules. These companies were: the German AEG and Siemens; the British Thomson-Houston, English Electric, GEC, and Metropolitan Vickers; the American International General Electric and Westinghouse Electric International. In May 1932, the leading Swedish firm (ASEA) joined the cartel, and, in 1933, even the leading Swiss firm (Brown Boveri) joined the agreement.

They agreed to notify the association secretary of all inquiries for 15 classes of electrical and auxiliary apparatus in countries outside Western Europe, the USSR, Canada, the United States, Japan, and French and Spanish colonies. The secretary would determine whose turn it was to take the order and the price that the winner was to bid. All other members bid above this price. The winner of an award was required to pay into a compensation fund held by the secretariat itself. The payment was designed to help defray the costs of preparing tenders by the losers. This fund was to ensure the competitive power of all the members of the cartel.

The procedures for obtaining a bid were minutely described and included four phases: notification, submission of tenders, report of orders, compensation.

Notification. Every member was required, upon receipt of an enquiry, to notify immediately the secretary of the agreement, and the secretary was required to advise immediately by means of an advice card all members who had been similarly notified. Only the members who received advice cards with reference to an inquiry submitted notification forms with reference to the same project. This practice confined the competition to those members who obtained information concerning the project from their own outside sources, giving them an opportunity to get together to discuss the project, to agree among themselves as to which members should be permitted to obtain the order, and to agree among themselves as to what quotation they, respectively, would make.

Submission of Tenders. The agreements stated that no tender for the plant coming within the scope of the agreement should be submitted by a member unless and until he has submitted a notification to the secretary and until he has received an advice. The only members to receive advice cards relative to a particular project were those who submitted notifications with reference to it and, further, that not even the member first notifying might submit a tender until after receiving an advice card with reference to his own notification.

Report of Orders. The agreement stated that every member will immediately, on receipt of any order coming within the scope of the agreement, report to the secretary that he is in receipt of such order; the secretary will notify all tendering members of the name of the successful tender and the number and size of each plant ordered. The member would also be advised that the order under a particular transaction had been placed with a nonmember.

Compensation. The agreement defined for each class the rate of compensation or a mathematical formula to be applied in the computation of the amount of compensation to be paid by the successful tenderer. The administration fund's portion of each compensation was to be 5%.

The agreement provided for the creation of a deposit fund that was to be formed by payments out of (a) compensation payments made by members; (b) fines or penalties imposed upon and paid by members for violations of the agreement; and (c) such other sums of money as may be unanimously agreed upon by the members. The fund was to be the property of the members equally, and it could be used for a variety of purposes: e.g., it could be used to support cutthroat competition against a non-member competitor in any of the territories coming within the scope of operation of the agreement. The fund remaining after withdrawal of a member could be used also to support competitive warfare against that former member.

The main point that has to be underlined is that the agreement did not include a specific price agreement among the parties to the agreement. This exclusion was due to the severe antimonopolistic legislation of the United States that regulated the domestic market. Anyway, the purpose of a cartel was to regulate shares and prices, and a way to establish price indirectly was clearly included in the agreement through the very detailed procedures for notification arrangement. Through them each interested member could ascertain the identity of the potential competitors and get together to agree on the division of total business in each class of apparatus. The *Report on International Electrical Equipment Cartels* by the Federal Trade Commission relates an example of how this agreement worked by an actual case in which General Electric and Westinghouse allocated business between themselves and agreed both as to the prices at which the successful tenderer was to be permitted to obtain the contracts and as to the prices the unsuccessful tenderer was to be permitted to quote.

An obvious difficulty of this kind of arrangement is the extension of this way of allocating business. If two or more notifying members would agree among themselves on prices, terms of payment, and conditions of the contract, any member who subsequently would notify the same enquiry could be obliged to adhere to the arrangement under the same conditions. This practice was mildly contested by German and Swiss members who were generally farther than American members from the territories of the agreement. On the other hand, the German enterprises too could rely on the clause of the exclusion from the agreement of the orders on reparations account, which allowed some orders in Mexico, Brazil, Argentina, etc., to be placed by Germans on their reparations account.

The original INCA was to expire on December 31, 1932, but it was extended practically automatically. With the extension, however, the form of organization was changed without any change in the basic method of operation. The omnibus agreement was replaced by two separate agreements, i.e., a notification agreement and a compensation agreement. The association was divided into sections, each having a separate notification agreement, and each participating concern was a member of as many different associations and signer of as many different agreements as it saw fit. On May 26, 1936, an International Electrical Association integrated the INCA agreement. The operation of this agreement is beyond the scope of this paper. Anyway, this association grew up after a long period of stagnation that, according to the minutes of association, did not prevent a steep fall of prices and growing competition among the members of the original agreement; for this reason this body was more strongly devoted to establishing explicit compulsory price-maintenance and quotas. The problem was that German and Swiss producers had an aggressive policy of penetration in markets covered and excluded by the original agreement, essentially lowering the prices of goods. The other members of the agreement, especially the American and British firms, could not sustain this competition on prices and proposed an explicit agreement on greater quotas for the Germans in exchange for raising price levels. German and Swiss members were very wary of this proposal and, according to the Federal Trade Commission report, these arrangements developed very slowly.

V. The Italian Cartel Agreement

This policy of international market regulation was accompanied by agreements also on national markets. In Italy, for example, on April 1, 1931, an agreement called ANIEM was signed by five companies—CGE, TIBB, Ercole Marelli, Ansaldo, and San Giorgio—to divide the national market and to halve the lowering of prices.[12] This agreement had been preceded by an outline of the agreement signed on November 5, 1929.[13] The agreement regulated the production and sale of electrical machinery and of transformers according to an accurate classification and according to a more detailed description included in the General Rules.

The Italian agreement was essentially established to fix the prices. The agreement distinguished between small and heavy machinery. Only the first type of machinery had really established prices. Nevertheless, no detailed procedures were established in order to fix them. The agreement said only that they would be fixed by common consent. The other rules regulating the cartel were very similar to those of the international cartel, but they were much less detailed. For example, it did not distinguish between inquiry or order from customers, at least for small machinery.

Notification. Every member was required, upon receipt of an order or inquiry from a purchaser, to notify the secretary. The enterprise inquired could also ask for protection and propose the date of discussion. The secretary was responsible for the protection.

Submission of Tenders. Each member of the agreement had to tender according to the general supply conditions established periodically by a special commission, pointing out the name of the purchaser, the date of inquiry, and a very detailed description of the machinery requested both in weights and prices. The secretary had to control all the tenders submitted verifying that they were conformable to the official list or to the specific resolution of the secretary. Any difference had to be pointed out. Finally, the secretary had to inform the other members of the agreement of the tenders that he had received.

The General Rules included also a part on the negotiations following the notification or the submission of tenders. This was intended to limit competition on prices and/or on the conditions of supply among the members of the agreement. This part also included an item on the rules that had to be followed to compete with a firm outside the agreement. This stated that, in such cases, the tenderer had to inform the secretary in order to accept onerous conditions of supply, and in exchange receive compensation from all the parties to the agreement.

Report. For any order placed with a member, the member had to proceed to advise the secretary on the prices, conditions, etc., and on the eventual transfer of the order to other competitors. The secretary had to advise the other tenderers of this order. Finally, the tenderer had to let the secretary view the original drawings and visit the construction plant of the machinery in order to ascertain that the submitted contractual conditions were regularly fulfilled.

As we have said above, the Italian agreement, unlike the international one, included price and quota conditions.

Prices. The agreement was very mild about the price, which could move up and down referring to a reference price, the level of which had a generic fixing procedure. The price had to be fixed periodically with reference to market conditions and especially to the behavior of firms outside the agreement.

The second class of equipment covered by the agreement included heavy machinery. Members who received inquiries from a purchaser had to immediately notify the secretary, who would call a meeting to establish the tenderer and the price of supply. Members could not tender a bid to the purchaser before this meeting.

Quotas. The secretary had to collect, each month, a list of the orders received and proceed to determine the eventual surplus or deficit in respect of the fixed quota. The compensation quota amounted to 25%. Of this, 10% was assigned to the firm in deficit, and the remainder had to be subdivided among all the members according to their stated quota.

Generally speaking, the Italian cartel was less formal than the international one. For example, it provided for a special meeting of members to establish at any time the price of the heavy equipment to be tendered; or for very rough procedures of compensation for surplus or deficit firms; or for the establishment of quotas. Primarily, this was due to the relatively small dimension of the Italian demand in this period, which favored informal collusive agreement. But probably this was also a way by which the smaller firms of the agreement could exercise a major role. This was a recurring point of disagreement among the members of the cartel. For example, the affiliates of the international concerns, CGE and Tecnomasio, favored on many occasions a more formal way to determine quotas or a more accurate formula to revise prices according to the changes in costs of materials and of labor.[14] On the other hand, Marelli and Ansaldo opposed that, saying it was not suitable to let the members of the agreement know each other's costs. The high prices also favored the growth of the quota by smaller enterprises—S. Giorgio, and later Savigliano, Breda, and Cantieri Riuniti dell Adriatico (CRA)—that grew from 9% of the original agreement to 15%, in 1938. The major firms, CGE and TIBB, strongly opposed this effect, trying to fix their share at 15%.

This asymmetry in power and costs structure among firms obstructed, despite the existence of the cartel, the restructuring of the Italian electromechanical industry, which, in the 1930s, was still very fragmented. For example, the concentration ratio of enterprises (Herfindhal-Hirschman index and the four leading firms, referring to plants), in the period 1929–39, was 416 against 662 for 1906–39 (see Table 4).

Many attempts to build up joint ventures or to concentrate and rationalize production failed. For example, a joint venture between Siemens and Ansaldo in the field of high voltage failed at the end of the 1920s. A much more significant example comes from the prolonged attempt to build up a national electromechanical network of enterprises.[15] This attempt began in 1932 and involved firstly Ansaldo and CGE and, later, Ansaldo, CGE, and Marelli. The first tentative agreement was between International General Electric and Ansaldo. This proposed the

TABLE 4 Concentration Index (Herfindhal-Hirschman)

Year	Number of firms	Total capital (thousands of current lire)	HHI	Value of plants (thousands of current lire)	HHI
1904	3	8580	3939	4138	3735
1905	5	9916	3605	4336	2976
1906	10	19216	1667	7776	1734
1907	14	33687	1117	17933	995
1908	21	53822	867	29453	839
1909	23	59501	847	35361	840
1910	24	59516	842	31477	829
1911	24	62241	824	37807	876
1912	23	53577	833	44472	854
1913	26	59395	729	53858	818
1914	31	70316	567	61623	669
1915	34	70039	562	56080	631
1916	24	47951	690	41955	720
1917	17	52475	1017	31255	1007
1918	22	85401	892	40476	1103
1919	32	122634	612	58160	863
1920	41	222277	613	111310	730
1921	48	263164	670	154450	608
1922	62	326863	592	171870	579
1923	63	327256	586	171902	612
1924	70	375310	510	199323	512
1925	65	437001	493	238879	557
1926	72	467841	470	264665	543
1927	75	478510	479	271718	545
1928	82	510996	450	305301	484
1929	93	607725	413	356209	404
1930	93	672293	375	398634	379
1931	96	680325	368	423529	354
1932	91	663649	368	419402	364
1933	93	659209	372	427661	354
1934	91	655037	368	432466	398
1935	92	662492	351	500545	540
1936	98	746024	358	538371	488
1937	93	788229	379	730506	464
1938	96	881358	354	867222	428
1939	99	948747	361	942003	404

Source: Same as Table 2.

constitution of a new company, the Stabilimenti Elettrotecnici Riuniti, which would include Ansaldo Elettrotecnico and CGE plants. The agreement reserved to General Electric the supply of the electric components and to Ansaldo the supply of the mechanical parts of the equipment. General Electric would hold the majority of the new company.

In a first phase, Ansaldo Elettrotecnico refused to join the agreement, judging the evaluation of its share to be too low. Later, in 1934, when Ansaldo was part of Istituto per la Ricostruzione Industriale (IRI)—the newly formed holding company to manage the industrial shares of the German-type bank swept away by a financial crisis—it rejected the agreement in order to establish, in the new "nationalistic climate," a completely Italian electromechanical company. In 1934, International General Electric attempted to establish a new company with the same characteristics with Marelli, which was overcommitted, like many Italian enterprises at that time. These negotiations also failed, probably again because of the low evaluations of the Italian company made by GE. Later, IRI attempted to concentrate and rationalize the sector, which was in serious difficulties, proposing to establish a new company with the three companies involved. This agreement also failed because CGE refused to let the IRI hold the majority of the company. The strategic perspectives of IRI and International General Electric were radically different. IRI's strategy was to involve the Italian branch of the international concern to exploit its know-how in the field of electric components of electrical machinery and build up an integrated national enterprise, while General Electric considered the new company a way to reinforce its share in the Italian market.

VI. The Economics of Electromechanical Cartels in the 1930s

Following this exposition of the main features of the international and Italian cartels, we shall now discuss the economic effect of these cartels. Technically a cartel is formed when a group of independent firms join forces to make price or output decisions. The principal problems facing a cartel are reaching agreements, detecting deviations, deterring such deviations, and limiting entry by outsiders.

Reaching an Agreement. Sellers who recognize their mutual interdependence will have an incentive to cooperate as long as the profit that each can obtain acting jointly is higher than it would be acting independently. The asymmetries in product and cost are the main obstacle to reaching an agreement. Instead of agreeing on a single price or industry output, therefore, it becomes necessary to agree on a whole schedule of prices and output, thus multiplying the possible points of disagreement. The solution is to provide a list of prices for a prespecified product, but this can both obstruct technical change and favor cheating, changing only some characteristics of the product. One way to avoid this difficulty is to respond to one another's price announcements, which states a price through a series of iterations that involve no actual sales. This is the reason that electromechanical cartels adopted the "inquiry-notification-tender" method to share the market. Obviously, in the case of international cartels, this procedure was first adopted to overcome public regulation, which in the United States and in Great Britain forbade price and quota agreements, but this was not the case in Italy, where public regulation has never been adopted.

With cost heterogeneity, also, difficulties with the division of profits arise. If industry profit is maximized, marginal revenue is equated to each firm's marginal cost. When firms have different marginal cost curves, therefore, joint profit maximization requires that firms produce unequal output, earn unequal profit, and may even require that some firms close down altogether. The way to escape from this problem is to divide the market by market or geographically, as international cartel did, and distribute side payments, as both international and, more roughly, Italian cartels did. This involves complex bargaining problems, such as establishing quotas, as happened in Italy in a case that opposed the major firms, TIBB and CGE, to the minor ones that wanted to increase their share.[16]

These problems increase when uncertainty increases. Once uncertainty is introduced, agreements must be reached more often, thereby increasing negotiation costs. For example, the costs of administration of tenders and of the activity of the international secretary were very high; this latter absorbed 5% of the fund. In addition, divergence of opinion about future conditions becomes likely. Firms can disagree about costs, demand, and many other factors. This happened, for example, in the Italian case in 1935, when a disagreement arose on materials' price dynamics and on the way to provide for an indexing mechanism. Also, rapid technical change can hinder an agreement, but this was not the case for this sector, which was relatively mature in the 1930s.

Incentives to Cheat. Reaching an agreement is only the beginning of a cartel. When a collusive arrangement has been consummated, the mere facts that the price is above the noncooperative level and that the marginal revenue for a firm is greater than its marginal cost give the firm an incentive to cheat. The incentive to increase output or to cut the price in the case of a price-setting cartel is not the same for all firms in an industry or for all industries. The elasticity of the individual-firm demand curve is an important factor affecting incentives to cheat: the greater the elasticity the greater the temptation to cut prices and increase sales. Very small firms are most apt to take the price as parametric and therefore to expect large profits as a result of defection. In Italy, the number of firms that joined the cartel was very small and their size large, so defection never occurred. But this situation favored the persistence of a very fragmented supply outside the cartel.

Detection. Because incentives to cheat are pervasive, firms that enter into a collusive agreement must be able to detect secret price cuts or output increases initiated by rivals. Generally, collusion is more successful when sellers are few, and this is the case for both the international and national cartels in this industry. Detection is facilitated when sellers have ample information about competitors' behavior, i.e., they establish a pool of sales information which lets prices be common knowledge—for example, buyers' offers are made known to all members of the agreement. Such a body was present both in INCA and in ANIEM, which collected inquiries and orders to have long-term information on sales. Anyway, we were not able to find out what the incentive was for buyers to reveal their offers.

Penalties. This is a topic about which we know very little. We did not find any explicit reference to penalty strategies as, e.g., "long-term contracts with buyers," or "most favoured customer," or "meet or release." Both INCA and ANIEM had clauses to use the common fund (INCA) or subdivide the expenses (ANIEM) to penalize eventual cheating.

Limiting Entry. As we saw above, both INCA and ANIEM enlarged the number of participants in the agreement. Generally, collusive behavior leads to higher industry profits, which induces entry. But entry, in turn, depresses profit if demand is low and costs are asymmetric. This seems to be the case for the INCA agreement after Swiss and Swedish firms joined the cartel. On the other hand, in Italy, profits increased after the agreement (see below), showing that, in this case, an equilibrium between the two contrasting forces was reached.

VII. Collusion, Efficiency, and Welfare Losses

Despite the considerable economic literature on the effects of cartels, there is no agreement on the ways to measure their detrimental effects in terms of welfare loss and efficiency trade-offs. But the main difficulties come from the fact that adequate historical data are lacking, or are practically impossible to obtain, so we were not able to test general and partial equilibrium models, rent-seeking or X-inefficiency approaches, or game theoretic models.[17] Therefore, we are obliged to limit ourselves to some very rough observations on concentration and on profits, drawn from very poor accounting data for the Italian case.

Concentration. The expected effect of a cartel is an unchanged rate of concentration of the market. This is confirmed in the Italian case. Between 1931 and 1940, the rate of concentration of capital was relatively stable around the value 360 of the HH index[18] and the four leading enterprises covered around 30% of the market share.[19] On the other hand, this was a very low value for a supposed oligopolistic market.

Profits. The expected effect of a cartel in the field of profits is to raise them. If we observe the return on investment (ROI)[20] of the Italian enterprises in the five years before the establishment of the cartel and in the five following years, we can see that the average ROI of the three enterprises of the cartel (TIBB, CGE, Ercole Marelli) increased from 0.6% in the period 1925–30 to 3.3% in the period 1931–36, and the variance too decreased to near zero. On the other hand, the firms outside the cartel decreased their ROI from 0.1% to −1.7%, benefiting from the higher prices imposed by the cartel. In this case the variance remained unchanged at 0.7, for both periods (see Table 5).

Therefore, we can conclude that the Italian cartel made a difference.

VIII. Conclusion

The first conclusion that we can draw from the observation of the heavy electrical equipment cartels in the 1930s is that a technologically complex, multiproduct industry, where the relation among producers and customers is very tight, favored collusive behavior. This expressed itself

TABLE 5 Profits of Italian Electromechanical Firms before and after Cartel Establishment (%)

Mean and variance of all firms

	ROI	RCI	ROI	RCI
1925 to 1930			1931 to 1936	
Mean	0.3684	−1.414	−1.586	−9.152
Variance	0.7086	3.9787	0.7081	18.2159

Mean and variance of firms in the cartel

	ROI	RCI	ROI	RCI
1925 to 1930			1931 to 1936	
Mean	0.6221	0.4361	3.3146	5.5878
Variance	0.2362	1.3304	0.0889	0.2206

Mean and variance of firms outside the cartel

	ROI	RCI	ROI	RCI
1925 to 1930			1931 to 1936	
Mean	0.105	−2.111	−1.687	−9.876
Variance	0.751	4.3544	0.7607	19.6102

Source: Same as Table 2.

primarily in the exchange of patents and standard linkages among enterprises and in explicit cartel agreements prompted by a general decrease in demand. Generally, these cartels, both international and national, were successful. All this did not completely prevent competition in price, as in the above-mentioned case of German and Swiss producers vis-à-vis American and British producers, or in other factors, i.e., service and reliability, as in the case of pre-existing ties between customers and heavy equipment producers.

The second point concerns the role of the international oligopoly in hindering the rise of a national heavy electrical equipment industry. The Italian experience shows that this was not a major hindrance. The most important difficulties arose from the fragmentation of the "system of utilities," from the absence of an R&D policy for small improvements, quality, and reliability of products by enterprises, and from the contradictory policies of the Italian government regarding tariffs, legislation, and subsidies to industry.

In spite of this, the Italian market was relatively competitive due to the simultaneous presence of major international concerns and an abundance of small enterprises that favored high profits with a low concentration ratio.

NOTES

1. For this reconstruction, see British Electrical and Allied Manufacturers Association (BEAMA), *Combines and Trusts in Electrical Industry: The Position in Europe in 1927* (London, 1927); Eric Hess, *Elektropolitik und Welt Verstrung* (Amsterdam, 1931); Andrcas Gebhard, *Die Expansion der Amerikanischen Elektrokonzerne in Europa* (Heidelberg, 1932); Board of Trade, *International Cartels and Internal Cartels*, vol. II (Washington, D.C., 1944).

2. On these strategies see, for example, Peter Hertner, "Il capitale tedesco nell'industria elettrica italiana fino alla prima guerra mondiale," and Luciano Segreto, "Capitali, tecnologie e imprenditori svizzeri nell'industria elettrica italiana: il caso della Motor (1895–1923)," both included in Bruno Bezza (ed.), *Energia e sviluppo: l'industria elettrica italiana e la società Edison* (Turin, 1986).

3. On these aspects, see Renato Giannetti, "Engineers and the Rise of Standards in the Italian Electrical Network (1900–1930)," in *Actes du troisieme colloque sur l'energie électrique* (Paris, forthcoming).

4. See Renato Giannetti, "Tecnologia, scelte d'impresa ed intervento pubblico: l'industria elettrica italiana dalle origini al 1921," in *Passato e Presente* 2 (1982); on the Swedish case, see Jan Glete, *Storforetag i starkstrom: Ett svenk industriforetags omvarldsrelationer—en sammanfattning baserad pa "ASEA" under hundra ar* (Vasteras, 1984). There is a highly abridged edition in English published by the company: *Electrifying Experience: A Brief Account of the First Century of the ASEA Group of Sweden* (Vasteras).

5. On this, see Giannetti, op. cit. (1982), p. 61.

6. See Renato Giannetti "L'electrification des chemins de fer italiens (1899–1940)," in *Histoire, Economie et Societé*, forthcoming.

7. See BEAMA, op. cit.

8. On the origins of this strategy, see Claudio Pavese, "La naissance et le développment de la Société générale italienne Edison d'électricité jusq'à la constitution de son groupe: 1881–1919," in Fabienne Cardot (ed.), *Un siècle d'électricité dans le monde* (Paris, 1987).

9. On this matter, see Renato Giannetti, *La conquista della forza: risorse, tecnologia ed economia nell'industria elettrica italiana (1883–1940)* (Milan, 1984).

10. On the rise of cartels, see Robert Liefmann, *Kartelle, Konzerne und Trusts* (Stuttgart, 1927), English edition, *Cartels, Concerns and Trusts* (London, 1932); Laurence Ballande, *Essai d'étude monographique et statistique sur les ententes économiques internationales* (Paris, 1937); George W. Stocking and Myron Watkins, *Cartels in Action* (New York, 1946); Giuseppe Scagnetti, *Cartelli industriali internazionali* (Rome, 1928).

11. I drew extensively for this part on Federal Trade Commission, *International Electrical Equipment Cartels* (Washington, D.C., 1948).

12. For this part, I drew on various files kept in the Ansaldo archives in Genoa. The original of the Convention and the Rules are in ASA, *FSB 46/2*, April 1, 1931.

13. ASA, *FSB, 46/5*, November 5, 1929.

14. See, e.g., ASA, *FSB, 45/5*, November 19, 1935.

15. On this see Marco Doria, *Ansaldo: l'impresa e lo Stato* (Milan, 1989), chaps. 5–6.

16. ASA, *FSB*, 45/5, June 2, 1938.

17. For the equilibrium model, see, for example, Arthur C. Harberger, "Monopoly and Resource Allocation," in *American Economic Review* 44 (1954): 77; for the rent-seeking literature, see, for example, Robert A. Posner, "The Social Cost of Monopoly and Regulation; in *Journal of Political Economy* 83 (1975): 301; Harvey Leibenstein, "Allocative Efficiency vs. X-efficiency," in *American Economic Review* 56 (1966): 392; William. P. Rogerson, "The Social Cost of Monopoly and Regulation: A Game-Theoretic Analysis," in *Bell Journal of Economics* 13 (1983): 453.

18. This is the value of the Herfindhal-Hirschman index:

$$\sum_{i=1}^{n} x_i \left\{ \frac{y_i}{x_i} \middle/ \sum_{i=1}^{n} y_i \right\}^2$$

19. The formula for this index is: $C_a = \sum_{i=1}^{n} P_i (i = 1, \ldots, m, m - 1, \ldots, n)$

20. ROI (return on investment) is the ratio of total revenue to total assets according to the following formula:

$$\frac{Rn}{\dfrac{At_0 + At_1}{2}}$$

Comment

Etsuo Abe

Professor Giannetti's paper is composed of the following sections. Sections II and III deal with the development of the heavy electrical equipment industry between the 1880s and the 1930s, describing the changes from the competition at national levels to international penetration. Section IV explains how the international cartel, INCA, was formed and what its functions were. In Section V, he focuses on a national cartel, ANIEM, in Italy. In addition to these sections, he examines rather theoretically the economics of electromechanical cartels in the 1930s. Lastly, he concludes, "these cartels, both international and national, were successful."

For whom, however, were these cartels successful? For enterprises or consumers? Or for society as a whole? Admittedly, a competitive equilibrium gives optimal results to producers and consumers, that is, to society as a whole. If the price is set on the upper level by a cartel, it is sure that producers can gain more than before, but consumers lose more than the producers get. Accordingly, society, which is composed of both producers and consumers, eventually gains less than under the previous condition. So cartels generally have bad reputations. Also cartels are criticized because in the long run they might hinder R&D activities and cause the slowing of investment because of relative easy mass profits. It is probably true that cartels did not completely prevent competition in price and in non-price, i.e., service and reliability, in the Italian heavy electrical equipment industry. Yet they might have done damage to buyers' interests to some degree even if some competition still worked. But as Giannetti wrote, we do not have ways to measure the detrimental effects of cartels in terms of welfare and of efficiency trade-offs. We are thus in a situation where judgment cannot be given.

The international situation presents another problem: The question whether international oligopolies, such as GE, Westinghouse, Siemens, and Brown Boveri, hindered the development of rather undeveloped countries' electrical industry. Giannetti argues that the Italian experience shows that the role of the international oligopoly was not a major hindrance but that other factors, e.g., the contradictory policies of the Italian government, were. And finally, did the Italian heavy electrical equipment industry develop in a full-fledged way or not?

Let us look at Table 4. From the early 20th century up to 1939, the number of firms increased steadily and the value of plants, too. Also the percentage of the leading four and the HH index decreased secularly. This all means that the industry is not a mature industry but a newly growing industry. When we consider functions of cartels, we should distinguish whether the industry belongs to a mature industry or a developing one. If it is the latter, then combined with the character of a technologically complex multiproduct industry, a cartel might not have a bad effect on the industry in terms of R&D and investment activity. This is because the role of cartels can change either positively or negatively according to the character of products, development phase, and structure of competition of the industry.

Finally, I would like to raise the question of the comparison of Italy with Japan. Both countries were latecomers to the industry. On that account, the associations with foreign companies like GE and Westinghouse were critically important in each country. In Japan, at the early stage, foreign firms had major equity in joint ventures. But later on, Japanese firms were successful in getting majority, partly owing to the rise of nationalism. They assimilated foreign technology and managed to develop competitive power. Such electrical firms continue to flourish today and have become global enterprises. Did Italian electric firms take the same path? If not, why did they fail to do so?

Response

Renato Giannetti

Professor Abe asked if the cartels were successful for enterprises or for consumers. In the Italian case, they were successful for the enterprises because their profits increased. I could not estimate its effects on Italian consumers because of the lack of adequate historical data.

He also inquired whether international oligopolies hindered the growth of the Italian electrical equipment industry. They did hinder, in different periods and in different manners, the development of a full-fledged Italian electrical equipment industry. In the long run, they favored the specialization of Italian firms in supplying mechanical parts instead of electrical ones.

Another question addressed specifically the role of cartels in hindering or promoting the Italian heavy electrical industry. The Italian cartel did not promote the growth of a fully integrated industry. It helped to stabilize prices in a period of general deflation, and this favored the growth of many small- and medium-sized domestic enterprises.

On the other hand, this favorable environment crystalized the industry, which maintained a very fragmented structure of supply and, unlike the Japanese case, was not able to enlarge its competitive power in the post–Second World War period.

General Electric and the World Cartelization of Electric Lamps

Leonard S. Reich

I. Introduction

Like many other commodities during the late 19th and early 20th centuries, electric lamps ("light bulbs") were the subject of intense efforts to control markets in the United States and elsewhere. The American company General Electric (GE), the largest and most powerful electric company in the world, was at the center of these efforts, establishing cartels first in the United States and then in Europe. Because of increasingly strict American antitrust laws, GE carefully constructed its market-sharing agreements to avoid the appearance of market control when in fact the company worked very hard to acquire and maintain that control—and the high profits that went along with it. Always concerned foremost with its position in the very large American market, GE acquired equity in foreign concerns in order to influence their policies. This made them more willing to cooperate in joint ventures with each other and with GE, in most cases dividing markets and preventing direct competition.

In the paper that follows, I will describe GE's electric-lamp policies, which were based on both technological leadership and financial control. Particularly in the early years, the company was willing to invest whatever resources it took to develop advanced lamp technology or to buy it from others. GE used this technology along with its overwhelming market power (relative to most smaller competitors) to dominate the American sales of electric lamps. It then turned to Europe, not to gain market entry, but primarily to assure that the European producers stayed out of the United States. Its European activities resulted in formation of a powerful cartel that lasted from the mid-1920s to the Second World War and which, together with GE, controlled about three-quarters of the world's output in electric lamps.

II. The Early Years

When the Edison General Electric Company and the Thomson-Houston Electric Company merged in 1892 to form GE, the new company was the largest in the field and sought to dominate the American electrical industry. During the mid-1890s, GE and its smaller rival Westinghouse together controlled about 75% of the electrical industry but stymied each other through competitive pricing (and underpricing) and through hundreds of patent infringement suits. As profitability declined, accommodation became more desirable for them both. Thus, after extensive negotiations, GE and Westinghouse reached an agreement in March 1896 whereby they exchanged licenses to all of their patents except the ones for electric lighting. The value of production was to be in the ratio of five-to-three, GE's favor. If either company exceeded its share, it paid the other a substantial royalty.[1] Through this arrangement, GE institutionalized its dominance of Westinghouse.

Next, GE gained control of the American incandescent lamp market in an agreement that involved Westinghouse and sixteen of the smaller manufacturers. Together, they controlled 95% of lamp sales. In early 1897, GE established a cartel called the Incandescent Lamp Manufacturers Association (ILMA) that was based on improvement patents held by Westinghouse. The Association fixed proportional output keyed to GE's sales and set prices based on GE prices. GE held 50% of the market, Westinghouse about 12%, and the remaining 35–40% went to all the others. Lamp prices immediately increased about 30%.[2]

In 1901 GE developed a scheme that allowed it to more completely dominate the lamp market without crushing its small competitors. The Sherman Antitrust Act had been passed in 1890, and although the act had not yet been used to discipline large corporations for anticompetitive behavior, GE management realized that they needed to be careful.[3] Thus, while buying out most of the independent manufacturers, they maintained the charade that these companies continued to be independent. This was done through the auspices of F.S. Terry, president of the Sunbeam Incandescent Lamp Company, and B.G. Tremaine, head of the Fostoria Incandescent Lamp Company, both members of ILMA. Terry and Tremaine saw that GE kept all the independents weak and dependent under the ILMA agreements. Why not make them strong and dependent instead? With resources supplied by GE, Terry and Tremaine acquired most of the independent manufacturers between 1901 and 1906, setting up the National Electric Lamp Company to control the overall business. By 1911, they ran 18 subsidiary companies that continued operations under their own names, with coordination and technical services supplied from

Cleveland headquarters. To maintain the appearance of competition to its fullest, companies sometimes filled orders under the brand of another affiliate, putting the other's markings on the product and billing the customer on its letterhead.[4]

To further solidify its control of the industry, GE entered into agreements with manufacturers of lamp-making equipment and glass bulbs. In the former case, GE provided expertise and patent rights in exchange for the ability to dictate to whom lamp-making equipment could be sold. In the latter, it contracted to purchase most of the bulb output of the major suppliers in return for guarantees that they would charge the smaller producers more.[5]

During this early period of GE's American electric-lamp market domination, lamp technology changed significantly. GE maintained control of it through purchase of patent rights combined with in-house technical development. At the time of the company's formation in 1892, the basic form of Edison's original invention had changed little: a carbon-thread filament in an evacuated glass bulb. The major problem with this technology was its inefficiency; 5% of the power that went into a lamp came out as light, the rest was lost as heat. So long as GE maintained control of the American lamp market through its ILMA cartel during the 1890s, there seemed small reason to work for improvement.

However, considerable lamp development went on outside of GE, both in America and abroad. In the United States, several researchers were working on gas-discharge lamps that created a bright glow from ionizing gases rather than filaments. Westinghouse even supported one of the best of them, Peter Cooper-Hewitt. In Europe, strong physical-science programs at the universities and long-standing university-industry connections led to research on a number of promising filament materials. Certain metals, inherently more efficient than carbon because of their higher operating temperatures, became the focus of research efforts. In 1898, Austrian electrochemist Carl Auer von Welsbach developed a filament made from the metal osmium that was 60% more efficient than GE's carbon filament and lasted longer as well. Although its fragility and expense limited the osmium filament to the European market (where electric power was considerably more expensive), this advance served notice that the carbon filament's days were numbered.[6]

GE paid attention. At the urging of its most creative engineer, Charles Steinmetz, the company in 1900 established a research laboratory whose primary purpose was to work on lamp development.[7] GE's new lab had mixed success in developing electric-lamp technology during the following decade, but the company was able to purchase all of the important patent rights that it did not produce itself. GE lab scientists did make some minor advances within a few years; however, bigger things were happening abroad, where researchers succeeded in making filaments of metals like tantalum, titanium, molybdenum, and tungsten. With the highest melting point of all, tungsten promised the most efficient lamp, and in 1907 GE purchased rights to the tungsten-filament patent application of Austrians Alexander Just and Fritz Hanaman for $250,000. This turned out to be an extremely valuable investment. When GE researcher William Coolidge fabricated a ductile tungsten filament in 1909 that was both more efficient and more rugged than the Europeans' metal filaments, GE had a virtual lock on state-of-the-art lamp technology.[8]

As the situation with metal-filament lamps has made clear, GE needed to be concerned about foreign companies coming into the U.S. market or selling commercially valuable patent rights to American competitors. It lessened this likelihood by initiating agreements with a number of foreign firms, some of which it partially owned as a result of Edison's and Thomson-Houston's earlier forays abroad. By 1905 it held equity in and contracts with British Thomson-Houston, Compagnie Française Thomson-Houston, Tokyo Electric Company, Allgemeine Elektrizitäts-Gesellschaft (AEG), and Canadian General Electric. These contracts provided for the exchange of patent rights and set out exclusive sales territories—in each case reserving the American market for GE. As of 1905, GE maintained holdings in the above-named companies valued at more than $4.4 million.[9]

GE had no interest in invading foreign lamp markets for a number of reasons. First, it already received income from foreign lamp sales through its equity positions described above. Second, it wanted to maintain mutually beneficial relationships with would-be foreign competitors to keep them out of the American market, which comprised about half the lamp sales in the world, year after year. And third, lamp prices elsewhere had fallen due to competition between manufacturers. There had been an attempt to run an international cartel in carbon lamps—the International Incandescent Lamp Cartel, founded by the German firms AEG and Siemens & Halske in 1903—but it soon fell victim to metal-filament lamps and to competition from outside producers. Decidedly unappealing low lamp prices resulted.[10]

In 1911, GE's position in the American incandescent-lamp market may have appeared unassailable, but it was subject to attack from one quarter: the U.S. government. Antitrust action was brought against the company because of its web of contracts, which, in the words of the Sherman Antitrust Act, "restrained trade" in the lamp market. Rather than fight the suit directly, GE management decided to accept the government's requirements that it abrogate the contracts and purchase outright its national subsidiaries, so long as GE was able to exercise its rights of control under the lamp-related patents that it held. But, as things turned out, that was enough.[11]

III. The Middle Years

Stripped of its disguises and barred from its special agreements, GE made formidable use of its patent position. In fact, when all was said and done, the government agreement had little effect on GE's domination of the American electric-lamp market.

Coolidge's ductile-tungsten patent, granted in 1912, became the backbone of GE's position, and the company soon added many improvement patents, from techniques for making non-sagging filaments to tipless and frosted glass bulbs. Patent-licensing agreements alone now became the vehicle of GE's dominance. For example, as of March 1912 Westinghouse held licenses under 216 GE lamp patents, but on highly restrictive terms. Westinghouse was limited to 17.25% of the two companies' combined lamp sales on a patent royalty rate of 2%; for sales exceeding that amount, it paid 10%. Westinghouse could export lamps only to those countries where GE exported them, and only with GE's permission. Westinghouse also granted royalty-free licenses to GE under all its present and future lamp patents for the duration of the contract, permitted GE to sublicense those patents, agreed to share relevant technical information, and admitted the validity of all GE patents and patent applications. This took away Westinghouse's incentive to conduct lamp research on its own or to go after new inventions. GE offered similar arrangements (with far smaller sales limits) to other manufacturers, although they were not permitted to export. They were also required to provide GE with royalty-free licensing for the life of any patents they acquired during the term of the agreement, irrespective of whether that agreement was later terminated. GE had the right to sublicense any of these patents. By 1915, less than 5% of American lamp sales lay beyond the company's grasp.[12]

With the passing of the government consent decree and the consequent patent-licensing agreements, GE entered a new phase in its domination of the American electric-lamp industry. The company concentrated its efforts on expanding the entire market, while preventing the emergence of major new competitors. This pleased its licensees, whose production quotas were linked to GE lamp sales. Still smarting from the antitrust suit, which targeted GE as a "bad" corporation, the company worked diligently to improve lamp efficiencies while lowering their prices. These actions,

combined with decreases in electric power rates, lowered the cost of lighting to American consumers by a factor of four between 1910 and 1930.[13]
This helped expand the market, transforming the incandescent lamp into
a true mass-market product during the 1920s.

The 1920s was a very good decade for GE's lamp-market interests.
Based largely on rights to the Just-Hanaman and Coolidge tungsten-
filament patents (which did not expire until 1930), GE controlled the industry with ease. To assert its patent rights, the company brought a series
of infringement and injunction actions in 1923, even threatening a few
large purchasers of unlicensed products with contributory infringement.
Whatever sizes and types of lamps GE chose to produce became the industry standard, as the company worked to limit the number of base
types, power ratings, and line voltages in order to boost the efficiency of
lamp production and distribution. Improvements in lamp-making
machinery emerged regularly from its development laboratories, increasing labor productivity by a factor of more than four during the decade. Its
licensees obtained most of their equipment from GE or from manufacturers licensed under GE's patents. In the latter case, GE controlled to whom
the equipment could be sold, and in both cases it required that the equipment be returned to GE should the license expire. Given the structure of
the lamp market, bankers were extremely hesitant to provide capital for
lamp producers not incorporated under the GE umbrella. Unlicensed
competitors thus lacked the resources to challenge the leader in issues of
production and costs, product technology, and especially in marketing,
where the greatest inroads might have been possible.[14]

If this seems a little too good to be legal, the U.S. Justice Department
thought so as well and in 1924 brought another antitrust suit against GE.
However, a federal district court quickly dismissed the case, and the
government's appeal to the Supreme Court brought the same result. The
high court's ruling stated that GE owned patent rights that "cover completely the making of the modern electric lights with the tungsten filaments, and secure to General Electric the monopoly of their making, using
and vending." In other words, with these patents in force, GE could do
most anything it wanted in tungsten lamp production, distribution, and
sales.[15]

IV. World Cartel

One reason it enjoyed this freedom was that over the previous two decades
GE had worked out a number of international agreements that effectively
divided the world market. Mention has already been made of contracts
dating from the early 20th century, of GE's equity positions in foreign

electrical firms, and of a generally unsuccessful attempt by European concerns to form a lamp cartel prior to the First World War. After the war, GE's interests became more international in scope, and it is important at this point to consider the American company's role in the worldwide electric-lamp industry.

Compared to GE's well-organized U.S. market, the European situation was chaotic. The struggling International Incandescent Lamp Cartel of 1903 was strengthened somewhat in 1911 when the three leading German firms pooled their metal-filament patent rights (including ductile-tungsten rights acquired from GE) in an attempt to control the German market. They also made agreements with non-German cartel members for rights within their home countries, including Philips in Holland, Watt in Austria, United Incandescent Lamp in Hungary, and Compagnie Française Thomson-Houston (in which GE held a large interest). Nonetheless, the years after 1910 saw an inrush of new metal-filament competitors, and the beginning of the world war in 1914 destroyed the cartel completely. The two strongest European companies before the war, AEG and Siemens & Halske (both German), suffered considerably by the appropriation of their foreign subsidiaries in England, Holland, and Russia during the war and by the absence of strong capital markets in Germany afterwards. In addition, foreign competitors such as Philips had expanded their facilities during hostilities, resulting in significant worldwide over-capacity in electric lamps at war's end. So bad was the situation that world demand for lamps could have been supplied by half of the existing production capacity.[16]

To offset these difficulties, the German firms in 1919 combined their lamp business. AEG, Siemens & Halske, and Auergesellschaft (founded by the chemist Carl Auer von Welsbach during the 1890s) merged their lamp operations into a company called Osram. Osram quickly acquired several of the lesser German electric-lamp manufacturers, leaving only one of importance beyond its control. To re-establish a German presence internationally, Osram during its first five years purchased or established subsidiaries in Czechoslovakia, Sweden, Poland, Switzerland, and Austria. This made it by far the strongest lamp company in Europe, with Philips in second place.[17]

Osram and its major competitors caused GE some concern. The size of the American market was so great and the profits to be made there so large that one or more of the aggressive European concerns were bound to be attracted to GE's home market sooner or later unless barriers could be erected to keep them out. And even if these companies did not invade America themselves, they might still sell their own patented lamp-making equipment to GE's unlicensed American competitors, removing one of GE's important advantages over the smaller companies. Thus, accommodation was very important.

Accordingly, GE set out to deal with the lead firm, Osram. Using its International General Electric (IGE) subsidiary, the American company pursued contacts in 1920.[18] However, negotiations did not go smoothly because Osram wanted to establish and dominate an international cartel, whereas GE held equity positions in a number of European producers with conflicting interests, including Philips. Osram intended to regain some of the market that Philips had taken during the war. As the largest and most powerful electrical company in the world, GE was used to getting its way and acted accordingly in dealing with Osram. This approach caused resentment among the Germans. IGE's head negotiator, on being questioned about provisions in a proposed agreement, replied to his Osram counterpart, "But after all we [GE] have to control the light bulb business in the world."[19] The Germans did not see it that way. The final outcome of these talks was a nonaggression pact between the two companies to exchange patent rights, provide each other with technical assistance, and set out "exclusive sales areas for the two contracting parties, and thus set territorial limits to the competition between [them] for the . . . protection of the home market."[20] But that was all; no other manufacturers were involved.

Extremely concerned about excess lamp capacity among the European manufacturers, Osram moved to establish a cartel for the maintenance of lamp prices. In 1921, working with Philips and six other central European lamp makers—and having a separate contract with the British—it established the International Union for Regulating Prices of Incandescent Lamps. However, this group soon succumbed to internal bickering (especially between the Germans and French), and to external opportunism. By February 1924, the International Union had "broke[n] down utterly."[21]

At this point, GE stepped in. Believing that its interests were best served through stability and expecting the Germans to be more compliant because of the chaotic situation and because GE had recently acquired a major equity share in AEG, IGE negotiators suggested reopening talks on a full-fledged cartel. Discussions began that April, with J.M. Woodward, head European representative for IGE, serving as coordinator. Agreements between Osram and Philips were especially difficult to achieve, as each believed that it deserved a larger share of the market. GE sweetened the pot for Osram, lending the company $1.5 million on excellent terms to help it pursue its business plans.[22] On December 24, 1924, with everyone finally accommodated, the Convention for the Development and Progress of the International Incandescent Electric Lamp Industry was signed into existence. Lest there be any question about GE's role in its creation, let me quote at length from Woodward's report to his supervisor:

> Circumstances and luck having brought about almost the precise situation which we have from the beginning desired, and the proposition having been made, I have given my adherence to it in the belief that you would approve it. . . . I have taken advantage of the entire freedom of action which you left me, to develop the affair into a living partnership. For a long while it appeared as if the only thing which it would be possible to achieve would be a naked agreement between the parties as to quota. . . . Gradually the European owners and managers came to like the idea of a permanent relationship . . . and we took advantage of every opportunity offered to advance this idea. . . . Also they have become impressed . . . with the fact that they must cooperate in what we call the Business Development program, and have become educated not so much in the morality of this cooperation as in the necessity for it. . . . I may say without being misunderstood that the European parties are entirely amateurish[!], for reasons which arise from their historic division of interest. They realize this, and that realization coupled with their still active mistrust of each other has caused them to accept our leadership and to invite its continuance.[23]

Cartel members established a Swiss corporation called Phoebus S. A. Compagnie Industrielle pour la Developpement de l'Eclairage to administer production quotas, prices, exchange of technical information, and sharing of patent rights. Within Phoebus, the General Assembly set policy, the Administrative Board issued rules to carry out that policy, and the Board of Arbitration adjudicated disputes. In addition, a testing laboratory worked to assure consistent quality among members' products, and a marketing division promoted the use of electric lighting, particularly the lamps of cartel members instead of those of outsiders. Companies' production was tied to the share of the lamp market that they held during the 1922–23 fiscal year. These production rights could be traded or sold among members. The cartel's original members included Osram, Philips, Tungsram (Hungary), Associated Electrical Industries (Britain), International General Electric of New York (Britain), Compagnie des Lampes (France), and the Brazilian, Chinese, and Mexican subsidiaries of GE. Other important lamp makers, such as Societa Edison Clerici Fabbrica Lampage (Italy) and Tokyo Electric (Japan), joined later. Conspicuously absent from the roster was GE itself, though Phoebus's operations were for some time managed on its behalf by IGE's J.M. Woodward[24] (see Figure 1).

Why did GE not become a member of Phoebus? The answer is that joining would have been politically unwise within the United States and that GE did not have to join to enjoy the cartel's main benefits: division of markets, maintenance of prices, and sharing of technical information.

American antitrust laws of the late 19th and early 20th century reflected a very different philosophy about corporations' role in society than existed in Europe. In the United States, big business had preceded big government, and as governmental power grew, lawmakers tended to take an adversarial position toward large corporations, usually because of past abuses. Rather than working in concert with government for the national good, American corporations were seen as benefiting mainly their owners and managers, often at the public expense. Perceived as the "Electric Trust," GE had come in for more than its share of scrutiny and animosity. In addition to the antitrust suits already mentioned, the U.S. Senate initiated a Federal Trade Commission investigation of GE's role in the electrical industry, with an eye toward dismembering the company. This happened at about the same time that Phoebus was being formed. In such an environment, appearances were very important, and joining Phoebus would have been quite inexpedient.[25]

Because of the agreements that GE had already made—and continued to make—with the major lamp producers, it had no need to join Phoebus in any case. Through its IGE subsidiary, the company adjusted its existing agreements, bringing them into line with cartel operations and using language similar to the cartel's in exchanging patent rights and technical information, limiting competition geographically, and maintaining prices.[26] Because its patent position was considerably stronger than those of the cartel members, GE did insist on certain patent-based royalty fees and service charges, taking in about $5 million from cartel members during the 1920s and 1930s. It thus benefited from the export of lamp technology where agreements barred it from exporting the lamps themselves. All such agreements with cartel members fully protected GE's home interests (which continued to account for nearly half of world sales through the 1930s) and set out secondary markets in which it was permissible for both parties to sell lamps. However, restrictions often applied there. For example, IGE's late 1920s agreements with Philips and Osram permitted them to do business in South America, but only at minimum prices set by GE, while GE could sell for whatever prices it chose.[27]

GE also interwove its operations with the cartel by purchasing substantial portions of the principal members' stock and by entering into joint

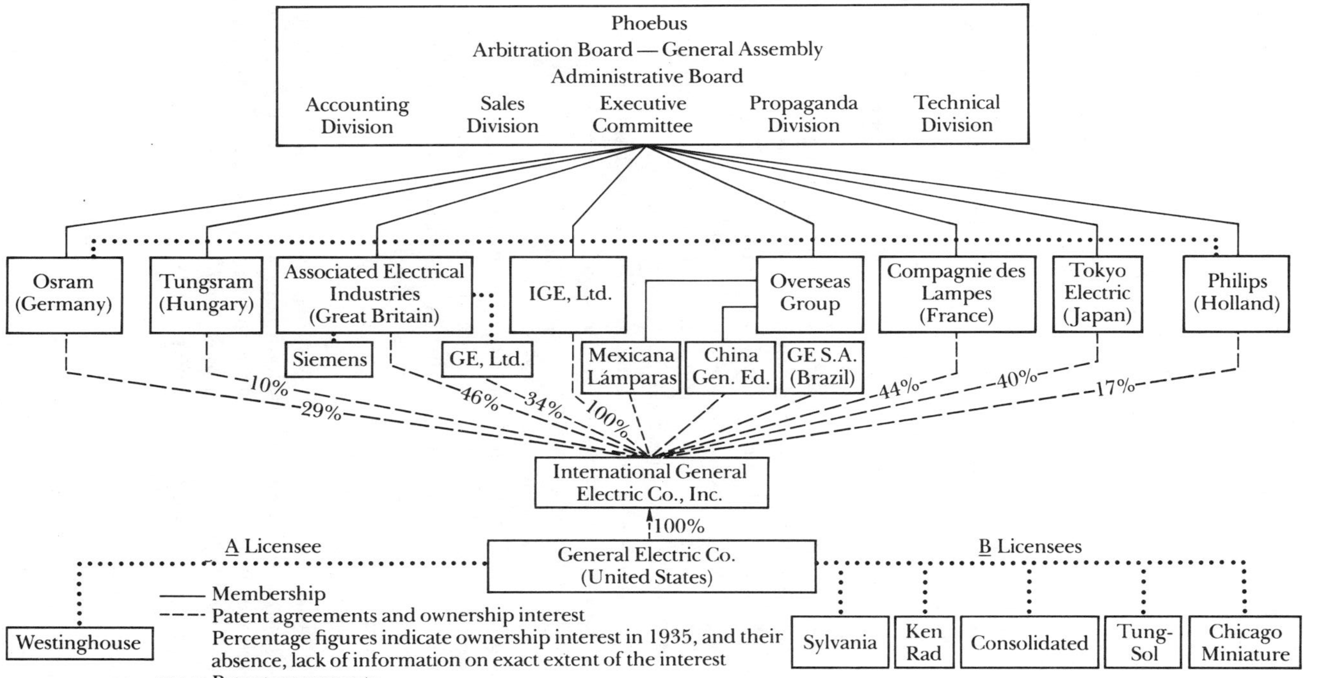

FIG. 1 Structure of the Phoebus Cartel, 1925–39
Source: George Stocking and Myron Watkins, *Cartels in Action* (New York, 1946), p. 334.

ventures. Its 1929 holdings, expressed as a percentage of the companies' outstanding stock issue, were: Osram 29%, Philips 17%, AEG 25%, Compagnie des Lampes 44%, Tungsram 10%, Associated Electrical Industries 46%, International General Electric of New York, Ltd. 34%, and Tokyo Electric 40%. Usually the largest single shareholder by far, GE had a very strong voice in company policies. Thus, it was not difficult for the American company to enter into joint ventures, for example, making lamps together with Osram and Philips in China and with Osram in Mexico and supplying lamps to these companies for sale under their names to other places in the world. Economists Stocking and Watkins claimed that "Phoebus plus General Electric" resulted in a "world cartel," and it is not difficult to see why.[28]

The purpose of the cartel was to assure each company as much of its home market as it could handle plus a fixed share in other (common) markets. The fixed share came from a quota system based on the ratio of its sales to total cartel members' sales during the fiscal year 1922–23. A company could distribute its sales in common areas as it saw fit, so long as it stayed within its overall quota. Total production above quota resulted in increasingly severe penalties payable to Phoebus.

How effective was this cartel in controlling output and market shares? Within the United States, where GE reigned supreme, it was very effective, although by the mid-1930s the amount of business outside cartel (i.e., GE) control had risen to about 10%. However, GE kept its lamp prices considerably below those of the cartel members, for both competitive and political reasons.[29] Elsewhere, the loss of market control was far higher; usually about 40% of lamp sales came from nonmembers. There were two major reasons for this. First, the most important metal-filament patents expired by the early 1930s, and producers everywhere were free to sell lamps that gave efficient service with reasonably long life. And second, the cartel held lamp prices artificially high (as do all successful cartels), and this made entrance into the industry quite attractive. Given conflicting corporate and national interests as well as the welter of laws affecting manufacture, transshipment, and sale of lamps worldwide, it is actually quite impressive that Phoebus held on to so much of the market for so long. By the late 1930s, as international tensions increased, Phoebus's effectiveness declined, and the Second World War destroyed it.[30]

V. The Later Years

Although GE had protected its American market from major European and Japanese producers, it nonetheless had to work very hard to control domestic and foreign competitors during the later 1920s and the 1930s. As before, its efforts paid off handsomely, bringing the company regular and substantial profits during a time when other industrial lines sometimes provided it with losses.

During the late 1920s and early 1930s, GE renegotiated its license contracts with Westinghouse and the smaller American companies. Westinghouse pressed for more sales, and GE responded by increasing its market share from 17.25% to 25.44%, with a royalty rate of 1% in lieu of the earlier 2%. At the same time GE imposed greater restrictions on Westinghouse, for example, substantially increasing penalties for going beyond quota (up from 10% to 30%), setting the prices at which Westinghouse could sell lamps, and claiming right of refusal on Westinghouse's choice of distributors. Hence, GE gave up some sales and base royalties in return for an even tighter control of the competition. Contracts with the smaller licensees remained essentially unchanged at a royalty rate of 3%.[31]

The greatest threat to GE's American market domination during the 1930s came from unlicensed foreign competitors, particularly the Japanese. When the tungsten-filament patents expired in 1930, non-cartel Japanese manufacturers, who benefited from extremely low labor costs and a recently devalued yen, actively pursued the American market. At a time when GE priced its 60-watt lamp at \$.20, the Japanese product sold for \$.10 even with an import tariff of 20%. Although these lamps had low efficiency, short life, and uneven performance, they appealed to some consumers. GE combated the Japanese in three ways. First, it introduced an "economy" lamp, called the Type D, that went head-to-head on price while providing considerably better efficiency. Then it successfully prevailed upon the courts to bar the lamps of certain Japanese manufacturers because of markings that confused them with GE products. Finally, it brought suit against selected U.S. distributors (and threatened others), claiming that the imported lamps infringed GE patents. As a result, many distributors desisted. Japanese share of the U.S. market, which soared from 1% in 1929 to 9% in 1932, fell continuously through the remainder of the decade, back to 4% in 1937 and to 2% in 1940. The invasion had been rebuffed. This was one important case where GE's financial and market power prevailed in the face of Phoebus's inability to protect it from foreign competition.[32]

VI. Conclusion

Over the course of half a century, GE maintained control of the large, profitable American market in electric lamps while realizing lamp revenues abroad and protecting its home market against foreign invasion. It accomplished this in a number of ways: research and development, both in science and engineering, to improve the lamp and the processes by which it was made; purchase of strategic patent rights; control of contracts with domestic competitors and suppliers; legal maneuvers of various kinds to avoid antitrust suits and to prevent competitors' access to free markets; large equity positions in electrical manufacturers worldwide; and international nonaggression agreements bolstered by the Phoebus cartel that it brought into existence.

The company's desire to maintain control of the American market had significant international impact. Unable to establish an effective cartel by themselves because of antagonisms, jealousies, and conflicting interests, the other major electrical manufacturers in the world were brought into an enduring arrangement because of GE's efforts to secure its own markets. Largely because of antitrust activities in the United States, GE never joined Phoebus, but its continued direction was strongly felt. When Phoebus finally broke down with the coming of the Second World War, its members, under GE's de facto leadership, had successfully maintained production quotas and prices far longer than any comparable cartel in the electrical industry. GE, still then the largest and most powerful electrical company in the world, had accomplished its goal.

Notes

1. Harold Passer, *The Electrical Manufacturers, 1875–1900* (Cambridge, Mass., 1953), pp. 331–33.

2. The Association was based on Westinghouse patents because GE's contracts with some utility companies precluded licensing its lamp patents to others. Arthur A. Bright, *The Electric-Lamp Industry: Technical Change and Economic Development from 1800 to 1947* (New York, 1949), pp. 103–4; United States Tariff Commission, *Incandescent Electric Lamps*, Report No. 133, Second series (Government Printing Office, Washington, D.C., 1939), pp. 32–33. Since GE's production costs were lower than those of the smaller competitors and all parties sold lamps for about the same price, GE made greater profits per lamp on a far higher sales volume.

3. Standard Oil was not so careful and found itself dismembered within the decade.

4. T.K. Quinn, *Giant Business: Threat to Democracy* (New York, 1953), p. 50. Quinn worked at the National Electric Lamp Company and later rose to be a vice president of GE.

5. Bright, op. cit., pp. 52–53.

6. Leonard Reich, *The Making of American Industrial Research: Science and Business at GE and Bell, 1876–1926* (New York, 1985), pp. 62–64.

7. On the establishment of the General Electric Research Laboratory, see Reich, op. cit., pp. 62–69; see also George Wise, *Willis Whitney, General Electric, and the Origins of U.S. Industrial Research* (New York, 1985), pp. 66–94.

8. Willis Whitney, "Research as a Financial Asset," *General Electric Review*, vol. 14 (1911): 327. The Europeans' filaments were brittle, which made it difficult to adapt them to high-speed lamp-making equipment. However, the Just and Hana-

man patent remained basic; that is, one could not make use of the Coolidge patent without also having rights to the Austrians' invention.

9. Thomas P. Hughes, *Networks of Power: Electrification in Western Society, 1880–1930* (Baltimore, 1983), p. 179; George Stocking and Myron Watkins, *Cartels in Action* (New York, 1946), pp. 321–22; General Electric Company, "Fourteenth Annual Report," January 31, 1906, p. 17; Bright, op. cit., p. 155. It is of interest to note that AEG began as an Edison subsidiary (Deutsche Edison Gesellschaft) and always maintained close ties with GE as a result. Economist Robert Liefmann claimed that GE "stood godfather" for the smaller German company. Robert Liefmann, *Cartels, Concerns and Trusts* (London, 1932), p. 248.

10. Founded by two German firms, the cartel included the major producers in Austria, Germany, Hungary, Holland, Switzerland, and Italy. It was intended to fix prices and establish quotas but had trouble doing either. See Bright, op. cit., pp. 160–61.

11. Tariff Commission, op. cit., pp. 33–34; "Electric Trust Must Dissolve," *New York Times*, October 13, 1911, p. 8; for a general discussion of the antitrust proceedings, see Bright, op. cit., pp. 156–59.

12. "General Electric Lamp Information," John W. Hammond File, Hall of History Foundation, General Electric Company Building #2, Schenectady, N.Y., item L3438 (hereafter Hammond File); Bright, op. cit., pp. 236–37, 239–40; Kendall Birr, *Pioneering in Industrial Research* (Washington, D.C., 1957), p. 147; Frank Kottke, *Electrical Technology and the Public Interest* (Washington, D.C., 1944), p. 57; Floyd Vaughan, *The United States Patent System* (Norman, Okla., 1956), p. 76.

13. GE Lamp Engineering Report for 1925," p. 15, quoted in Wise, op. cit., p. 157.

14. By 1927, output of independent companies had been forced down to about 3% of the market. Bright, op. cit., pp. 243, 348–60, 388n; Tariff Commission, op. cit., pp. 40–41; Witt Bowden, *Technological Changes and Employment in the Electric-Lamp Industry*, Bul. 593 (Washington, D.C.: Bureau of Labor Statistics, 1933), pp. 30–32.

15. Confident in its legal position based on earlier rulings and agreements, GE actually challenged the government to bring suit after hearings in the New York legislature brought forth numerous allegations. *Electrical World*, vol. 83 (March 29, 1924): 637; Bright, op. cit., pp. 253–55; *United States v. General Electric Co.*, 272 U.S. 476 (1926), pp. 480–81.

16. Bright, op. cit., pp. 303–4; Harm Schröter, "A Typical Factor of International Market Strategy: Agreements Between the U.S. and German Electrotechnical Industries up to 1939," in Alice Teichova et al. (eds.), *Multinational Enterprise in Historical Perspective* (Cambridge, 1986), p. 161; overcapacity based on estimates of the British Committee on Industry and Trade report of 1928, referenced in Stocking and Watkins, op. cit., p. 323.

17. "Osram" is a contraction of the metal-filament types osmium and wolfram (tungsten). Ibid., pp. 23–24.

18. IGE was established in 1919 as the center for foreign operations. Its creation signified growing concerns about international trade in the postwar era as GE's businesses expanded. On IGE, see David Loth, *Swope of GE* (New York, 1958), pp. 93–105.

19. Stocking and Watkins, op. cit., p. 331n. The quote is from the notes taken by the Osram negotiator. Another of his entries, indicating GE's position, is as follows: "The Americans will supervise and control the whole light bulb business

with some kind of paternal interest, helping and advising every partner. But finally there must be an agreement about the right of decision-making, and this right could only be with the Americans because of their position." Both quoted in Schröter, op. cit., pp. 165, 170n.

20. United States Federal Trade Commission, *Supply of Electrical Equipment and Competitive Conditions*, 70th Congress, 1st Session, Senate doc. no. 46 (Washington, D.C., 1928), p. 143; League of Nations, *Review of the Economic Aspects of Several International Agreements* (Geneva, 1933), p. 70, quoted in Tariff Commission, op. cit., pp. 57–58.

21. Stocking and Watkins, op. cit., p. 330; J.M. Woodward to A.W. Burchard (both of IGE), April 7, 1924, quoted in *United States v. General Electric et al.*, 1364 D.N.J. (1943), Ex.2112-G.

22. Stocking and Watkins, op. cit., pp. 331, 340.

23. Woodward to A.W. Burchard, December 23, 1924, quoted in *U.S. v. GE*, 1364 D.N.J., Ex.2117-G.

24. Stocking and Watkins, op. cit., pp. 332–35; Bright, op. cit., pp. 305–6; Quinn, op. cit., p. 74. Woodward became a Phoebus employee.

25. A resolution in the U.S. Senate on February 9, 1925, officially initiated the FTC investigation, but Senate debate had been ongoing for some months at the time.

26. As a result of the agreements, GE voluntarily restricted itself from doing business in the following countries: Austria, Belgium, Brazil, Bulgaria, China, Czechoslovakia, Denmark, Estonia, Finland, France, Germany, Great Britain, Greece, Holland, Hungary, Ireland, Italy, Japan, Latvia, Lithuania, Luxemburg, Mexico, Norway, Poland, Portugal, Romania, Spain, Sweden, Switzerland, Turkey, and Yugoslavia. Of course, some of its subsidiaries or companies in which it held large equity shares did business in many of these countries. List from Stocking and Watkins, op. cit., p. 330.

27. Ibid., pp. 337–39; Bright, op. cit., pp. 310–11.

28. General Electric Company, "Annual Report for 1929," p. 12; George Stocking and Myron Watkins, *Cartels or Competition?* (New York, 1948), pp. 82–83; Stocking and Watkins, op. cit. (1946), p. 339, 341.

29. For example, the 1938 price of a 60-watt lamp, sold in the U.S. by GE for $.15, retailed for $.22 in France, $.34 in Belgium, $.39 in Britain, $.48 in Germany, and $.70 in Holland. Tariff Commission, op. cit., p. 49.

30. Stocking and Watkins, op. cit. (1946), pp. 342–43; Bright, op. cit., pp. 310–11.

31. Westinghouse quotas were based on combined GE-Westinghouse sales. Bright, op. cit., pp. 256–59; George Morrison to Gerard Swope, April 28, 1926, quoted in *United States v. General Electric*, Ex.64-G.

32. Tariff duties on tungsten lamps remained at 20%. Tariff Commission, op. cit., pp. 61–66; Bright, op. cit., pp. 261–65; Stocking and Watkins, op. cit. (1946), pp. 346–50. Throughout the 1930s there were over 200 electric-lamp manufacturers in Japan, and Japan became the second largest lamp-producing country in the world behind the United States. The Japanese manufacturers had been invited to join Phoebus in a block but declined.

Comment

Hiroshi Itagaki

Professor Reich's paper examines GE's strategies and methods for dominating the American incandescent lamp market and explains the reason for its high profitability. Reich's description of GE's strategies for controlling the domestic market backed by the strength and patents of process technology and product technology is persuasive enough that I agree with the gist of the paper. Nevertheless, there remain, I think, some points to be questioned. My questions are related to the following two points: (1) the significance for GE of the international incandescent lamp cartel in Europe; and (2) the characteristics of GE's financial power.

In addition to those points, I would like to pose two other questions, which are, I believe, significant to consider, though they seem to be somewhat beyond the theme of his paper. They are: (3) why did GE choose capital participation in major foreign competitors rather than establishment of its own subsidiaries? (4) What is the "legacy" of these international activities for GE's multinational operations in the post–World War II period?

The significance for GE of the international incandescent lamp cartel in Europe. Reich emphasizes GE's leading role in the formation of the cartel. However, as the author himself remarks, GE had already made licensing agreements with major lamp producers abroad and owned stock in them in order to protect the domestic market and to do business in secondary markets favorable to GE. If this is true, and I agree with him that it is, what was the major motivation of GE to form another such international cartel outside the United States in addition to its existing close relationship with cartel members, and how did GE benefit from the cartel? In other words, I think we need further explanation of the effect and influence of the international cartels outside the United States on the domestic market.

The characteristics of GE's financial power. An elaboration of the characteristics of GE's financial power in the 1920s would be helpful. When Reich discusses GE's financial strength, does he mean that GE had plenty of its own funds, such as retained earnings, or the ability to raise funds from leading banking houses? In the case of the former, is it possible that GE's financial power was not the "cause" of the domination of the market but rather the "result" of it? In the case of the latter, we must consider that GE did not rely on outside bankers so much during the 1920s when GE's domination of the market reached its peak.

Why did GE prefer to participate in the capital stock of major foreign competitors rather than to establish its own subsidiaries? I think the purpose of GE's capital participation was not the control of managerial power, but rather the reinforcement of license agreements. This strategy is quite opposite of that of American automobile manufacturing companies, which set up their own subsidiaries and embarked on local production in Europe. Why? One possible interpretation could be that GE's dominant position against foreign competitors, especially European ones, was not so strong as to allow GE to operate and maintain its competitiveness under unfamiliar managerial circumstances.

What is the "legacy" of foreign activities represented by license agreements and equity holdings in the pre–World War II period? Superficially there was none, as GE terminated all of its license agreements and released its capital equity of foreign competitors. GE's multinational activities in the postwar period had to start from zero. Nevertheless, experience accumulated within the company might somehow have served its foreign activities after World War II. This is, I think, related to the issue of how we can evaluate the significance of international cartels in the interwar period from the historical perspective.

Response

Leonard S. Reich

GE was concerned that the individual contracts it had made with the European producers were too fragile. That is, if some producer, say Osram, perceived that at a particular time it was in that company's best interests to either abrogate or fail to renew its contract with GE in order to invade the American market or sell lamp-making equipment to GE's American competitors, it might do so. If, however, that company were tied up in a whole web of contracts that involved not only GE but also other major producers in a cartel, such apostasy was much less likely.

GE used its financial strength in a number of ways. One was to buy substantial equity in European producers to realize a share of their profits and to gain some say in their operations. It also spent large sums to purchase important patent rights (e.g., Just-Hanaman) and financed large-scale research and development efforts of its own. The company loaned Osram $1.5 million on lenient terms in 1924 as part of the negotiations to form Phoebus, and it spent large sums in legal costs to discourage importation of non-cartel Japanese lamps during the 1930s.

GE financed its operations entirely out of retained earnings. It *never* went to bankers for funds—that was a fundamental company policy until the Second World War. I think it is fair to say that GE's financial power was both a cause and a result of its market power. Financial (and other types of) power led to strong profits, which then were used to augment the financial power, etc.

GE's primary concern was to protect the American market, not to sell large quantities of its goods in foreign markets (which the American auto manufacturers intended). As Professor Itagaki suggests, GE management recognized that it lacked the expertise to operate in unfamiliar circumstances, did not want to overextend itself, and so preferred to avoid subsidiary arrangements where possible.

The "legacy" of GE's international activities of the 1920s and 1930s on the postwar environment is difficult to assess, in part because the Europeans and Japanese were eliminated as strong rivals for some years. However, I should mention that the difficulties GE had maintaining control of electrical markets before the war led the company's management to a fundamental policy shift: away from concentration on electrical (and secondarily chemical) goods to a broad diversification, including everything from financial services and real estate to medical imaging equipment and jet engines.

Summary of the Concluding Discussion

Terushi Hara and Akira Kudō

I. A Recapitulation
Four Key Questions
The concluding discussion, held on the final day of the conference, began with a recapitulation of the six themes addressed by the participants and was followed by a summary of the contributions each paper made in shedding new light on these issues. For a final debate, questions concerning the reasons for the formation of international cartels, the formation process itself, the management of international cartels, and the effects of international cartels were suggested.

The Reasons for the Formation of International Cartels. Why were international cartels created? And why were international cartels formed mainly in the interwar period? Was the formation of international cartels an alternative policy to direct investment and licensing? A theoretical question concerning the relationship between international cartels and multinational corporations needed to be answered. The issue of whether member companies sought security, diversification, or maximization of profits also needed to be discussed.

The Formation Process. How were international cartels created, and what was the relation between international and domestic cartels. Differences in the type of relation between international and domestic cartels are apparent in the case of Germany, as on international cartel leader, and France and Japan, as followers. The role the government played in the formation, by enacting laws, imposing duties, and granting subsidies, etc., also needed clarification.

The Management of International Cartels. What functions did the international cartels have? A discussion on the management strategy and typology of international cartels was proposed. As this particular conference was taking place in Japan, which was a newly industrialized nation in the interwar period, it was suggested that international cartels be analyzed not from the center but from the point of view of the nations and corporations that found themselves on the periphery. Following a description of the typology of horizontal- and vertical-type cartels, an analysis of the informational functions of the cartels and their influence on corporate decisions was proposed.

The Effects. What actually did the formation of international cartels give rise to? What influence did international cartels have on technical transfers, international trade, costs and selling price, as well as on the business strategy of individual companies?

Horizontal and Vertical Typology

Following Terushi Hara's four issues for discussion, Akira Kudō classified the arguments raised at the conference by their horizontal and vertical typology. He related this to the questions on the management and effects of the international cartels. The typology seemed appropriate in the case of Japan. In the joint Hara-Kudō paper, seven cases concerning Japanese companies had been presented, four of which were discussed at the conference in relation to Japan. These were: dyestuffs (Schröter), nitrogen fertilizers (Ōshio), incandescent electric light bulbs (Hasegawa, Reich), and the heavy electrical industries (Hasegawa).

In the case of dyestuffs, an agreement on indigo was signed between the international cartel and Mitsui Mining. Furthermore, I.G. Farben (acting as representative for the interests of the international cartel) reached an agreement with Nihon Senryō Seizō Co. and Mitsui Mining. In the case of nitrogen fertilizers, agreements were signed between the CIA and members of the Japanese nitrogen fertilizer industry. Thus within the dyestuffs and nitrogen fertilizer industries, vertical relations, i.e., the agreements between the international cartels and Japanese corporations, were of central importance.

On the other hand, in the incandescent electric light bulb industry, no agreement between the British and Japanese industries existed, but a horizontal-type relationship, in the form of the international cartel Phoebus, assumed greater importance. Regarding the heavy electrical industry, the most important point to be considered was the indirect regulations concerning the Japanese market imposed by the international cartel, INCA. In the case of the incandescent light bulb and heavy electrical industries, horizontal relationships were central; in other words, relationships at the cartel level were based on agreements concerning the Japanese and other Asian markets and aimed at excluding Japanese corporations.

Within the incandescent light bulb and heavy electrical industries, there was fairly active direct investment in Japan by European and American companies, and relations were controlled through this. The international cartels' agreements regarding the Asian markets (including Japan), in other words horizontal-type relations, were established to help these investments. In contrast, in the Japanese dyestuffs and nitrogen fertilizer industries there was hardly any direct investment carried out by European and American companies. As Harm Schröter had made clear, I.G. Farben, which was at the very center of the international dyestuffs cartel, saw security as the most serious consideration and was negatively disposed to direct investment, seeing Japan as no exception here. As control over the Japanese market and corporations was not exercised by direct investment, this was where the vertical-type international cartels needed to function. As pointed out by Takeshi Ōshio, the fact that the international cartels made constant concessions with regard to Japan was worthy of attention. This was also evident in the dyestuffs industry. In both of these cases, Kudō stated, the responses needed to be explained as part of the global strategies of the American and especially the European companies belonging to international cartels.

The growth of Japanese companies in the 1920s was achieved basically without the protection of the Japanese government. As Ōshio had emphasized, during this period there were no fundamental measures regarding duties, subsidies, or import controls for nitrogen fertilizer. Moreover, as Shin Hasegawa had pointed out, the imposition of import duties in 1926 had only a modest effect as far as the Japanese electrical industry was concerned. Hara and Kudō stressed that even within the dyestuffs industry, in which the government played a fairly important role, it was the entrepreneurship of Mitsui Mining that was crucial in the development of indigo dye. In every case, a desire and strong capacity for growth had been shown by the Japanese corporations. This, therefore, precluded attempts by European and American companies to draw Japanese corporations into the sphere of influence of the international cartel.

Detailed reports had been presented on a number of cases from Europe and America: dyestuffs (Schröter), pharmaceuticals (Liebenau), nitrogen fertilizers (Chadeau, Devos), incandescent electric light bulbs (Reich), the heavy electrical industry (Giannetti), and polymers (Smith). By way of answering the question of how far the typology could be applied to countries other than Japan, Kudō asked which was the more dominant, horizontal- or vertical-type cartels. At the beginning of the conference the assumption had been made that in countries other than Japan emphasis was placed on direct investment by European and American companies, and that thus the phenomenon of horizontal relationships could be more widely observed. This hypothesis held true in the case of dyestuffs, nitrogen fertilizer, and incandescent light bulbs, but in the case of pharmaceuticals, heavy electrical goods, and polymers, it was not necessarily so. We had thus made too simplistic a supposition. There was, therefore, a need to refine the Hara-Kudō hypothesis, taking into account the proposals for improvement put forward by the conference participants.

The fourth point concerning the effect of the international cartels was divided into the following parts: (1) the connection between the hope placed in the international cartels and their actual outcome; (2) their effect on individual enterprises; and (3) their effect on business as a whole (production, sales, and technology). As far as four cases involving Japan were concerned, the three points could not be said to have been dealt with in a comprehensive manner. But both the European and American companies on the one hand and Japanese on the other were to some extent satisfied, although the European and American companies were unable to control the growth of Japanese corporations. Furthermore, there was virtually no technical transfer made by the international cartels, but, despite efforts to the contrary, Japan's development as one of the first NIEs was also unrestricted. Thus from an evaluation based on these points the hypothesis as put forward in the joint Hara-Kudō paper (see p. 20, Table 3) could be assumed to be correct to a certain extent.

II. The Discussion

Topics and Typology

Leonard S. Reich proposed a fifth theme for discussion in addition to the original four. This was that the success or failure of the international cartels should be examined in relation to the type and quality of the goods that they produced. Emmanuel Chadeau suggested that the relation between the international cartels and the international trade mechanism, in particular, should be discussed.

John Smith commented on Kudō's point that the number of American participants in international cartels was very small. He explained that during the interwar period, the amount of imports and exports as a total of U.S. products was only around 10% and that the U.S. economy was thus mainly domestically based. Therefore, American corporations did not show a great deal of interest in the international cartels. A debate on the Hara-Kudō typology began with Schröter questioning its accuracy. He pointed out that in view of the greater complexity of the actual situation, by applying this simplistic typology there was a danger of omitting those cartels which fell into the grey area between the two categories. Also, participation of Japanese companies in the international cartels was minimal, and thus by using only actual examples from Japan the classification of international cartels was made extremely difficult, as was the application of this to the analysis of international cartels on a global scale. There was a gentleman's agreement in August 1926 between Japan and Germany, and more details about the actual situation regarding participation in the international dyestuffs cartel might be helpful. Hiroshi Itagaki, in response to the Hara-Kudō typology, which placed great importance on investment in the electrical companies and thereby pointed out the differences between Japan and Europe, stressed instead the similarities between the two. He agreed on the importance of the licensing agreements, observing, however, that foreign direct investment was nothing more than a means to licensing. In response to the above points, Kudō replied that he took as his academic principle "simple is beautiful."

Reasons and Process of Formation
The discussion then moved on to the question of why the international cartels were formed mainly in the interwar period. Smith acknowledged himself as an adherent of Chandler's theory and stated that what induced the formation of international cartels could be explained according to the economies of scope and scale as proposed by Chandler. International cartels were made necessary by the constant growth tendency of capitalism, bringing with it the need to develop new products, acquire larger markets, and expand into foreign markets. But in the case of the United States, the domestic market in the interwar period provided sufficient growth potential for its corporations. Schröter agreed with this explanation based on Chandler's theory and said that in Germany cartels are considered "the child of necessity."

Seiichirō Yonekura, while giving recognition to Chandler's theory, said that a new interpretation was also necessary. From the point of view of Japan's participation in the international cartels, the presence of such factors as the introduction of technology and information and the protection of the domestic market should be emphasized. In this sense, the informational function of international cartels, as pointed out by Jonathan Liebenau, was a point worthy of attention. Regarding the fact that the formation of international cartels took place mainly between the two world wars, Smith asserted that this period should not necessarily be regarded as anything exceptional. Jun Sakudō stressed that it was moves

                    T. Hara and A. Kudō

within European countries from competition to cooperation, and the intervention by governments in economic activities, that contributed to the formation of international cartels after the First World War.

The discussion on the formation process of the international cartels centered around the relationship between leaders and followers, as well as the domestic and foreign markets. Liebenau said that there were cases where a distinction could not be made between leaders and followers, and in the case of the British chemical industry, the members participating in the international cartel were all followers. This indicated that the response by the British companies to the international cartels was similar to that of the Japanese. In Germany, the case was probably the same. Schröter declined making too simple a classification of leaders and followers and was of the view that the leadership in the international cartels had been taken not by the United States but by Europe. I.G. Farben took the initiative in the formation of the international cartel, but the situation in the dyestuffs industry was in fact much more complex. Before I.G. Farben, Swiss companies had taken the lead in forming a binational agreement with French companies, and there were also moves in the same direction in Great Britain—an indication that there was a circumstantial inevitability pertaining to the formation of international cartels.

On the relationship between domestic and international markets, Chadeau saw the domestic markets in Europe as reaching a saturation point during the interwar period, and thus exports abroad assumed importance for European companies. At this point, as can be seen from Greta Devos's paper, each country adopted policies of depreciation to boost exports. Even in France, in 1926, the franc was devalued. In view of this situation, even if I.G. Farben had made plans to invest in and export from France, it probably would have faced difficulties in obtaining a return on its investment. Moreover, it had probably also been difficult for French producers to draw up import plans. Devos added that in the 1930s an exchange rate control policy was implemented with regard to the export of saltpeter from Chile.

The Effects

In the discussion on the extent of the influence of international cartels, Smith asked what Japanese researchers saw as the effect of the international cartels on the Japanese government, technology, and business. Hideaki Miyajima responded that participation in the international cartels was a disadvantage for Japan as a developing nation. The leaders of the international cartels saw cartels as a rational move leading to an increase in profits, but for Japan this was not the case. The best policy for

Japanese companies was not to join the international cartels but to promote industrialization and increase exports instead. Moreover, even if they did join they had to try to reduce the restrictions imposed on them to a minimum and to allow room for unrestricted growth. Tsuneo Suzuki emphasized that in the European chemical industry cartels of the 1920s and 1930s, Japan's importance as an export market varied. In the 1930s, for the British, the Japanese market should have assumed an importance such as to make it worth defending to the last.

Renato Giannetti spoke on the influence of international cartels on the prices of the follower nations, based on the situation in the Italian electrical machinery industry. As the international cartels generally fixed prices at levels higher than those achieved through free competition, initially participation was greatest by those corporations seeking higher profits. But after two or three years the situation usually changed. International cartels collapsed due to the implementation of more aggressive policies by new participants, and following this, lower-cost producers joined to form new cartels.

A discussion was held on Reich's point about the influence of international cartels on technology transfers to Japan, in which three Japanese scholars participated. Hasegawa cited the example of the heavy electrical industry to give the following interpretation. The basic strategy of General Electric was either to form an international cartel with Siemens, etc., or else to carry out direct investment in developing nations like Japan. Of course, General Electric held the monopoly in advanced technology, but in order to compete with rival companies it was prepared to provide know-how on other technology to its subsidiary company in Japan. The Japanese then used this to promote their industrialization.

In the case of the electrical light bulb industry, as Miyajima made clear, the Japanese side could not see any benefit in participating in an international cartel. Following this, Hiroaki Yamazaki, using the rayon industry as an example, explained the situation regarding technical transfers to Japan. At the end of the 1920s, there were six large rayon companies in Japan. The largest company sounded out the idea of obtaining technology from the international cartel, but as it did not receive a favorable reply, it proceeded to carry out technological development on its own. The second largest company in the industry acquired technology through licensing from Germany. Three out of the remaining four corporations introduced technology through consultant companies. Therefore, there was no case of any company in the rayon industry introducing technology through an international cartel. Moreover, Ōshio, who had studied the nitrogen industry, pointed out that the situation was similar in that industry too.

Finally, Liebenau warned that in theorizing that the international cartels brought only negative results, we are unconsciously acting on the presumption of inevitable moves in a specific direction by certain industries. In other words, we are considering the development trajectory of these industries. Therefore, we should base our theory on the actual process of industrialization of each industry and the effect that this had on international cartels.

Organizing Committee and Conference Participants

Chairman:	Yuzawa Takeshi	(Gakushuin University)
Vice Chairman:	Udagawa Masaru	(Hosei University)
	Abe Etsuo	(Meiji University)
	Hiroyama Kensuke	(Nagasaki University)
	Kawabe Nobuo	(Waseda University)
	Kikkawa Takeo	(Aoyama Gakuin University)
	Kudō Akira	(University of Tokyo)
	Sakudō Jun	(Kobe Gakuin University)
	Yonekura Seiichirō	(Hitotsubashi University)
Advisers:	Wakimura Yoshitarō	(University of Tokyo)
	Nakagawa Keiichirō	(Aoyama Gakuin University)
	Yasuoka Shigeaki	(Doshisha University)
	Morikawa Hidemasa	(Keio University)

Project Leader and Editor for the Third Meeting:

Hara Terushi
(Waseda University)

Kudō Akira
(University of Tokyo)

Participants:

Abe Etsuo
(Meiji University)

Chadeau, Emmanuel
(Université Charles de Gaulle–
Lille III)

Devos, Greta
(University of Antwerp)

Giannetti, Renato
(Università di Firenze)

Harumi Namiko
(Miyagi Gakuin College
for Women)

Hasegawa Shin
(Shizuoka University)

Itagaki Hiroshi
(Saitama University)

Kawabe Nobuo
(Waseda University)

Liebenau, Jonathan
(London School of Economics,
University of London)

Miyajima Hideaki
(Waseda University)

Ōshio Takashi
(Meiji Gakuin University)

Ozawa Katsuyuki
  (Takachiho University)
Reich, Leonard, S.
  (Colby College)
Sakudō Jun
  (Kobe Gakuin University)
Schröter, Harm G.
  (Freie Universität Berlin)

Smith, John Kenly, Jr.
  (Lehigh University)
Suzuki Tsuneo
  (Wako University)
Yamazaki Hiroaki
  (University of Tokyo)

Secretariat: Kikkawa Takeo   (Aoyama Gakuin University)
  Yonekura Seiichirō   (Hitotsubashi University)
  Ichikawa Fumihiko   (Toyama University)
  Clahsen, Hans-Jürgen   (Hitotsubashi University)
  Tamura Chikako   (Hitotsubashi University)
  Yongue, Julia   (University of Tokyo)

Index